Hitless Wonder

A Life in Minor League Rock and Roll

Joe Oestreich

LYONS PRESS
Guilford, Connecticut
An imprint of Globe Pequot Press

Lyons Press is an imprint of Globe Pequot Press.

Cover photo: Jayna Wallace
Project editor: Meredith Dias
Layout: Justin Marciano

Library of Congress Cataloging-in-Publication Data

Oestreich, Joe.
Hitless wonder : a life in minor league rock and roll / Joe Oestreich.
    p. cm.
Includes bibliographical references.
ISBN 978-0-7627-7924-6
1. Watershed (Musical group) 2. Rock musicians—United
States—Biography. 3. Rock groups—United States—Biography. I. Title.

ML421.W27O47 2012
782.42166092'2—dc23
[B]
                                2011050510

Printed in the United States of America

10 9 8 7 6 5 4 3 2

To Kate, for living this twice.

Joe (left) and Colin (right) prepping newspapers in Colin's garage and walking to a gig at Lifestyles Communities Pavilion, in both cases almost certainly talking about Cheap Trick.

Contents

PROLOGUE

Columbus, Ohio

"I'M NOT HAPPY ABOUT THIS," MY WIFE KATE SAYS. I'M DRIVING HER parents' old Chrysler, hustling her to Port Columbus for a 6:00 a.m. flight back to Sea-Tac. Even though it's still dark, she slides on her Jackie Onassis sunglasses and turns to the passenger window. We speed past the soccer stadium, the fairgrounds, the skyline. She gathers her black hair into a ponytail. "Not one bit."

Christmas and New Year's are over, so now Kate is flying away from Columbus—the city that, until five months ago, we'd always called home—to Tacoma, where we now live. But that's not why she's unhappy this morning. She's unhappy because I'm not going with her.

Airport traffic is heavy for pre-dawn, and I follow a long line of droppers-off to the departing curb. "Where's your boarding pass?" I say as I pop the trunk.

Kate climbs out of the car, waving her pass between her fingers. "Where's yours?"

Tonight my band Watershed starts a two-week tour that will take us to Detroit, Milwaukee, and Chicago, then to Cleveland, New York, Baltimore, and down the East Coast. We'll finish with a big homecoming show in Columbus. Kate's the one with the plane ticket, but it feels like I'm the one leaving.

The airport cop blows his whistle, trying to keep traffic moving. From the trunk, I lift the backpack I once gave her as a birthday present. We've packed it for trips to Vienna, Paris, and Caracas. She wore it on our honeymoon in Turkey. "Got your I.D.?" I say.

She digs through her purse and nods at her license. "You're lucky," she says, "to have so much time to waste."

While I spend the next two weeks in mop-bucket bars, she'll be busy writing a chapter of her PhD dissertation on fashion and sexuality. What she doesn't say, but surely means, is that my bandmates and I have grown too old to load ourselves into an Econoline and live on beer and pretzels. The band has been together for twenty-three years—fifteen years longer than Kate and I have been married.

The cop puts more air into his whistle, and it hits me that if somebody were to bet him which of the two people clogging traffic is a rock star—the bald guy in the sweats and slippers or the long-haired beauty with the big sunglasses—he'd lay his money on Kate.

"Why are you doing this, Joe?" she says, pushing her shades to the top of her head.

"We write songs and make records," I say. "Then we go out and play. That's how it works." I hold the backpack up for her. It's stuffed heavy with Christmas gifts and dirty clothes.

She puts her arms through the straps and shimmies it into place. "We were supposed to spend these two weeks together. You promised."

Add this to a long list of broken promises.

Setting her jaw tight, she stares blankly into the terminal. Her breath makes smoky plumes. "Nobody gives a shit about a Watershed tour," she says, "except the guys in Watershed."

There was a time when all sorts of people cared, people with power and money. There was a time when even the airport cop might have recognized me.

Kate shakes her head, almost laughs. Maybe everyone looks their best the minute before you put them on a plane, but standing here in the idling exhaust, my wife is more beautiful than she's ever been.

"I'll miss you," I say.

She turns to me with dead eyes, a half smile. "I know you will."

I stretch one arm out to her, and the cop yells, "Come on, guy. Move it."

Kate starts toward the sliding doors, steadying herself under the backpack. "This better be worth it," she says. Just before she disappears into the concourse, she hitches the pack higher on her shoulders, jerking the straps as if cursing the weight of everything she's carrying.

THE FIRST LEG

1

The Headliners
Detroit, Michigan

FIRST THING YOU LEARN IS THAT YOU ALWAYS GOTTA WAIT.

Wait to get noticed. Wait to get signed. Wait to get famous.

I'm standing backstage, behind black velour curtains, waiting to go on. Pre-show jitters have me shifting from my right sneaker to my left and back like a kindergartener ten kids deep in the restroom line. A Pabst longneck sweats in my hand. I take a pull, and I dry my palm down the thigh of my girl-cut jeans. Then I lean against a cinder block wall heavily Sharpied with graffiti (CALL FOR A DISCREET BLOW JOB) and clever rebuttals from the graffiti annotators (WHAT'S A DISCREET BLOW JOB? WILL I NOTICE IT?). And I wait.

Biggie pokes his head between the curtains, a Maglite stretching from his mouth like a metal cigar. "We're set to pop," he says. He aims the beam at my bass. "Let's do this."

"Where's everybody else?" I say.

He takes the light from his mouth and draws figure eights across the backstage area. "They aren't back here?"

Before I can shake my head no, Biggie has pulled the curtains shut and disappeared.

I take a drink and imagine what waits on the other side: a sports arena, the floor sold out from row A to ZZ. And girls smelling like fruit-flavored perfume and bummed cigarettes, wrapped tight in low-slung jeans, their belly buttons pierced, their breasts defying gravity thanks to the tautness of youth and the bra engineers at Victoria's Secret. The girls put one hand on each other's shoulders and boost themselves onto the folding chairs to see over the heads of the boys standing in front of them. The dough-faced boys—in their new concert T-shirts, half-drunk on parking lot beers—thwack each other and point out which steroided-up security guards to avoid when, the second the lights go down, they'll ass and elbow up to the front row.

Until then everybody keeps an eye on the stage, studying a roadie as he puts the gear through the final tweaks—*the testing, testing, one-two-threes* and *waaaank-waaaank* power chords—to make doubly and triply sure the guitars and amps are wired for sound. The digitally reproduced voice of AC/DC's Brian Johnson blasts through the PA at 102dB—*FIRE!*—saluting those about to rock. Marijuana smoke wafts to the ceiling trusses. And every few minutes the crowd noise swells when a whole section thinks they've seen a band member mingling with the stagehands, VIPs, and contest-winners who huddle in the wings.

Just before the houselights drop, the stage manager appears. He walks coolly from rig to rig, giving the microphone cables, speaker wires, and blinking red lights—the tangled landscape of rock—a final once-over. Then he pulls a Maglite from his back pocket and shines it toward the mixing board, across the sea of the floor, over the backwards ball caps of the boys in row J, over the hairsprayed heads of the girls in row K, through the rising smoke and devil-horn fists and AC/DC—*FIRE!*—commanding one and all to stand up and be counted for what we are about to receive. The message the Maglite carries fifty-two rows back to the soundman and the light tech and an arena full of kids who've paid fifty bucks and waited months for this very moment is this: *It's showtime.*

It is showtime. But from my spot backstage—in this Detroit bar, on this Thursday night—here's what I see when I pull open the curtains: twenty by twenty feet of wide-open floor. No chattering girls in row K. No blustery boys in row J. There aren't any rows. Hell, there aren't any seats, so, no, there's not even one security thug on duty. The spot right in front of the stage is anyone's for the taking. But there aren't any takers. Tonight in this club, dishearteningly named Small's Bar, the front row is empty.

I walk through the curtains and out to the floor. There are exactly five people in the audience. Five people who've paid five dollars each to see Watershed play a fifty-minute set. All five are excruciatingly well behaved, standing in the back, politely waiting for us to start. Everyone seems hyper-aware of his voice, speaking in hushed tones, not wanting to disturb the peace. The soundguy has cued up the Foo Fighters, but quietly. Detroit may be Rock City, but Small's Bar is as loud as a library.

I move toward the stage, where the opening band—a local act that was supposed to help fill out the crowd—should be tearing down their gear. But earlier, when we were checking into the Fairfield Inn, we got an e-mail from the guy who owns Small's: "Opener dropped off the bill. Tonight doesn't look promising. I'm okay with canceling." We shook our heads and laughed. What else could we do? This is the first night of the tour. The launch party. Headlining in Detroit, baby. Home of Motown Records and the MC5, The Stooges and The White Stripes. If we drove two hundred miles to play for five people, so be it. No way we were canceling.

Still, as I scan the back wall, where the crowd is leaning like a police lineup, it depresses me that I know four of the five by name. There's Joe The Animal, a semi-pro football player who is probably borderline autistic. Thankfully he's a *hulking* probably borderline-autistic semi-pro football player, and he always helps us load and unload the van. In fact, a few hours ago, when we pulled up to the club for load-in, The Animal was standing on the sidewalk wearing weightlifting gloves, doing torso twists and knee bends. "I got here early," he said, holding the door open for me. "'Cause I know you guys will sell out a dump like this."

I didn't want to undermine his optimism, so as I hefted my basses past him, I said, "We'll find out soon enough, Animal."

He followed me into the bar, taking in Small's and all its, well, smallness. "This joint doesn't sell advance tickets or anything," he said.

I didn't tell him that we rarely play venues that sell tickets of any kind, let alone in advance. A hand stamp? Absolutely. Wrist band? Sure. But *tickets?* "This is a real rock club, man," I said. "We love playing shows like this."

Now, as I'm walking toward the bar to see if Biggie has found my bandmates, The Animal spots me. He checks his watch and gestures toward the mostly empty room as if to say, *You love playing shows like this?*

Compared to lots of bars we play, Small's isn't so small. It's divided into two separate spaces: the band room and the barroom. The band room, with its painted cinder block and high ceiling, has the feel of a warehouse. Like Detroit itself, the room is industrial, utilitarian. If not for the wooden stage along one wall, it would be a perfect spot for silk-screening T-shirts or polybagging hex nuts. The barroom was built in 1923 as a bank, and the current incarnation recalls the original captain-of-industry–era design. Art deco lamps hang from the coffered ceiling, and stained-glass windows throw colors on a mahogany bar top. Connecting the two sides is a border zone with pool tables, a nook for bands to sell their merchandise, and two tiny and well-graffiti'd restrooms (think airplane lavatories with cocks drawn on the walls).

The beauty of Small's two-room layout is that you can isolate from whatever misery awaits on the band side by camping out in the bar side. And there, elbows bent on the mahogany, is where I find my bandmates—everyone but Colin, anyway. Dave Masica, the drummer, is trading a five for a Budweiser, his salt-and-pepper hair spiked high as the second cut at Little Turtle Country Club, where he works as a cook. One stool over is Mark "Pooch" Borror, the rhythm guitar player. He's chatting up the bartender, who, with her bangs and tattoos, has got to be a jammer on a roller derby squad. Pooch wears horn-rimmed glasses, so if it was late enough and you were drunk enough, you might catch this scene and swear you saw Buddy Holly making time with Bettie Page.

So there's Pooch, chewing gum and smiling the smile that makes girls in the crowd—when there are girls, when there is a crowd—gather at his side of the stage and yell "Poochie!" But Bettie is focusing on our roadie, Ricki C., who's winding through one of his greatest road story hits, about the night he met David Johansen of the New York Dolls.

"So I say to Johansen," Ricki says, "'I was at the Dolls show in Columbus in '74.' And Johansen pauses for a second. Starts walking away like he didn't hear me. Then turns back and says, 'That's funny. You don't *look* queer.'"

"Wow," Bettie says, her lips shaped into a red O. "That's *perfect.*"

Now Biggie's waving the Maglite in our faces. "You ladies gonna play sometime tonight?"

I set my empty bottle on the bar. Without taking her eyes off Ricki C., Bettie twists a new one open for me. "You find Colin?" I say to Biggie.

"You three—" He nods toward Dave, Pooch, and me. "Get your asses to the stage so we can start the minute I do." And he walks away, in search of the AWOL guitar player.

Dave laughs and says, "Playing in a rock band is stupid." He and Pooch order up another round of Buds and settle deeper into their stools.

By most quantifiable standards, playing in a rock band *is* stupid. Five paying civilians at five bucks a head means come 2:00 a.m., Watershed will make twenty-five dollars at the door. Divided by the four guys in the band, that's $6.25 each. But nobody will pocket his six-and-a-quarter. We almost never see any cash. Instead *we* pay. For the gas. For the hotels. For the trips up and down the Wendy's Supervalue Menu. We dig into our pockets to cover five or six shows in a row, hoping to eventually land a high dollar gig that will get us all reimbursed. Sometimes this gamble works, sometimes not. On our most lucrative tours, we come home with a hundred bucks or so. Usually we lose twice that. So we bankroll the gigs the American way: with credit cards. Rock now, pay later. Even Biggie, the tour manager, is out here on his own nickel. The only member of the Watershed camp guaranteed to land in the black is Ricki C., who works for the cut rate of twenty-five dollars a day. And he only turns a profit because he can eat for a week on Hostess cupcakes and skim milk.

When Biggie filled up the tank in Columbus this afternoon, he paid $3.09 a gallon. The drive to Detroit was two hundred miles. At fifteen mpg—and fifteen is a generous estimate considering the Econoline is loaded with four band members, two crew guys, our bags, and all the amps, drums, and guitars—we've already burnt $41.19 in fuel. We haven't yet played a note, and the one thing I know for sure about tonight's show is that we'll lose money. At closing time, Biggie will settle up with the doorman, and then he'll stuff the bills into the gray pouch he keeps stashed in the dashboard. Tomorrow, tonight's twenty-five dollar take will get us a third of the way to Milwaukee. Here in the minor leagues, bands don't play for sex, fame, and fortune. They play for gasoline.

An economist would tell us that by driving three hours to perform for five people, we have not behaved in our monetary self-interest. It's Econ 101, supply and demand. There clearly isn't much demand for Watershed in Detroit, so we would have been smart to cut off the supply by staying home. Get a good night's sleep. Wake up tomorrow and commute to our real jobs, jobs that actually pay. I used to think of gigs like this as investments in the future. *We're paying dues now,* I'd tell myself, *for the big rockstar payoff later.* The trouble is I'm now thirty-eight years old. So is Colin. Dave is forty-three. Pooch is the youngest at thirty-five. By music business standards, we're too damn old for the rockstar payoff. So now I have to wonder, *what future?* Besides, we already had a shot at stardom. And we whiffed.

Remember your crappy high school band? The one you formed after you finally got that guitar for your birthday? You practiced down in the basement, learning "Smoke on the Water" and "Ironman" and "You Really Got Me," crossing your fingers you'd stick together long enough to write a song that some other crappy high school band might one day cover. A couple years later you called it quits, bowing to the entropic forces that went to work starting with that very first practice: egos, insecurities, differing motivations. Because crappy high school bands are supposed to break up, like the Bryan Adams song: *Jimmy quit. Jody got married.*

My crappy high school band is headlining Small's tonight.

Colin and I started it the summer before our junior year. We didn't know Dave and Pooch back then, but Biggie was with us, setting up gear and getting us to the stage on time. In the years since, we've played over a thousand shows, in thirty-four states and 116 cities. We've humped our amps through the doors at CBGB ten times. We've played the House of Blues on the Sunset Strip, The Metro in Chicago, The Rat in Boston. We've played on South Street in Philly, on Sixth Avenue in Austin, at the 7th Street Entry in Minneapolis, and above a gay bar called Rod's in Madison. We've played fifty-eight different venues in Columbus alone.

Small's Bar is the fifteenth place we've played in Detroit. We've released six full-length albums; a batch of cassettes, 45s, and EPs; a couple videos; and a DVD. Colin, Biggie, and I have been together longer than The Beatles, The Doors, and Nirvana combined.

Watershed's long haul hasn't been all sparse crowds and dive bars. At one point we almost made it. We were limo'd around Manhattan. We recorded in the same studio as AC/DC, Aerosmith, and Springsteen. We played arenas and amphitheaters, headlining shows in front of thousands, opening for bands everybody's heard of. We were treated to fancy dinners and promised by insiders that we were the Next Big Thing. But we never had a hit song. Never had a video on MTV. Never won the notoriety that comes measured in songwriting residuals or on the *Billboard* Hot 100. And yet somehow we've stayed in the game for two decades, like a hustling utility man with a great glove but no bat, a hitless wonder.

By now, most musicians we've shared the stage with, famous and not, have packed away their guitars and decided to sell real estate or insurance. In the Fifties, in fact, "selling insurance" was a euphemism for quitting. *Hey, what's Bill up to?* Bill could be a shoeshine boy or a CEO, but if he was no longer rocking, he was selling insurance. Then again, in the Fifties, one nickname for the guitar was the "starvation box," so it should surprise no one that rock and roll has always been a struggle. The story here is not that Watershed has had it tough; every band has it tough. The story here is that most bands with Watershed's career arc quit long before they're reduced to playing for crowds they can count on one hand.

So maybe doing this show is a little stupid. Maybe we've booked this tour because we've built an inertia that's stronger than our better judgment. But I suspect the real reason is a million times simpler and more complicated. Watershed has dragged ourselves up to Detroit because we're a rock band, and playing live—whether it's for five people or fifteen thousand—is what rock bands do. Stupid or not.

Here at the bar, Dave is catching Pooch and me up on the gossip from the country club. "My Percocet dealer calls me Frankenstein now," Dave says. He goes wide-eyed and zombie-like, his arms straight and stiff. "He's created a *monnnn*ster."

Biggie's silhouetted by the jukebox, rubbing a dollar on his jeans to iron it flat. He's given up the search for Colin.

Joe The Animal has wandered over from the band side. "Still no Colin?" When none of us answer, he smiles and says, "I'll hunt 'em down for you." And even though The Animal's voice is pure Michigander, something in that smile is reminding me of Quint, Robert Shaw's character from *Jaws*. And I'm bracing for him to follow up with, *and I'll catch him and kill 'em for ten.*

"Forget Colin, Animal," I say over The Replacements' "Bastards of Young," which Biggie has blasting from the bar speakers. "See this?" I motion toward Dave and Pooch, toward Biggie at the jukebox and Ricki C. down the bar. "The five of us? *This* is the band."

Pooch and Dave nod at this, one of our regular bits. Whenever two or three of us are separated from the rest, we badmouth the other guys. Say that *we* are the real band, regardless of who *we* happen to be at that moment. For all I know, Colin is standing out on the street right now telling anyone who will listen that *he's* the band.

Who could blame him? The whole operation was his idea, after all, sparked in the eighth grade, the year he talked me into buying a bass. Colin and I spent our afternoons that summer sitting on the floor of his garage, prepping copies of the *Columbus Dispatch* for our paper route. His hair was short and blond, the color of a Pony League infield baking in the August sun. Mine was feathered rusty brown—that same infield, but sprayed with a hose. Our hands were newsprint-stained and, *snap,* lined with rubber band welts. As we folded and rolled the papers, we'd talk Ohio State football, Reds baseball, and Georgia Championship Wrestling. But mostly, with Q-FM-96, *Ohio's Best Rock,* cranking from Colin's jam box, we talked Aerosmith, Bad Company, Blue Öyster Cult. *Snap.* Rainbow, Billy Squier, Bob Seger.

We lived in the Columbus suburb of Worthington, named, as the Ohio-shaped signs at the city limits said, for Thomas Worthington, the

Father of Ohio statehood. Despite the historical pedigree, Worthington was a fairly run of the mill FILL IN THE BLANK*ington* suburb. Town planners and real estate developers are suckers for _____*ington*. _____*ington* promises quiet charm, class and distinction. When you walk through the threshold of an _____*ington* home, you enter a community of ox-roasts on the village green and sticky block parties where the fire department brings a hook and ladder to spray down the kids. _____*ington* city councils pass zoning laws that mandate neo-colonial architecture for retail outlets and offices. Downtown _____*ington* is a painfully cozy strip dotted with a hardware store, a dress boutique, a flower shop, an art gallery, an ice-cream shop, and an old-time pharmacy. There are no golden arches in _____*ington*. Instead there's a tasteful wooden sign that seems to announce apologetically, um, *McDonalds*?

You know the place. If not a _____*ington* then maybe a _____ *Hills* or a _____ *Heights,* cul-de-sac–pocked towns your punk ass couldn't wait to bolt from. The cops had nothing to do but harass you and your buddies for ding-dong-ditching or TP-ing or for whatever good old-fashioned, neo-colonial trouble you could get into. When you were growing up there, you hated _____*ington.* You hated it almost as much as you hated those spoiled pricks from your biggest sports rival, *Upper* _____*ington.*

Our subdivision was called Worthington Estates, but don't let the name fool you. The aluminum-sided houses sat on quarter-acre plots and were nowhere near estate-like. My house was indistinguishable from at least five others on my street.

One afternoon in the garage, Colin flipped though the Arts section and read that Cheap Trick was coming to Columbus. "Oh, we're going to this," he said.

For months I'd been cranking *At Budokan* loud enough to make my sister slam her bedroom door shut. I can still hear the opening seconds: Japanese girls in high howl, Tom Petersson checking his bass, the goose bump–inducing introduction, "*All right, Tokyo! Are you ready? Will you please welcome Epic recording artists . . .*"

Hell yes, I wanted to go see Cheap Trick. But mostly I wanted to go see Cheap Trick with Colin. He was cool, and I was not. He had a fort in his backyard. He had Atari. And unlike anyone else I knew, he'd already been to a rock concert. For his tenth birthday, his mom had taken him to Cleveland to see KISS.

Now she walked from the side yard onto the driveway. "If you boys get hungry," she said, exhaling cigarette smoke, "I'll put a couple cheese dogs in the microwave."

I watched Mrs. Gawel turn the spigot that fired the lawn sprinkler. Even late into the summer, Colin's lawn was deep green, Chem-Lawned to perfection, and so unlike my dandelioned and dog-shitty backyard. My mom was convinced that microwaves caused cancer, so she boiled our Oscar Mayers until the casings split open. She was also certain that TV rotted the brain, so we didn't have cable. We made do with *Masterpiece Theatre*.

Like all kids, I thought my parents were weird, but they seemed even weirder when compared to the Gawels. Colin's dad sold wood products. His mom stayed home. Solid, suburban citizens. My dad was an ex-priest. And my mom was an ex-nun. They'd met in grad school and then left the church to get married. Now my dad was directing a facility that trained blind folks in employment skills, and my mom was teaching English part-time at Columbus Tech. They were both finishing PhDs at Ohio State. Given that my sister and I were the only kids in Worthington with an ex-priest and -nun for parents, we were weird by definition, but if I went with Colin to see Cheap Trick, maybe I'd pick up some residual cool.

Colin and I scored seventh row seats, then rode the COTA bus downtown to the Ohio Center for the show. It was even more jaw-dropping than I knew it would be. Rick Nielsen's guitar blew my hair back. Bun E. Carlos's kick-drum socked me in the gut. Tom Petersson's twelve-string bass knocked my balls into my throat. Split-second eye contact from debonair frontman Robin Zander had the girls next to me screaming like they were seeing The Beatles at Shea. The arena smelled like perfume, cigarettes, and weed. Piss and puke soaked the bathroom floor. When the band launched into their new single, "She's Tight," the arena rained panties.

On the bus ride home, Colin said, "We have to start a band."

Like so many life-changing moments, this one came as an afterthought: six throwaway words tucked inside sixty thousand others as we talked a mile-a-minute on that bus. The lack of fanfare with which it was said was a testament to the inevitability of my answer. There was no internal debate on my part, no deliberation. Following Colin into battle was already my specialty. Earlier that summer he'd decided that I should take over half his paper route. Then he recruited me as his aide-de-camp in a campaign to terrorize his neighbors with Cottonelle and rotten eggs. So when Colin told me we were starting a band, I shrugged and said okay and that was that.

As the bus rolled up High Street, past the Ohio State campus, Colin laid out his plan for rock domination. For Christmas his mom had bought him a Gibson Melody Maker, so naturally he'd be the guitar player. The only instrument I owned was the clarinet I'd played in third grade orchestra. But my dad kept a guitar in his closet, a Martin acoustic he'd strummed when presiding mass. As soon as I figured out how to play that church guitar, Colin and I would be a two-headed monster.

Colin looked confused. "But *I'm* the guitar player."

"We need two, don't we?" I caught our reflection in the bus window. We were all knees and knuckles, draped in the bootleg concert shirts we'd bought for five bucks in the parking lot. "Like Paul Stanley and Ace Frehley."

"Any schmuck can play the guitar," he said. Then he flashed the same smile his dad surely used when selling his line of cedar hangers and shoe trees to department stores. "*You* get to play the *bass*."

I cringed. Bass was only slightly cooler than clarinet.

"No, man," Colin said. "Bass players are the *coolest*. Like Gene Simmons. Like Tom Petersson."

By the time the bus eased into The Estates, Colin had given our band a name: *Sudden Shock!* And a logo: *SS* in two stylized lightning bolts. We drew this logo all over the bus seat. *SS*. Lightning bolts. The next passenger must have thought the seat had been occupied by Hitler Youth.

The bus pulled away from the curb, and we slapped each other five. Then Colin took off toward his house, and I headed toward mine, playing air-bass to Cheap Trick's "Gonna Raise Hell" the whole way home.

Now, as if on cue, Colin walks into Small's. He's met by the doorman, who's asking for five bucks and a look at Colin's I.D. Slim-shouldered and 140 pounds, give or take a few Budweisers, Colin's not much bigger now than he was on that COTA bus. Smiling his son-of-a-salesman smile, he explains that he's with the band, and then he beelines for the bar. "So, Biggie," he says. "What's the beer situation?"

Biggie pulls twenty wooden tokens from his pocket. "Free domestics."

"Beautiful," Colin says.

Dave and Pooch divide the tokens into four stacks of five.

"Look at us," Colin says. He's holding a to-go coffee with one hand, mussing his hair with the other. "Out on tour. All set to rock." He puts his hand on my shoulder and says, "We've got our balls back."

What he means is, *You've* got *your* balls back.

Watershed hasn't played a show in five months, not since the August night in Columbus when we celebrated the release of our live CD, *Three Chords and a Cloud of Dust II*.[1] A couple days later I committed the cardinal sin. I moved away. Far away. Kate and I packed our furniture into a freight-sized Penske and drove across the country to Tacoma, Washington, where I'd taken a job as a visiting English professor at Pacific Lutheran University. For one year I'd teach and write, and Kate would finish her dissertation. Colin was hurt, disappointed, pissed off. As far as he was concerned, I'd checked my balls at the state line. Still, we promised to keep the band together despite the 2,500 miles that separated us. And sure enough, before Kate and I had unpacked in Tacoma, the e-mails from Colin were flying.

Subject: Rocking
We owe it to ourselves to work the live album. When does your school let out for Xmas?

Rock,
CG

I deleted the first few messages, because I knew everybody was too busy at home to head out on tour. I was acclimating to a new city, a new time zone, a new job. When we weren't on campus, Kate and I were cruising up to Seattle for dim sum or hiking Mount Rainier or ferrying to islands in the Puget Sound. Biggie was newly married and knee deep in planning his honeymoon. Dave and his wife, Sarah, had just brought home their second child, a son. Pooch and his wife, Christy, were potty training their daughter. And Colin had finally scraped together enough cash to buy the coffee shop where, for ten years, he'd worked as a barista. Now he was clocking sixty hours a week at Colin's Coffee, working to keep up with the tuition at his five-year-old son's Montessori school. And yet somehow he found the time to call the clubs, e-mail the booking contacts, and send the promo packages. By December this tour was on the calendar.

One Saturday morning, while Kate was at her 8:00 a.m. yoga class, I sat at my desk in Washington State—a continent away from my best and oldest friends—and I read the e-mail from Colin that spelled out the itinerary. There were ten shows all told in a span of sixteen days. I scrolled through the list. Detroit, Milwaukee, Chicago. Cleveland, Toledo, New York. Then down to Baltimore, Charlotte, and Raleigh. We'd cap it all with a headlining show at Columbus's Lifestyles Communities Pavilion, a venue that—despite its unfortunate, vaguely prophylactic-sounding name—held 2,200 people. Playing the LC would be a high profile homecoming, for Watershed and for me, but more importantly, a room that size would let us know where our career stood. A huge crowd would be evidence that we still mattered. An empty house might convince us to finally hang it up, to spend more time with our families, our day jobs. Either way, booking the LC was a gutsy call by Colin, like going all-in in Texas Hold 'Em.

I scanned through the tour dates one more time, and then walked to Kate's office and stood before the US map she'd hung on the wall. I ran my finger eastward from Tacoma, over the Cascades and the Rockies, across the Great Plains and into Ohio, then northbound up US 23 toward the mitten of Michigan. If Kate had been home, I would have said to her the same thing Colin just said to me: *We've got our balls back.*

"Order-up quick, ladies," Biggie says, tapping his Maglite on the bar. "Time to make with the rock."

Colin rakes his stack of drink tokens. "Joe The Animal isn't going anywhere."

Biggie and Ricki C. beat it to the band side to run the guitars through one last tuning, and Bettie the bartender raises her eyebrows to ask who wants what.

"I'll take five Budweisers," Dave says. "How many you want, Pooch?"

"Four," Pooch says to Bettie. Then he flips his last token toward Dave. "And one Percocet."

While the drummer and rhythm guitarist negotiate their buzzes, I slide over to Colin, who's alternating between coffee and beer. A poor man's speedball.

I ask him where he found the coffee. Small's Bar is in Hamtramck, a part of Detroit you wouldn't want to explore at night on foot.

"King Video and Convenience Mart," he says. "Across the street." He makes a wafting motion over the cup. "It's not bad. I'm getting notes of beef jerky and pork rind."

Bettie is lining up beers two at a time, and Dave is reaching into his coat pocket, fulfilling Pooch's painkiller prescription.

"On the road again," I say to Colin.

"We needed to get out of the house and rock a little bit," he says.

"You made it happen." I raise my beer to him. "Credible bars. Visible cities."

"I don't give a shit about the gigs. It's great just to be hanging out with my friends."

Like Colin, I'm jacked to be back with the guys. But as we stand here, sipping beer, I have no doubt he does give a shit about the gigs. We all do. We need this tour to tell us there's still a place in rock and roll for old lizards like us. But neither of us can say as much. Not out loud. Not when we're about to take the stage for five people.

Soon Biggie's heading our way. He looks ready to beat somebody down. "Seriously," he says. "Let's go-fucking-go."

I shoulder my bass and walk to my usual spot in front of Dave's drums. Pooch stands to my left, plugging his Les Paul into his amp. Colin's bending to his overdrive pedal at stage right, tweaking the knobs. Satisfied, he twists the volume on his Telecaster and hits two searing D-chords. *Wank-wank.* Then Pooch flips his amp's standby and joins in. *Wank-wank, wank-wank.* I thump a couple eighth notes to make sure my rig is working, feeling the low rumble in my scrotum. After five months grading essays and keeping office hours, these noises, distorted and raw, add up to a beautiful racket.

Dave pops his snare a few times, tightening the lug nuts until the drum cracks the way it ought to, and then he looks to Colin, who nods and mouths *Go, Dave. Go.* And the drummer launches into "Suckerpunch," tonight's opening song. Colin jukes up to the mic and counts "*one, two, one-two-three-four.*" Watershed is off and rocking.

I sing the first line, and with the houselights down and the PAR cans shining in my eyes, I can't see the audience at all. I can almost fool myself into thinking we're headlining for twenty thousand up the road at The Palace of Auburn Hills, for the boys in row J and the girls in row K and the poor suckers back in row ZZ. I know that as soon as I take two steps to the left, where the lights aren't directly in my face, I'll look out and see Joe The Animal and *BAM,* I'll be right back at Small's. Playing for five people. But that's okay. There's no point worrying about the 19,995 who didn't show up tonight; our job is to play for the five who did.

So Dave will chuck his drumsticks to the ceiling and catch them without missing a beat. Pooch will jump like a young Pete Townshend, putting the exclamation mark on a big chord. Colin will hop across the stage like the bastard son of Chuck Berry and Angus Young, spitting beer into the lights and urging the audience to clap and sing along. And the show will end with Colin and Dave flat on their backs, the stage littered with guitars and cymbal stands and beer bottles. All the while I'll be thinking, go ahead. Call it a comeback. Watershed's back in the van, back on the road, aiming toward Chicago and New York and a big-ass room in

Columbus. But first, tonight. Topping the bill in Detroit. The main event in Motown. Arena or no, we're *headliners.* And the word will rattle around my skull, carrying me through the between-song silence, until the moment immediately after the show, when I'll take the piss I've been holding for an hour, and there, on the wall above the toilet, I'll read graffiti that says, Some nights you headline, some nights you just play last.

2

Happy Days
Milwaukee, Wisconsin

"THANK YOU! GOODNIGHT!"

I take off my bass and raise it high in the air, as I've seen so many MTV-caliber rock stars do. I stand there, proud as a torchbearer, sweating like a sparring partner, holding my guitar by the neck, headstock nearly touching the lights, and I want so badly for the crowd to chant our name. To cheer for one more song. To stomp their feet and slam their seats and not let us go anywhere. I want them to want me. I'm begging them to beg me.

But this is the minor leagues, buddy, so here's what we get: We get golf-applause. We get a "yeah!" or two. We get five minutes to get our shit off the stage.

What do you do for an encore when there is no encore?

I head to the merch table, where some kid with multiple piercings walks up and says, "You guys rocked. Where you from?" And he looks over our CDs and asks what album that last song was on, but he doesn't buy because ten bucks is ten bucks and beer ain't cheap. Then he pulls a CD from his coat pocket, hands it to me, and says, "If you ever want to trade gigs with us, man, look me up." I don't want to open for this guy's band. I don't want his band to open for us. But for some reason I feel guilty about taking his CD, so I swap him one of ours, quid pro quo, even though we can't afford an even swap because our record company charges us five bucks per disc. Now, thanks to a trade I didn't ask for or want, we're down five. We'll have to sell another CD to get back to zero. But nobody else is showing the slightest interest. They're grabbing their coats and purses and filing toward the door.

I beat it to the bar, and no, beer isn't cheap. I drank through my drink tokens by mid-set, so now I have to crack my own wallet, and this gets me thinking there ought to be a law, some equity-in-the-workplace statute that mandates unlimited beer for bands. Free draft at least. And food too. At 50 percent off, minimum. Because it suddenly occurs to me that the last thing I ate was a truck-stop banana and a granola bar, and that was about ten hours ago. Since then I've had two cups of coffee and six beers.

I ask Bettie the bartender if anybody's serving this late, and she tells me about a diner that cooks up a furiously good omelet. It's just ten miles down the expressway. Take the second exit. Or is it the third? No, the second. Then go though two lights, make a left and another left and it's right there. You can't miss it.

But we can miss it. We will miss it. And I don't want to drag everybody on a wild omelet chase anyway. They'd all be asleep by the time we reached this house of furious eggs. So I ask Bettie, whose cleavage, I'm just now noticing, is dotted with freckles, how 'bout Taco Bell? She pulls a ballpoint from her back pocket, and I force myself to maintain eye contact as her wifebeater slides up her belly, revealing three inches of milky skin and a string of panty elastic. Scratching directions on a napkin, I think: This is rock and roll, right? Instead of charting a course to a cheese chalupa, shouldn't I be drawing a map back to her apartment? Shouldn't she be sliding me four quarters to drop into the ladies' room condom machine? Isn't *rock* = *sex* a universal law on par with Newtonian physics?

Never mind that I'm married and I'd never cheat on Kate. Even if I weren't wearing a ring, the odds of me bedding the bartender or anyone else tonight are roughly as long as me launching our van to the moon.

One: The crowd's light. From a sheer numbers perspective, if there are only two or three women in the bar, how many of them are realistically looking for casual sex with an obscure musician from out of town? Casual sex with a rock star maybe, but it's tough to make a case for your rockstardom when you've just played for fewer people than are at this moment idling in the Taco Bell drive thru.

Two: Say there exists in the world a woman who fantasizes about hooking up with little-known bass players. Say she's in the bar tonight.

Even say she walks up, grabs me by the shoulders, and says, *Fuck me, you four-stringed beast.* Where would we do it? Her place? Okay, but how would I get there? Chances are she doesn't sleep in a cot above the bar. She probably lives across town, in the suburbs. And even if she's sober enough to drive me to her pad (forgetting for the moment that sober women rarely shake you by the shoulders 'til you fuck them), and even if she doesn't have a boyfriend/roommate/parent that might nix the deal, and even if we could manage to wrangle a condom and do the deed before either of us passed out, then still, how do I get back to the van before the band takes off for tomorrow's show in Milwaukee? Straying too far from the herd, making the band drive hell's half acre in search of your horny ass is a surefire way to get 'em all strangling mad. Bands break up at those velocities.

So why not do it *in* the van? After all there's a whole bumper sticker genre dedicated to that very act: IF THE VAN'S ROCKIN', THEN DON'T COME KNOCKIN' etc., etc. Thing is, the van is the sun around which a band's galaxy rotates, so except for the forty-five minutes we're on stage, somebody is always holed up there—Dave calling his wife, Pooch swigging a beer, Colin tuned in to the last inning of the ballgame. Assuming I could carve out ten minutes when the van is empty, and assuming this bass-fetishist and I could pull off the gymnastics required to get our pants down and our pelvises close enough to physically do it without hitting our heads on the ceiling or falling off the bench seat and onto the floor, then we'd still have to compensate for the frigid weather; the various and sundry smells (sweat, smoke, flatulence, *last* night's Taco Bell leftovers); the backpacks, duffel bags, and wet clothes heaped on the seats; and finally, the used water jugs and beer cans and Gatorade bottles scattered everywhere—some of which now contain tobacco spit or urine. Overcome these disincentives and I'd bump up against a single hard truth: A woman who consents to sex in a van littered with spittle and piss is not a woman you should have sex with.

What about the hotel? Sometimes there isn't one, so the plan is to drive through the night to the next gig, in the next town, where we have booked a room. And when we get there at nine or ten in the morning, we'll try to convince the desk clerk to let us check in early. If he doesn't, then the unshowered, unshaven band will raid the continental breakfast and snooze in the lobby, drawing suspicious looks from the well-scrubbed business-types, until the clerk finds us a clean room. Then we'll sleep the eight hours until soundcheck, and we'll sleep again after the show, giving us two "nights" for the price of one. As thrifty as this strategy is, it doesn't ease the logistics of romantic liaisons.

Tonight happens to be a night when we do have a room in town, but it's just that—*a* room. One. For six people. Four on the beds, two on the floor. Bettie would make seven. True, a lack of comfort and privacy has never stopped anyone who really wants sex from forging ahead, but any woman who'd fuck me on a hotel carpet, next to five snoring guys . . . well, this'd be much more an indictment of me than her.

On this night when there is no encore, when nobody seems to care if we play one more song or not, I can fantasize about pursuing the Apollo-size project that is getting laid. But I won't do it. Because I am married. Because I'd never cheat on Kate. Because I'm probably just a few years younger than Bettie's mom. Besides, I've played in a band long enough to know that after-show sex really only exists for MTV-caliber rock stars, and even for them it has pretty much dried up. Rock and roll is old. Music played by dads, for dads. The official soundtrack of Viagra.

Still there's one further obstacle keeping my hands on the safe side of Bettie's panties. It's stacked near the back door, and unlike some mythical bass-loving, spit- and pee-tolerant sexpot, it's not going to load itself into the van. Here in rock and roll's trenches, the show might be over, but the work isn't done. So I fold the Taco Bell directions into my back pocket and hand Bettie her pen. I smile and say thanks. See you next time. I move down the bar to where the guy who gave me his CD is finishing his beer, and I say, thanks again, dude. Can't wait to check out the disc. Then I put on my coat, slide on my gloves, and walk toward the seven hundred pounds of speaker cabinets, amplifiers, and drum hardware that are always waiting to be humped.

Click-click-click. "Housekeeping." *Click-click-click.*

I wake with a sore throat.

"Housekeeping."

And the maid tapping her key card on the door. *Click-click-click.*

I swallow thickly, my soft palette on fire. One day on the road and I'm already sick. "Housekeeping," she says, easing the door open.

"Need a few minutes." My voice is as gruff as a longshoreman's.

"Sorry, baby." And she pulls the door shut.

Daylight slices through the gap in the blackout curtains. Pooch, who six hours ago passed out next to me, is gone. I look down to the floor between the two beds: Colin's up and out too. And Dave's sleeping bag lies limp. Ricki C. doesn't drink, so he's always awake early. What self-respecting band makes the continental breakfast? Sleeping as late as you want is one of the best things about being on tour. Then again Colin, Dave, and Pooch are dads. To them 7:30 or 8:00 must feel like Mötley Crüe–style hedonism.

Across the horizon of the bed, I see the snoring lump that is Biggie. Keeping this train on the rails has got to be exhausting. The guy has put in twenty-three years as Watershed's accountant, business manager, tour manager, publicist, booking agent, graphic designer, lighting tech, merch man, sound guy, electrician, technology guru, webmaster, mechanic, housekeeper, designated driver, and all-around *consigliere.* He's designed enough great flyers to fill a coffee table book, logged more miles than a NASCAR driver. He's been the first and best audience for our songs, and quick to check our egos when they needed checking. Biggie has earned his sleep.

Like Colin and me, Mike "Biggie" McDermott was an Estates kid. We met him in seventh grade, on one of those Sundays when we were playing football on the front lawn of the elementary school. Colin had an arm as skinny as a Wiffle ball bat, but he was usually the quarterback. He'd draw a post pattern on the front of his shirt, and I'd be running the route, waving my arms to show him how open I was, when suddenly I'd hear Aerosmith screaming through the autumn afternoon. Jogging back to the huddle, I'd see the stocky kid carrying a jam box across the grass.

"Hey, McDermott," Colin would say. "Get out here and even up the teams."

Biggie was squat and strong, built like the UNIVAC. And like a supercomputer, he always seemed to be calculating something that none of us was smart enough to understand. But Biggie never played. With his radio blasting *Toys in the Attic,* he was perfectly happy standing on the sidelines.

Managers, agents, record companies, and even Herb—our first drummer—have come and gone, but Biggie's been watching from the side of the stage the whole time. For what? There's not much glory in this for any of us. For Biggie, there's even less. Whenever I ask him why he's stuck with the band for so long, he says, "Same reason as you."

I'm never quite sure what that reason is. I've always felt vaguely unqualified for a life in rock and roll.

"It's got nothing to do with rock and roll," Biggie says. "Could be a bakery, could be a bait shop." He presses a fat pinch of Copenhagen into his lower lip. "I do this because I do it with you and Colin."

A bowl of fruit is all that's left of the continental breakfast. The khaki-and-loafers set has already banged down the Raisin Bran and mini-muffins. They're out doing whatever business they've come to Warren, Michigan, to do, so there's nobody in the lobby who isn't in Watershed. We've spent many nights on couches and floors[2], but these days, because Kate's sister works for Marriott, we get the employee rate at Fairfields and Courtyards. So we stay in the suburbs, near office blocks and airports, where parking is cheap and gear thieves are scarce. Last night's room cost thirty-five dollars, which is more than we made at the door, but it's a sound investment in our health and happiness. Even the trivial amenities—a bowl of fruit, free coffee, a lobby where we can spread out before packing shoulder to shoulder in the van—go a long way toward keeping everybody sane.

I grab an orange, hoping the Vitamin C will get to work on my throat. Ricki C. is bopping around the lobby in the sneakers of an emo kid, but he's got the paunch and jowls of that kid's dad. Colin, in his sag-in-the-ass jeans and bleach-splotchy shirt, is eating dry Cheerios with his fingers and reading *USA Today*. For a small guy, he takes up a lot of space. He's sitting at one table, but his backpack rests at a second table, his jacket at another table still. His unzipped bag waits in a corner near the front desk, where the clerk is eyeing it suspiciously, as one might a collarless dog. Me, with my bald head and Eastern Bloc cheekbones, I'm wiping my nose on the back of my hand and clearing my throat like a wino. The clerk shoots me a look that says *I'm going to have to clean up after you guys, aren't I?*

Two tables down, Dave and Pooch, both of them January pale, are staring up at the TV, where Mitt Romney appears, looking genetically engineered for focus group appeal.

"There's your boy, Pooch," Colin says.

Pooch is the one guy in the band that fancies himself a Republican, one of those fiscally conservative/socially liberal half-assers.

"Which means you want everything, but you don't want to pay for it," Colin and I always tell him.

"You guys want everything even though you *can't* pay for it," he answers, which, considering all the expenses that loom between now and the tour finale in Columbus, sounds like a fair summation of the philosophy of Watershed.

While Colin and Ricki C. give Pooch political hell, Dave takes a call from Sarah. They've got two kids. Their son, Charlie, is five months old and was born with an underdeveloped gall bladder and testicles that hadn't dropped. He was jaundiced and incubated for so long, he needed physical therapy to strengthen his neck. The kid has already had two surgeries, the most recent just a few weeks ago. Charlie has been suffering from flu-like symptoms ever since. So while Dave is here on the road, Sarah is home with a sick infant, worried about how she's going to manage her work schedule, arrange for babysitters, and get their daughter to ballet lessons on time. I peel my orange and skim the sports page, trying not to listen to Dave's end of the conversation. Something about medical expenses, bill collectors, and cashing in an IRA.

Biggie eases the Econoline to the lobby doors, our cue to get our asses in gear. As we shuffle out to the Michigan cold, he's tidying the van, gathering the empty water bottles and pretzel bags. I open the back doors and squeeze my duffel bag between the kick drum and the cymbal case. Dave pushes his sleeping bag into a slot between the basses and the ceiling. Colin, Pooch, and Ricki C. shove their suitcases against the gear, and as long as somebody holds all this stuff in place, it fits just fine, but as soon as Pooch lets go to shut the doors, Colin's bag drops to the blacktop.

"Help, Biggie," Pooch says, because Biggie is the best packer in the universe. In another life he could have been a NASA engineer, designing the International Space Station to maximize storage capacity, industrial efficiency, and general ergonomic awesomeness. But alas, he's stuck tour-managing Watershed. His job is to get Colin's bag from the curb to the cargo bay.

Biggie hands me the garbage, which I empty in the hotel's ashtray cans, hoping that dumping piss bottles doesn't violate the terms of our Marriott employee discount. When I come back, everyone is sitting in his usual spot: Biggie behind the wheel, Ricki C. shotgun, Dave and Pooch on the second bench, and Colin in the back row.

"Still got that old van smell," I say, scooting next to Colin. But actually this van is showroom new. Probably rolled off an assembly line not far from here. It now smells a little like Small's Bar, but we haven't yet soiled it too badly, which is good, because we don't own it. Hertz does. "A fucking rental," I say to Colin. "How the mighty have fallen."

A few weeks before Kate and I moved west, in a blinding flash of fiscal responsibility, Watershed made the tough decision to sell our van. We'd named it Sheldon "The Machine" Levine after Jack Lemmon's washed-up salesman in *Glengarry Glen Ross*. Like this Hertz, Sheldon was a fifteen-passenger Econoline, and he was the most luxe of the three vans we've owned. But we couldn't justify making payments during the year I'd be in Tacoma, so we let Sheldon go for $7,500 to an Amish guy from Holmes County, Ohio. The Amish dude owned a thriving business—barn building, naturally—and even though his religion kept him from driving, he needed a vehicle for his employees to get from barn to barn in. He showed up at my apartment with two non-Amish helpers: one guy to drive everybody down to Columbus, a second to drive our van up to Holmes County. After Biggie and I took his money and drew up a receipt, the Amish guy slid us his business card, complete with a cell phone number and an e-mail address.

"No offense," I said. "But are you, like, allowed to own cell phones and computers?"

He told us he couldn't own the technology himself—but his *business* could. Even the Amish have loopholes.

So now a bearded barn magnate is tearing through Holmes County in Watershed's van, and we're tooling around suburban Detroit in a stinking Hertz rental.

Biggie swings onto 696 West, and if this were a movie, now would be the time to cue "Born to Be Wild." Except I can't cue "Born to Be Wild" because I'm not driving. Driver picks the soundtrack. On this Friday morning, Biggie's punched up the Ricky Gervais podcast on his iPod, and it occurs to me that in 1990—the year we started touring—the words *podcast* and *iPod* didn't exist. Back then Biggie kept a milk crate filled with cassettes on the floor next to the driver's seat, and if there was one tape he really wanted to hear—The Cult's *Electric* or the first Georgia Satellites record, say—he'd lean over and dig through the crate at seventy-five mph, taking the steering wheel with him until the rumble strips finally barked, telling him to right the ship. Many times I braced for impact, figuring us for dead, all because Biggie had a hankering for Bob Mould's *Black Sheets of Rain*. Later, we bought a portable CD player with a cassette adapter, and Biggie'd have to balance it on his thigh to keep it from skipping. A pothole or sharp turn would knock the player to the floor, and the ensuing reach would send us back to the shoulder and the rumble strips.

Those were the technological dark ages. Biggie has outfitted this rental, like Sheldon before it, with an A-B-C-D switchbox that serves as a multimedia command center. Push the A button and we hear the radio/CD player. The B button gives us the iPod. Button C connects to the satellite radio. The D button controls the video system Biggie has rigged to the ceiling: a combo TV/VCR, with an Xbox attachment for video games and DVDs. We're also wired to the teeth with cell phones, BlackBerrys, and laptops—meaning that now, instead of fifty milk-crated cassettes, most of music history is at our fingertips. If somebody wants to hear a song that isn't already loaded on the iPod, we fire up the wireless card in Biggie's ThinkPad, surf to a Russian website that sells mp3s for a dime, and pluck the song from the sky—all in less time than it takes to boil water. No wonder the record companies are screwed.

Even mobbed-up with so much technology, everyone but Biggie is staring at plain-old written text this morning. I've got the deluxe, laminated *Rand McNally Motor Carrier's Atlas* spread across my lap. In the passenger seat, Ricki C. is plowing through Joan Didion's *A Book of Common Prayer* for the fourth or fifth time. Pooch thumbs a guitar magazine. Dave skims the Nikki Sixx autobiography. On the bench next to me, Colin's scanning the back cover of the new Replacements bio. A live Ramones DVD plays on the video screen over Pooch's head—on mute, like a moving poster. Nobody's paying the Ramones much attention, but it's good to know they're here when we need 'em.

As we slide into rural Michigan, Biggie's dividing his attention between the road and his newest gizmo: the GPS navigation system. Through the stereo speakers, the GPS voice is saying, "After five hundred yards, exit right" in an accent that sounds like a British Airways flight attendant who secretly wears nipple clamps under her pantsuit. We've dubbed her the Map Slut.

"You don't have to scream at me," Biggie says to her, but like all submissives, he finds the dominatrix's directives super hot. He went to Best Buy and paid good money for this abuse.

"After four hundred yards, exit right," the Map Slut commands. Her steadiness is both reassuring and creepy.

Biggie looks from the windshield to the GPS screen and back, confused. I-696 is about to intersect with both I-96 and I-275. "*Which* right?"

"After three hundred yards, exit right."

I could flip a few pages in the atlas and help Biggie out, but I'm busy looking at Utah, confirming that I-70 does in fact dead-end south of Provo. You never know when a detail like this might come in handy, and I like to store this information in my head, not in a box that suctions to the dashboard.

"After two hundred yards, exit right."

Colin looks up from the Replacements book. "We want *94*, don't we?" he says. "Toward Chicago." Like me, he's suspicious of the Map Slut.

Biggie's locked on the screen. "My choices are 96 or 275." He doesn't want choices. He wants marching orders.

"After one hundred yards, exit right."

Biggie is paying so much attention to the tiny, virtual GPS screen, he's blind to what is happening in the real, live windshield. Ahead is a full-scale, three-dimensional road sign that reads I-275 TO I-94 DETROIT/ CHICAGO.

I lean toward the front seat. "Get off here, Biggie."

Biggie finally looks through the windshield. We're almost past the exit. "Which—"

"Here!" I say, and Biggie swerves us onto the cloverleaf.

The centrifugal force pushes Dave into Pooch and me into Colin. "Whoa," says Dave, laughing as he tries not to lose his place in his book. Pooch holds onto his glasses.

Under my weight, Colin goes tense. He's doubly violated. He hates having his personal space invaded, and Biggie's driving scares him shitless. For our whole career he's ridden nervous, certain that the fatal crash waits round every bend.

As we flatten onto 275, Colin rights himself and says, "Catlike reflexes, Biggie."

I notice that Biggie, as usual, isn't wearing a seat belt. "You're married now, Biggie," I say. "A responsible citizen. You've got to buckle that shit in."

"Know why I don't wear a seat belt?" he says. "If I ever get us into an accident, I'd rather die than have Colin saying 'I told you so' for the rest of my life."

We all laugh harder than the line deserves. The mixture of alcohol, caffeine, and too little sleep is starting to make everybody squirrely. The Toll—a Columbus band Biggie once roadied for—called this squirreliness "The K Factor." *K* stands for *Keith,* as in *Keith Richards.* The Toll figured that Richards lives at 100K; anyone else would die instantly if they scored half as high. Watershed is probably only hitting 5K this morning, but it's enough that I'm buckled over, slapping the atlas, barely able to see the Ramones through the tears welling up in my eyes.

Past Kalamazoo, Biggie has switched off the Gervais podcast, and the rest of us have shut our books. Out the window there's nothing but acreage, fields and farmhouses.

"How's the stocks, Pooch?" Colin says.

Pooch's personal satellite radio is plugged into one ear, set to Bloomberg News. "Taking a beating," he says. "Google's down. Apple's down."

"The market is just gambling for rich people," Colin says. He once wrote a lyric that goes, *I don't trust a man who checks his stocks before the box scores.*

Pooch turns off his radio. "Good thing my latest investment's safe and secure." He points to his guitar magazine, which features the Foo Fighters on the cover. "A Dave Grohl signature Gibson."

"Your in*vest*ment," I say. "A guitar."

"That's ridiculous," Colin says.

"Comes with a certificate of authenticity," Pooch says. "Signed by Grohl himself."

"You're half a retard," Biggie says.

Ricki C. turns toward the back. "And you see this as a money-maker, Pooch?"

Pooch laughs. "Why not?"

"It's like investing in baseball cards," Colin says. "Or rare coins."

"Or Pez dispensers," Biggie says.

"The value is only going up," Pooch says.

"Why the fuck would you assume that?" Biggie says.

"Because Dave Grohl is the new Paul McCartney, Biggie," says Pooch. "What if you bought a McCartney Hofner bass in 1962? What would that be worth today?"

Biggie shakes his head. "Jackass."

"The new Mc*Cartney?*" says Ricki C. "Seriously?"

"Who else is there?" Pooch looks toward Dave, Colin, and me for backup. He didn't listen to rock music until college, when grunge hit big. Before that his favorite act was MC Hammer. He wore the Chess King parachute pants and everything.

"If Nirvana was the new Beatles," Dave says, "then I guess the Foo Fighters could be the new Wings."

"And Grohl is McCartney?" Biggie says. "Bullshit."

"Who the fuck is Wings?" says Pooch.

When the laughter dies down, Colin says, "The Foo Fighters are the new Van Halen."

"But David Lee Roth is back in the band now," Dave says. "That makes Van Halen the new Van Halen."

"Plus Van Halen is a *band*." I say. "The Foo Fighters are all Grohl."

"True," says Pooch.

I think for a second. "I'm calling Dave Grohl the new Bob Seger."

Dave and Ricki C. give me a "fair enough" nod.

Pooch looks confused. "The 'Like a Rock' guy?"

"Tons of radio hits. Just like the Foo Fighters," I say. "I bet Grohl would agree with me."

"Melissa Etheridge was already the new Bob Seger," Colin says.

Biggie breaks into the chorus of Melissa Etheridge's "Come to My Window," doing a little dance in his seat.

"No," I say. "Kid Rock is the new Seger."

"Exactly!" Dave says.

"Wait-wait-wait," I say. "I got it. The Foo Fighters are the new Journey."

"Daughtry is the new Journey," Dave says.

"Who's Daughtry?" says Colin.

"Who's Journey?" says Pooch. And so it goes until we stop to piss in Indiana.

I take over the driving duties, not because Biggie's tired[3], but because my sore throat has made it hard to concentrate on either the *Rand McNally* or *The Lay of the Land*, the Richard Ford book I brought along. Be it in 1:100,000 scale or in words and sentences, I'm too tired to read the land in miniature. I need the land writ large: ribbons of road, fields that stretch to the horizon, and 180 degrees of sky.

On the outskirts of industrial Gary, I ask Colin how's business at the coffee shop.

"Not bad," he says. Then he backs away from the pat answer. "It's been tight lately, I guess. But it's always tight. Hard to make a living on water and beans."

"That's why Starbucks is now a record store," I say.

Pooch the Capitalist chimes in. "What's the profit margin on, say, a regular coffee?"

"Not as much as on a double mocha macchiato," Colin says. "The fancy shit keeps me in business."

He tells us that to supplement the family income, his wife, Erin—a counselor who recently quit her longtime job at the Columbus AIDS Taskforce to open a private practice—has started holding wellness classes at Colin's Coffee. These classes are meant to enlighten people, sure, but they also increase traffic in the shop and build Erin's private client list. Colin and Erin both have to hustle.

This talk of enlightenment reminds Colin of a story one of his regulars—a hulking guy who played O-line for the Miami Hurricanes in the Nineties—recently told him. One year Miami was up by forty-something on Iowa. Late. The game was essentially over. But on every down the Miami lineman was just getting hammered by this big-ass Iowa farm boy. So between plays, Colin's regular said to the Iowa kid, "Easy, dude. We're kicking your asses."

The farm boy took out his mouth guard and said, "I don't care what the score is. I'm going to hit you as hard as I can. On every play. Until the clock hits zero."

"Because it's about *pride*, man," Colin says, as a way of putting a period on the story. "Pride's what keeps you going whether you're running a coffee shop or playing in a band."

Pooch laughs. He actually played college football, starting quarterback for the Denison Big Red. The game soured him, as it has done for many athletes. Now he thinks sports—and sports metaphors—are stupid and silly. "How much pride did we take in at the door last night?" he says.

"Doesn't matter," I say.

"The point is, we didn't phone it in," Colin says. "Most bands would have. We can be proud of that."

"Hey, Mark," Biggie says. He always calls Pooch *Mark*. "You think your buddy Dave Grohl gives a shit how many people are in the crowd?" Biggie then launches into a diatribe about how any band worth a damn plays to honor the long history of rock and roll that came before it. He draws an evolutionary line from Chuck Berry and Jerry Lee Lewis to Bruce Springsteen and Steve Earle. Circling back to the topic at hand, he says, "Don't play for the crowd; play for the twenty years we've put into this thing."

I ask Colin if he's talked to Thomas O'Keefe, our manager. I'm wondering how tickets for the LC show are selling.

"Last Thomas heard, we'd sold something like thirty," Colin says. "But it's early."

It is early. But jeez. It's gonna take more than pride to fill those 2,200 seats. And I need to believe that our twenty years together have added up to something more quantifiable than pride. Pride's important, sure. But it's the sucker prize. Sometimes you just want to be the team that's up forty.

WISCONSIN WELCOMES YOU, reads the sign at the border. True, true. The Badger State has been especially welcoming to Watershed. We're huge in Wisconsin. We used to be, anyway—in the mid-Nineties. Maybe not huge, exactly. And not in all of Wisconsin. Really just in the Fox River Valley—Green Bay, Oshkosh, and Appleton. And, yeah, okay . . . mostly just in Appleton. But, man, in Appleton, Watershed once was big enough to make a soundguy say, "Up here you guys are like Rush." All thanks to the airplay we were getting on WAPL—*The Rockin' Apple*. We were the station's pet project. DJs would interview us. The program director would add us to whatever festival he was promoting that season—The Summer Jam! or The Spring River Rally! Unfortunately the glory never followed us to Milwaukee or Madison, and nobody south of Fond Du Lac would ever mistake Watershed for Canada's finest Ayn Rand–inspired power trio.

Tonight's gig is at Milwaukee's Points East Pub, a neighborhood joint known for hot wings and Riverwest stein, the microbrew named for this part of town. Back in 1994, when we first played this bar, Riverwest was a workingman's neighborhood, heavy with taverns and package stores, places where the guys that clocked in at Harley Davidson or Miller could knock the taste of the factory out of their mouths. Now as I circle the block, it seems clear that, unlike Detroit, Milwaukee has made the turn into the post-industrial economy. Riverwest in particular feels newly buffed and polished. A Chipotle and a Buca di Beppo are open nearby. Two blocks away, Brady Street is lined with wine bars and $25-a-plate restaurants. There are as many galleries and boutiques as there are taverns.

I'm hoping the Points East won't fall victim to the usual dynamic: (1) Rock club goes into low rent neighborhood; (2) Rock club helps make that neighborhood cool; (3) Newly cool neighborhood now attracts high-end restaurants and shops that sell $300 jeans; (4) Bar owner can't afford the skyrocketing rent, so the club goes under. In Columbus we recently lost the long-standing and semi-legendary Little Brother's. Just before Kate and I came home for Christmas, the Crocodile Café in Seattle went dark. Even CBGB, the Taj Mahal of rock clubs, has pulled down its iconic awning. If the club that gave the Ramones, Blondie, and the Talking Heads their start isn't immune, what club is?[4]

I carry my basses up the icy stairs and see that the Points East has remodeled since our last gig here. The stage is bigger, the bar rebuilt.

There's good, polished wood everywhere. I try to imagine the club the way it was years ago, when we naively assumed that we'd be able to parlay the Appleton crowds into a huge Milwaukee following. One weekend we drove all the way here from Columbus, 450 miles, just to play one show. Drive up, play for two hours, turn around and head home. After that night's soundcheck, Colin, Dave, and I were walking toward Lake Michigan when we came upon Shank Hall.[5] A line stretched down the block, so we asked who was playing.

"Scrawl!" was the response.

A guy wearing a Scrawl T-shirt flashed his ticket. "Sold out."

Scrawl was from Columbus, and we were friends with them. We'd even covered one of their songs. But it was depressing to watch two hundred people line up to see a Columbus band that wasn't us. It got more depressing later that night when only ten people showed up at our gig. Heroes in Appleton. Zeroes in Milwaukee.

We made the best of it by getting absolutely bombed. Colin forgot chords. Dave dropped beats. I made clam after clam on the bass. Until that night we'd always taken Watershed so seriously, so professionally. We only drank after the show. Almost never smoked pot. Never did coke or acid. Wouldn't even consider heroin or meth. We'd always been the Richie Cunninghams of rock and roll, hardworking and earnest. But that night we didn't just phone in the show; we drunk-dialed it.

Biggie was furious afterwards, as he sat in the idling van, waiting for Colin, Dave, and me to pry ourselves from the bar. Eventually we stumbled out laughing, each carrying a sixpack we'd bought with the merch money.

By the time we hit the Illinois state line, I had a Budweiser in my crotch and Biggie's CD sleeve in my hands, but I couldn't get a song started because we were all giggling like Girl Scouts. Even Biggie. As bad as the show had been, we'd left it behind in Milwaukee.

"I got an idea," Colin said. "Next month, instead of hauling our gear all the way up to Wisconsin, let's load two cases of beer into the van, and just drive circles around Columbus all night. Fuck the gig."

Biggie shook his head and said, "I'm like a house mother for a freaking sorority."

Colin cracked open a beer and handed it to Biggie. "A sorority on wheels, Biggie. A sorority on *wheels*."

Now on the Points East stage, Colin spits beer into the lights. Pooch shakes his Les Paul to a wail of feedback. Dave stands on his kick drum, rocking the kit back and forth, surfing it, like it might collapse to splinters. I take off my bass and let it thump to the stage.

"Thank you! Goodnight!"

Tonight was a good night.

Because after soundcheck, Colin and I went for coffee, and we didn't have to settle for convenience store swill. In newly gentrifying Milwaukee, Starbucks is right across the street. Leafing through the local rags, looking for a preview of tonight's show, I came across a story about how Milwaukee citizens are debating whether to build a downtown sculpture of Arthur "The Fonz" Fonzarelli. The anti-statue faction argues that the city long ago outgrew its *Happy Days* image.

Meanwhile Colin was using his Sumatra to wash down two Stackers.[6] "Time to take my medicine," he said.

Tonight was a good night.

Because from the Starbucks sidewalk, I got Kate on the phone. She sounded settled, happy. She sounded glad to be home. "How's the show looking?" she said.

"I'm getting sick."

"You're worrying too much. Do a shot of whiskey."

"My voice is shot."

"Whiskey and honey then. And Joe?"

The lake wind blew down the street, biting hard.

"Kick their Milwaukee asses."

Tonight was a good night.

Because fifty people showed up. One kid drove all the way from Minneapolis; another came down from Appleton, another from Green Bay. A tableful of guys brought their girlfriends. Two of my Wisconsin cousins turned out. And one of Colin's. By the time we took the stage, Ricki C. had sold ten copies of *Three Chords II*.

Tonight is a good night.

Because now, in the bar, the thirty people who've stuck it out are still clapping. They want an encore. They're banging empty bottles on the tables, chanting our name, cheering for one more song. "Wa-ter-shed! Wa-ter-shed!" Maybe they're doing it in memory of a time when we were a little younger, a little more successful. But still, they're doing it.

Their voices take me back ten years and a hundred miles north, to Appleton. A club called Ryan's Ballroom. A night when we were bigger in the Fox River Valley than anywhere else on the planet. That night Colin, Dave, and I stood in the wings, ready to take the stage, and, like now, the crowd chanted "Wa-ter-shed!" Seven hundred Appletonians, who'd heard our song on the radio. "Wa-ter-shed!" Seven hundred Appletonians, who'd lined up in an icy parking lot to see the band that the DJs swore was the Next Big Thing. "Wa-ter-shed!"

From the side of the stage, Colin and I peeked out at the audience. Packed. We looked at each other and nodded *fuck yeah*.

Dave turned white as a hotel sheet. He was the new guy, just joined the band. He'd never played for a crowd that big, a crowd that loud. "Just *listen* to that," he said. "Wa-ter-shed! Wa-ter-shed!"

"Hey, Dave," Colin said, yelling to be heard over the chanting. "Let me give you a little advice." He took the drummer by the shoulders, looked him right in the eye, and smiled. "Don't get used to this."

3

Busload of Faith
Chicago, Illinois

CHICAGO IS A MONUMENT TO WHAT GELATINOUS BRAINS AND SOFT-tissued hands can build. The Great Fire of 1871 devastated the city, but those two thousand scorched acres became the slate upon which a new skyline was drawn in sheet glass and soaring steel. Chicagoans had faith enough in their own brass and muscle to start over. The only public building to survive the blaze was the Water Tower, and as Biggie steers us up Michigan Avenue toward the gig, the old tower is framed postcard-perfect in the van's windshield. *Tower,* of course, is a taller word now than it was 130-some years ago. Tonight Chicago's skyscrapers—those architectural Next Big Things for which the great fire cleared the ground—dwarf the castle-like structure, making it look like a Disney stage prop. The Tower doesn't tower over anything but Nike Town shoppers and taxicabs.

Looming black and massive over the Water Tower's slim shoulders is the biggest brother on the block, the John Hancock Center, a dual-antenna'd display of pure bravado. I can't look at the building without thinking of the day in 1995 when the program director at Chicago's WRCX elevatored us to a breathstoppingly high floor of the Hancock to be interviewed on the air by Mancow, the morning jock. The program director's office boasted a helicopter-eye-view of Lake Michigan. He stood before a bank of windows, against a backdrop of sailboats and lake chop, and nodded toward a gold record given to him by Collective Soul, the last band he'd taken under his wing. I squinted through the windows and imagined our voices—Colin's and mine—blasting from the building's twin antennae, carrying us into Chicagoland's car radios and onto the

Billboard charts. Like post-fire Chicago, Watershed's plan was always to build big.

The summer before our junior year at Worthington High, Sudden Shock! was still a two-man act: Colin and me jamming Kinks and KISS covers in his basement. If we were ever going to be a real band, we needed a drummer. But Colin insisted it couldn't be just anybody. To maintain the chemistry, the drummer had to be a guy we were already friends with. One afternoon in the basement he asked me, "You know Herb Schupp, right?"

I knew Herb Schupp. He was Colin's lab partner in biology class, and I was still chafed that the Gawels had taken Herb, and not me, to Ocean City, Maryland, that summer.

"He's our new drummer," Colin said.

But Herb didn't know how to play the drums. He'd never had a lesson, held sticks, or even sat down at a proper kit. All he'd done was beat hell out of school desks with his bare hands, banging out drum rolls during science experiments, his index fingers hammering paradiddles when they were supposed to be swabbing sodium-caked beakers and volumetric flasks. On the plus side, Herb listened to the same bands Colin and I did. Like Colin, Herb's favorite guitar player was Rainbow's Ritchie Blackmore. Six months earlier, Colin and Herb had each forked over fourteen bucks and mail-ordered a rare Ritchie Blackmore coffee table book. The book was rare because it was a Japanese import. And because it was a Japanese import, it was written entirely in Japanese. Colin and Herb paid almost thirty bucks for a book they couldn't read. They just looked at the pictures. Ritchie Blackmore shredding through a knuckle-busting solo. Ritchie Blackmore sipping a Guinness. Ritchie Blackmore in nylon shorts and knee socks, kicking a soccer ball. They shared joint custody, as the book spent one week in Colin's locker, the next week in Herb's. I was jealous of how close Colin and Herb were, but I was excited to finally fill out the band. So what if our new drummer had never played the drums? Colin had an eye for undeveloped talent. I was proof of that.

A few weeks later Colin and I were dragging our guitars and amps over to Herb's for our first practice. Both fifteen and not old enough to drive, we figured we'd just load our gear right onto the COTA bus. When the doors folded open, Colin squinted inside and said, "Can we bring these on here?"

The driver looked at us and our equipment. "As long as you got the bus fare," he said. "And as long as you do the liftin'." This is the great constant of rock and roll. Rock is heavy. Literally. Colin grunted under his amp, and my knees buckled as I struggled up the bus stairs with my fifty-watt Sunn. With our stalk-thin legs and farmer's tans, we were the most un-road-tested roadies in rock history. But we found seats for our amps and guitars, and we were on our way.

Herb was leaning against his front door, twirling a drumstick. The sleeves of his Polo shirt hugged biceps the size and shape of large lemons. He wore madras shorts and docksiders with no socks. His legs were well defined, country club tan. If not for the spinning drumstick, he might have been waiting for an afternoon tee time.

Colin looked around and said, "So where we gonna do this?"

Herb's mouth opened, but he didn't answer right away. Instead he pressed his lips together a few times before saying, "I-I-I." He stopped. Worked his lips again. His Adam's apple bobbed up, but no sound escaped.

Herb was a stutterer. But because he was built like a J. Crew model, he wore everything well, even a little verbal hiccup. If anything, his stutter made him more charming, like a strategically-placed mole or a cool-looking scar. "I-I was thinking we could try the space above the g-garage," he said. Once the first few words pushed away from the dock, he had smooth sailing. "But it's kind of a mess."

We walked up the creaky steps to the crawl space. It smelled of rotting wood and burnt tar, and the floor was littered with hundreds of unfolded, unrubberbanded *Suburban News* papers.

"The hell?" I laughed. "So many extras." On our *Columbus Dispatch* route, Colin and I had never had more than a paper or two to spare.

"W-what do you mean *extras?*" Herb said.

"All these," I said. "The leftovers."

Herb picked up a sun-faded *Suburban News* and chucked it against the wall. "This is all of them."

Colin crouched over a stack of newspapers. VILLAGE GREEN OX ROAST A BIG HIT, read one headline. The Ox Roast had happened over a year ago. "You don't deliver them? *Any* of them?" He peeled off a section, the pages stuck together in darkened clumps. "You just toss them up here?"

Herb shrugged.

"And nobody ever complains?" I said.

He laughed and kicked a stack of unread papers across the floorboards. "Not so far."

We decided to rehearse in Herb's bedroom, where he'd already set up his new kit. Because drums are such a pain in the ass to put together and tear down, most bands practice wherever the kit lives, hoping the drummer's parents can tolerate two hours of cymbal crashes and guitar feedback. But Herb's parents wouldn't be an obstacle. They'd split up a year earlier, and now Herb and his brother and sister lived with their dad, a banker who belonged to Brookside Country Club and owned a sailboat. Word was the divorce had been nasty. Colin's mom had told us not to tell anyone, but Herb was seeing a psychologist.

I knew how Herb must have felt. My parents had also divorced that year. I didn't understand how a priest and nun could leave the church to get married, only to get divorced sixteen years later, but there it was. My dad was now living in a townhouse, in a subdivision that had recently sprung from a soybean field.

Herb's house was much more impressive than my place or Colin's. Because it sat on a ravine, it expanded in the back, opening to rooms you'd never see from the street. As we walked from room to room, I noticed fist-size holes in the drywall.

"Check this out," Herb said, and he led us into the living room and toward the far wall, where a framed *Chinatown* poster was hung, off-center and too low. He took the poster off the hook. Behind it was another hole in the wall. "I did this yesterday," he said. Now I could see that the poster had been hung at perfect left-jab height. "My dad hasn't seen it, and I'm gonna keep it that way."

Up in the bedroom, Colin set his Vox amp between Herb's drums and the twin bed. I stood next to the dresser with my amp aiming out of the closet. No PA for the vocals, no stand for the microphone. Instead we plugged the mic into an auxiliary input on Colin's Vox, and we removed the shade from the floor lamp and draped the mic cord around the lightbulb. If Colin and I leaned into the lamp hip-first, we could almost get our lips to the microphone.

We tuned by ear. *Give me an A. Wait. No. Give me an E.* As long as Colin and I were in tune with each other, it didn't matter if our notes matched whatever frequencies constituted Es and As in the real world.

Herb sat behind the drum set and hammered out a kick-snare-hat beat. He was a natural lefty, but his drums were set up for a right-hander. For righties, the "coordinated" right hand is supposed to play the intricate hi-hat cymbal patterns, while the "uncoordinated" left hand smacks the snare. This means that when right-handers play drums, they hit the snare with their weak hand, *pop*. Not Herb. He was hitting the snare with his wall-punching hand, *POP!* It sounded huge.

Once everything was tuned and tweaked, Colin looked at Herb and said, "Can you play 'Heaven's On Fire' by KISS?"

Herb shrugged. "Probably."

"Who's gonna sing?" I said. Down in Colin's basement, the vocals were handled by whoever was coordinated enough to play and sing at the same time.

"We'll both try," Colin said. "But you do that Paul Stanley *whew* thing at the beginning."

I leaned into the lamp, counted four, and in my best falsetto, turned *whew* into a seventeen-syllable word. With the bedroom windows open to the summer afternoon, the neighbors must have thought H. Herbert Schupp Jr. had quit the country club to join an experimental art-rock outfit fronted by Yoko Ono. *Wheeeew–wheeeew–wheeeew–wheeeew–wheeeew–wheeeew–wheeeew–wheeeeeeeewooooooooo!*

Now the three of us would kick-in with a mighty cymbal crash and—

Herb fell off his drum stool with laughter. Colin doubled-over. All three of us were howling.

We weren't laughing at KISS or Paul Stanley or this idiotic intro. We were laughing at the idea that, holy shit, we'd started a band.

Colin and I eventually agreed to split the vocal duty 60/40 in his favor. Biggie signed on as roadie and manager, and the lineup was set: three skinny kids in Polo shirts and Jams shorts, with our husky-jeaned friend bringing the muscle.

We decided to call ourselves The Wire[7], and we printed up business cards that read IF WE CAN PLUG IN, WE'LL PLAY. Then we booked a gig in the basement of a kid whose parents were out of town, and we played 'til the Worthington PD chased everyone home. We played in the smoking section of the Bill Knapp's restaurant where Colin, Biggie, and I bused tables and washed dishes. We played in the backroom of a Subway sandwich shop, in the front room of an all-you-can-eat buffet, at the talent show and the rec center. We played at the community pool and the senior class dinner, at dances and canteens and teen nights. From Worthington Estates to Colonial Hills, from Old Worthington to Olentangy Highlands, The Wire plugged in, and we played.

Watershed is the opener tonight at the Beat Kitchen, a role we're very much accustomed to. After soundcheck, the manager hands me a stack of menus and says to order whatever we want, on the house. You might assume that a club with *kitchen* in the name would, as a matter of course, offer free food to its bands, but believe me, hospitality like this is a rare treat.[8] Still it's best to take the stage a little hungry. I try to eat at least two hours before we go on—like a Red Cross–approved swimmer. But when the food is free, I'll eat as much as I can, whenever I can. Colin has evolved beyond food. He eats almost nothing, toting around zip-lock bags packed with carrot sticks and almond butter sandwiches. Sometimes he breaks down and nibbles a few raw almonds and a handful of flax seeds. He's just short of a male anorexic—until last call. Then he'll tear through half a pizza and six tallboys.

Biggie mows his burger on a stool in front of the stage, with one eye on the *Chicago Reader* and one eye on our gear. Pooch, Dave, Ricki C., and I slide into a booth and dig in to our free sandwiches and beers.

"It's pretty cool your dad's coming tonight," Dave says to me.

It is cool. My old man's driving all the way from Ohio to see the show; then he's continuing on to Wisconsin to visit my aunts and uncles. I still remember the day, a few weeks after that Cheap Trick concert, when he drove me to Worthington's strip mall music store to buy my first bass. I brought a pocket full of paper route money, and he brought his checkbook.

"Now, you're sure you want to play the *bass* guitar?" he said.

"For sure," I said, and I pointed to a $139 Cort. "That one."

"I'm just worried you'll play this thing for a month, and then it'll end up buried in the closet." He put a hand on my shoulder. "Next to the clarinet."

I was thirteen then. According to my most recent Social Security statement I've earned more than $20,000 in only four of the twenty-five years since. I've never made $40,000. Still Watershed has had no fiercer supporter than my dad. Many times he's gone out of state to see us. He's watched bartenders throw ice at us. He's read reviews that have torn us to pieces. He's seen the full range of shows: the tight, the loose, and the drunken. And I know he's never once wished that Cort bass *had* ended up in the closet.

Dave's now been drumming with us for ten years—having replaced Herb, who would quit thirteen years after that first practice in his room— and as far as I know, his dad has only seen one show. His parents constantly hassle him for not being more like his older brother, a plastics executive who lives in a McMansion outside Ann Arbor. It doesn't seem to matter to them that Dave is happy, while his brother is miserable. In their eyes, a college dropout drummer, with two kids, who cooks at a golf course, couldn't possibly be happy.

I ask Dave if his parents are still trying to get him to quit the band.

He shakes his head. "They just ignore it. Over Christmas, I told my mom, 'Hey, Watershed's going back on the road.' She said, 'Oh.' So I said,

'Mom, we haven't played in five months.' And you know what she said?" Dave pops a few fries into his mouth. "She said, 'Oh.'"

Pooch laughs. "I think my parents have *forgotten* I'm in a band." In the five years since we added Pooch to the lineup as the rhythm guitarist, we've played Columbus about seventy times, and I've met his parents exactly once. His sister, who lives in town, has never come to see us.

"I think Colin's dad would like to forget," I say. Mr. Gawel has retired to Sarasota, where he drives a Buick and keeps a regular tee time. Whenever Colin, Erin, and Owen fly down to visit, Colin hears an earful from him. *I give you and Joe credit for sticking with it,* Mr. Gawel will say. *God knows, in business you've got to have guts. But when your business plan isn't working . . . I don't know, Colin. Don't you want to drive a nice car?* Mr. Gawel will then tell Colin that the best business move would be to put down the guitar and concentrate instead on the coffee shop.

"My dad would be thrilled to know I was out on the road," Ricki says, raking his Italian-poufy hair like a Jet from *West Side Story*. "When we drove to the club earlier, I was thinking: I wish he could have seen Chicago at night." When Ricki was a kid in the mid-Sixties, his dad worked as an usher at Veterans Memorial Coliseum. The old man snuck him in to see The Who, Hendrix, The Doors, and just about every other band that came through Columbus.[9] His dad died ten years ago, leaving Ricki a small inheritance that allows him to roadie for Watershed and for the folk-punk singer Hamell On Trial. Ricki's now fifty-five, and he's got a pacemaker planted in his chest. Every time he carries my amp up a flight of stairs, I'm hoping that gizmo is running on fresh batteries.

He sips a Diet Coke and says, "I'm lucky, I guess. I never had to worry about what my parents wanted for me."

"I don't know what my parents want," Pooch says.

"Mine want to say, 'I told you so,'" Dave says. "That's why I'll never stop drumming. Can't give 'em the satisfaction."

I can't imagine my dad ever saying *I told you so,* much less wanting to say it. "What would your parents do if we made it big?" I ask Dave. "What if an A&R guy signed us tonight? What if this time next year, we won a Grammy?"

Dave finishes his beer. "They'd brag about us to their friends. They'd say to them, 'I told you so.'"

A few minutes later, my dad walks into the bar, wearing his field-grade Cubs jacket. He sees me, waves, and smiles, and I notice the familiar chip in his front tooth, a chip I never paid attention to as a kid, until the day I found it in a photograph.

I was digging around in the basement that day, seven or eight years old, amazed at the odd treasures to be found. A tarnished Boy Scout pin—BE PREPARED. An antique pocketknife. A wooden footlocker packed with loose photos and papers. The footlocker was like a scrapbook, but it was all scraps and no book. Inside I found an old Polaroid: a black and white frieze of young men in sweatshirts and jeans, laughing, a football tucked in somebody's arm. One of the guys was a younger, leaner version of my dad. It was strange to see him engaged in some activity other than fathering.

I reached deeper into the box and picked up a clip of yellowing newsprint, a blurb about a community Shakespeare production. In the accompanying photo my dad's mouth was open mid-sentence, his body was hunched over, his arms were spread in a sweeping motion. I held the Polaroid and the newspaper blurb side by side, and tried to reconcile these images with the dad I knew. Playing football? Acting? I'd never considered that he lived a life that extended beyond me.

I dropped them into the footlocker, and I picked up a third photograph, a wallet-size portrait in muted color. Here was my young, lean dad again. Rectangular face, horn-rimmed glasses. He was smiling, but in this photo I noticed that one of his front teeth was chipped. Strange, I thought. But stranger was the get-up he was wearing: a black and white priest's collar.

I wondered if this was another role he was playing for the community theater. Or maybe a Halloween costume. It had to be some kind of joke, because "my dad" and "priest" didn't add up. Priests were the serious old men my mom dragged my sister and me to listen to every week. Priests droned in monotone and put stale crackers on our tongues. Priests were soft-handed and red-faced, smiling at us as we walked out of the dark church and into the bright Sunday morning. My dad was nothing like these men. He never even went to church with us. He'd stay home and watch *Meet the Press* and make doughnuts, while we sat and stood and kneeled and grew impatient with the ramblings of the priest. The real priest.

When I asked my mom about the photo I'd found, she sat me down at the kitchen table and told me that, yes, my dad had been a priest. And she'd been a nun. She'd grown up in a rough Milwaukee neighborhood, and her father had died when she was young. There was no money for college—not in a single-parent household, not with three brothers. So she entered a convent, mostly for the free education. She was in Madison working toward a master's degree when she met a fellow graduate student who was the pastor of a local parish and regional president of Clergy Against the Vietnam War. "This was your dad," she said.

She told me that he didn't like to talk much about how he ended up a priest. She didn't think he chose to enter the seminary, so much as the decision was forced upon him by his family. "I think your grandma dropped him in the collection basket," she said, laughing.

Later I asked my mom why she and my dad needed to keep these secrets. She said they weren't secrets exactly. But they worried that people would either condemn an ex-priest and -nun or hold them to unrealistically high moral standards. My parents wouldn't be allowed to make mistakes, to have regrets or lapses of faith, to get mad or jealous or depressed. Nobody can live up to those expectations, she told me.

Now I hug my dad in full view of the bar, knowing that my own happiness is the only expectation he's ever had for me. He hugs back hard, his latissimus dorsi muscles solid, his arms strong. At sixty-nine, he's in good shape. "Welcome back to the Midwest," he says, smiling wide, chipped tooth and all. "We missed you."

Colin walks in with his coffee, and my dad asks him about the shop, about Owen, about Erin's private practice. My dad likes Colin a lot. "Colin's a solid citizen," he once told me. "He's good people—even if he is a Reds fan."

Biggie walks up. "How are you, Mr. O."

"Hey, Michael." My dad squeezes his shoulder. "You keeping these guys in line?"

Biggie looks to the booth where Pooch and Dave are sitting, six or seven empty bottles lined up in front of them. "Doing what I can."

As my dad shakes hands with my bandmates, it really hits me, the level of faith he has in Watershed. He has no doubt whatsoever that our work has amounted to something more than what can be easily measured here in the Beat Kitchen. After all, he's a long-suffering Cubs fan. He's got faith in spades.

Anyone who plays in a band long enough knows that you can sort not only your families, but also your audience, into a loyalty-based hierarchy.[10]

On the lowest rung, you've got *The Skeptics*. Often members of other bands, they come to the show just to (a) see how many people you draw, (b) determine how badly you suck, and (c) complain about how many people you draw, given how badly you suck. They're often found in the back of the room, whispering in each other's ears. Occasionally, however, they'll approach the stage to shoot you an ironic devil-horn fist. Irony is big with The Skeptics.

Next are *The Handholders,* people who love listening to your albums, but usually can't get their shit together enough to make it out to a live show. They have legitimate reasons not to hang around a bar until 2:00 a.m. (read: kids), but when they finally do spring for a sitter, they'll seem needy and scared, and they'll expect you to lead them through the experience. Often they'll shoot you a string of panicky e-mails or phone messages: *How will I find the bar? Where will I park? Will it be loud? Will it be smoky? Can I get in on the guest list?*

Get a few drinks into Handholders, and they'll often morph into *Spotlighters,* that classification who won't be satisfied until you acknowledge them from the stage, give them a shout-out, sing happy birthday to them, etc. At some point during the show, a Spotlighter will probably say the hell with it and jump right on stage. Spotlighters aren't nearly as interested in seeing you as they are in making sure you see them.

Then you've got *The Base*. Reliable and self-sufficient, this is the bulk of your following. They always know when and where the next gig is, and they ask nothing from you except that you entertain them for the hour you're on stage. You owe it to them to make sure they get a show worth their time, but because they're so dependable, you risk taking them for granted.

The *Superfans* sit at the apex of the fan taxonomy. They travel. They see multiple shows per week. They know the names of your wives and kids. And pets. We found out early that you don't have to be as big as U2 to have Superfans. One couple, who met each other at a Watershed show, once wrote to tell us that our lyrics had saved their marriage. Another husband and wife sent a note asking if they could name their kid after one of us. A few months later, they dropped our names into a hat—then carried little Colin home from the hospital.

As the Beat Kitchen gets more and more crowded, I notice that Watershed Superfan attendance is high. Standing by the bar is Ken-from-Atlanta, who will always be Ken-from-Atlanta even though he moved to Chicago years ago. He once made a series of interpretive pencil sketches inspired by our songs. Next to Ken stand Kellie and Hot Sandy, moms in their mid-thirties who have followed us since the WRCX/Hancock Tower days. Kellie has a Watershed tattoo on her back, and her e-mail address is WatershedRocks@something-something.com. Hot Sandy isn't quite the Superfan Kellie is[11], but she did once ask me to sign my autograph on a bar napkin, which she took to her tattoo artist. Now my signature is permanently inked on her hot ankle.

Colin walks up with a blonde who looks like a *My So-Called Life*–era Claire Danes. "This is Katie," he says.

I shake her hand, and she says, "I hear you guys on the radio all the time."

"Then you must be from Columbus," I say.

She thumbs her hair behind her ears and says, "Yeah. But I just moved here."

Of course she did. Chicago is like a 50-Tesla magnet for gorgeous Midwestern girls, attracting every Wisconsin homecoming queen, every Indiana cheerleader, every beautiful bookworm from Detroit to Des Moines.

"Northwestern," she says.

"Good school," I say, wondering what kind of voodoo it might take to land a teaching job there.

"And we're giving her a ride home after the show," Colin says, "so she doesn't have to spring for a cab."

In any other band, this would be a transparent excuse to get the cute girl back to the hotel. But in Watershed, a ride is but a ride. I don't know this yet, but three days from now, we'll get an e-mail from Katie's mom, *thanking* us for getting her little girl home safe. So much for LOCK UP YOUR DAUGHTERS. Our motto should be WATERSHED: TRUST YOUR DAUGHTERS TO US.[12]

There's no denying that Colin is blessed with a kind of genius for the personal connection, but it sometimes feels like we're assembling a fan base one van ride at a time.[13] Still, Colin's gestures of inclusion have helped create a small but loyal cadre who rightly think of Watershed not as something they passively watch, but something they actively belong to. Look around the Beat Kitchen: Dave is chatting up Hot Sandy, much to the annoyance of her multi-pierced boyfriend. Pooch is cracking wise with Kellie, much to the annoyance of her scouring husband. Colin and Katie are calculating the added distance from the bar to her apartment, much to the annoyance of Biggie. And Ken-from-Atlanta is unpacking his video camera, intent on getting the whole shouting match on film.

I slide down the bar, to where my dad is nursing a beer and smiling over the proceedings. "Look at this thing you've built," he says.

Just before noon the next day, Biggie's steering us down Lake Shore Drive, away from Chicago's glass-skinned towers, toward Indiana and I-65 and Columbus, where we'll spend a few days off before the next show in Cleveland. My bones ache, and it hurts to talk. I need to build up the calluses on my bass-playing fingers, on my bass-playing body. Today is Sunday, and on the lakefront path, joggers are encased like sausages into space-age fabrics, yellow and orange paint flecks against the gray lake, the gray sky. There must be a hundred earmuffed and headbanded runners between our van and Soldier Field. Who are these just-do-it freaks, and how are they not as hungover as I am? A few years ago, I got a burr up my ass and ran a marathon, but after three days on the road, I can't imagine running 26.2 feet. I'm glad to have a little time to recover before the Cleveland show.

Last night's gig was the best of the tour. Ken, Kellie, and Hot Sandy sang along with every word, effectively telling the headliner's fans *It's okay to like this band.* Our Superfans were like shills we'd planted to help bring the rest of the crowd into the fold. Between our cut of the door and what Ricki C. sold in swag, we walked with $243. As we drove Katie to her apartment (and Ken-from-Atlanta to his), even Biggie was smiling.

Somewhere in the middle of the set we played "How Do You Feel," the song that the WRCX program director had pushed in 1995. When we got to the chorus, a few of the neutral crowd members seemed to recognize the tune. Maybe, in some small way, the Hancock Building's two antennae *had* blasted us into Chicagoland's consciousness.

After the show, a guy about my age walked up to the merch table and started looking over a copy of *Three Chords II.* "Who originally did that 'How Do You Feel' song?" he said to me.

"What do you mean?"

"It used to be on the radio all the time."

"Yeah, I know."

"Your version was spot-on, man. Sounded just like the original."

"That was us. Watershed."

He shook his head. "I think it was Marcy Playground or somebody."

"Trust me—"

"Or Silverchair."

"—it was Watershed."

He looked at me like I was speaking Mandarin. "That's your song? That wasn't a cover?"

"I'm telling you, that's our song."

"Man," he said, glancing down at the CD then back to me. "Whatever happened to you guys?"

4

Racing in the Street
Columbus, Ohio

AFTER DROPPING OFF THE GEAR AT THE PRACTICE SPOT AND THE VAN at the airport Hertz, Biggie and I head for his house, where I'll be crashing for the next five days. I could stay at my mom's, or with my sister and her family, but that would require flipping my sleep schedule and re-acclimating to a civilian agenda. It's much easier to bunk out in Biggie's attic, safe in the rock and roll bubble. I toss my bag onto the bed his wife, Jayna, has made for me, and then I snag a banana and the keys to his ten-year-old Saturn. There's a crack in the windshield and foam protruding from the dash. The door won't close true. This is the nicest car Biggie has ever owned.

I drive toward downtown, and for the first time in a long time, I notice how impressive the skyline looks. Columbus always seems to overachieve in this way, benefitting from low expectations—or maybe, no expectations at all.[14] And that, being snubbed, is a continual source of irritation for Columbus natives. The city is like a Triple-A ballplayer that bunts and hustles his way to a .310 average but still can't make the parent club for the playoff run. More than anything Columbus wants to be, deserves to be, major league. But nothing is quite so minor league as this desperate wanting. The metro area's population is 1.75 million. Nearly 750,000 live within the corporation limits. Columbus is the largest city in Ohio and the fifteenth largest in the USA. It's the state capital and home to Ohio State University's 53,000 students. Government and higher education insulate it from economic downturns and keep its collars Clorox white. While Cleveland, Detroit, and the other grand dames of industry have lost numbers in America's migration from Rust Belt to Sun Belt, Columbus has come of age.

Yet Columbusites can't shake the knowledge that we will always be an afterthought, the star in the middle of the heart-shaped state that's tucked away in our nation's meaty midsection. And we are meaty. Those of us who don't sit in cubicles stand behind cash registers, working to build you a better hamburger. We fight for the hometown teams: Wendy's and White Castle. We're not just round on the ends and high in the middle; we're pretty round in our collective middles too. We may be beer-bellied, but we're insured to the teeth. Grange Insurance, Motorists, State Auto: They're all headquartered here. Nationwide is not only on our side, they are responsible for three of our skyscrapers and our sparkly NHL arena. We spend our paychecks at Victoria's Secret, The Limited, Lane Bryant, New York and Company, Express, Abercrombie and Fitch, Hollister, Justice, and American Eagle—all of which call Columbus home. We've got the market cornered on ironic T-shirts and pre-teen thongs. We are responsible for your daughter's dangerously low-cut jeans, for the fact that your son's new ball cap looks like it's been run over by a lawnmower, for the word *tween*.

You'd think we'd sleep easy knowing our position in the national landscape is secure. But not in Columbus, Ohio. And it's all because of that damn comma, that unsightly gash that hitches city to state. Columbus can't ever ride solo, the way, to our great shame, even Toledo and Dayton can. So we self deprecate. We call our hometown Cowtown. We joke that it's a nice place to live, but you wouldn't want to visit. We take an ironic pride in being statistically average, the swing city in the swing state, test-market to the world.

Maybe this is because we've seen our city fathers pull a string of lame stunts meant to convince us of our own importance. In 1988 an exhibition called "Son of Heaven—The Imperial Arts of China" got the headlines. Three years later and with just as much fanfare, a replica of the *Santa Maria* docked on the downtown riverfront, and it has floated there like a lonely bathtub boat ever since. Five hundred years after the landing of the actual *Santa Maria*, Columbus hosted "AmeriFlora '92," an international flower expo that organizers hoped would rebrand us as a destination—land ho! Just as Christopher Columbus's voyage gave European cartographers a new continent to draw, these events were supposed to put Columbus, Ohio, on the map. But all they did was reinforce our small town-ness. Big cities don't need convincing; big cities just are.

I exit the freeway onto High Street, Columbus's jugular vein. It connects downtown with the OSU campus, the heart with the brain. From the day in 1979 when my parents relocated my sister and me to Worthington, to when Kate and I left Columbus for Tacoma, I've never lived more than a few football fields from High Street. I've simply moved up and down the strip, like a slide rule, following High Street out of Worthington and into neighborhoods like Clintonville, North Campus, and the Short North. To live anywhere else is to live in the provinces, to be invisible. Today, High Street feels familiar and comfortable as an old coat. Kate and I have been gone for five months, but driving down High, it seems impossible that I ever left.

Tacoma, on the other hand, feels like a dream I've blinked away. Only Kate—her absence here, her presence there—makes Tacoma real. I pull out the cell and try to reach her. No answer. It's early afternoon on the West Coast, so she's probably taking the walk we love so much. Our Tacoma apartment is in a beautifully restored, hundred-year-old building, two blocks from Puget Sound and across the street from a park thick with Douglas firs. In the afternoons we walk the hills of our neighborhood, past renovated Craftsmans and Victorians, each intersection offering a slightly different view of the Sound, the Port, and Vashon Island. Turn a corner and bam: the Olympic Mountains. Turn another: snow-capped Rainier and the Cascades, looking bigger, smaller, closer, farther, depending on the angle of the sun. "Goddamn," we tell each other on those walks. "We *live* here." In our thirties, we'd finally done what Kate had wanted to do since she was a girl: get out of Columbus. But it occurs to me now that the best hometowns—like the best homes—prepare you well to leave them, even as they exhibit a gravity that makes leaving hard as hell.

Hazards blinking, I pull in front of the Lifestyles Communities Pavilion, where in eight days Watershed's hometown will render a verdict on the state of our career. This has me thinking of something Kate recently said on one of our walks. "I know how important the band is," she said. "But I really think you should invest your time and energy where you'll get the best return."

Kate's not a band-wrecker. She's no Yoko. In the eighteen years we've been together, she's happily made sacrifices for Watershed. But she's also a practical woman, and as we walked the Tacoma hills she reminded me that we moved there because I am now—and the word sounded strange to my ear—a *writer*. Not a songwriter. Not a rocker. Several of my pieces have been published, which led to the teaching job.

"I hate to say it," she said, stopping to take in the view of the Sound. "But your writing career has all the momentum." She reached for my hand. "The band is petering out."

I wish she were sitting in the passenger seat right now, seeing what I'm seeing. Two stories above street level the LC marquee reads: WATERSHED. In big, block letters. Alongside the other upcoming acts: MARILYN MANSON, TODD RUNDGREN, ROB ZOMBIE. Watershed looks good up there. We look major league.

By senior year The Wire was the biggest band in Worthington—largely by attrition. All the other high school bands broke up as graduation neared. But Colin wasn't about to let diplomas and campus visits split us apart. He simply decreed, "This fall when we all start at Ohio State . . ." And after commencement Colin, Biggie, Herb, and I packed into Colin's Pinto and moved our base of operation from Worthington to campus—seven short miles down High Street. After class we'd walk past open storefronts and get blasts of air conditioning and Miles Davis. We'd shop for records at Magnolia Thunderpussy, Mole's Record Exchange, and Singing Dog's, loading up on used vinyl until our paper sacks split at the corners. We'd smack our hands on telephone poles plastered flyer upon flyer, thick as biology textbooks, and we'd run our fingers down poles that had been burnt clean to a reptilian skin of charred and rusty staples. Going to school on the High Street flyer trail, we learned that Willie Phoenix and Ronald Koal ruled campus. Soon they would be as familiar to us as Cheap Trick and KISS.

We wanted more than anything to wallpaper those telephone poles with flyers for our gigs. We'd been popular in Worthington, sure, but on campus we were one band among hundreds, thrown into the college stew like dethroned homecoming queens. Armed with a boom-box recording and a story that had been written about us in the *Suburban News,* Colin eventually booked a string of Wednesdays at Apollo's, a decaying joint where sickly gyro meat rotated on a spit behind the bar. The Worthington kids that came to those gigs were, like us, too young to drink. Combine that with our tooth-rattling stage volume, and Louie, the owner, told us he had no choice but to ban us from the bar—and the city. "You'll never play this town again!" he said, giving us the bum's rush down the fire escape. But by then we'd moved on to higher-profile clubs like Neely-B's and Ruby Tuesday.[15] We always played weeknights, and we were always the opening band, but still, by sophomore year we felt like we'd become a force on High Street.

We tried to prove it by getting ourselves voted Best Local Band in the *Ohio State Lantern* reader's poll. The morning the *Lantern* ran the ballots, we stole newspapers by the bundle and hauled them back to our apartment, where we had set up a ballot-stuffing assembly line. A week later, we'd beaten all comers, including the Royal Crescent Mob (who'd just signed with Sire), The Toll (who'd signed with Geffen), and The Best Damn Band in the Land, the OSU Marching Band (who, near as we could tell, had signed a deal with God). Columbus music scenesters who read the results must have thought, who are *these* jokers. But we didn't care that everyone knew we'd rigged the vote. If all it took to be Best Band was to stuff the ballot box, then why hadn't anyone else done it? The fact that we *had* done it *did* make us the best. So we blitzed High Street with flyers that said as much. We pressed stickers to the back of every stop sign on campus, and we spray-painted our name in five-foot block letters on the Olentangy River Road highway embankment—just as The Toll had done a year earlier. The *Lantern* win convinced us that the first step toward being big was shouting from the rooftops about how big you were.

We were Columbus boys to the marrow.

On New Year's Eve 1989, Colin, Biggie, Herb, and I stood in the kitchen of our college-ghetto duplex, each holding a champagne bottle by the neck. The *Lantern* win had seemed like a turning point, so we'd decided to literalize this new momentum by changing our name. Starting at midnight we'd be known as Watershed. This would be the marketing stunt (our "Son of Heaven," our "AmeriFlora") that would simultaneously cement our arrival on the campus scene and make clear our desire to transcend it.

Somebody switched off the stereo, which had been pumping Public Enemy's "911 Is a Joke" at cop-calling volume, and from the living room we heard fifty people counting down "*ten . . . nine . . . eight.*"

Biggie stuck his bottle between his legs and pulled Colin, Herb, and me into a four-man huddle, arms around each other, then tighter, until our foreheads touched. "This is it," he said. "This is our year."

"No retreat," Colin said, quoting our favorite Springsteen song. "No surrender."

"*Three . . . two . . . one!*" An eruption of "yeahs!" The clang and kazoo of Chinese noisemakers. From out on the front porch, the scream-bang of a bottle rocket. Inside, couples leaned in for slow, confetti-shower kisses. The four of us broke apart and thumbed our corks forward. "To Watershed!" Champagne cascaded down our forearms.

Then Colin took off to find Susan, his girlfriend. And Biggie's girlfriend Liz walked in and gave him a kiss. I stood there drinking straight from the bottle, jealous of my best friends, because at twenty I was still a virgin. I'd come close to having sex once—with Liz, in fact, a few months before she started dating Biggie. But now, watching her bite the tip of his tongue, watching her lick champagne from his lips, I knew exactly how little "close" counted.

Walking out to the back porch for another bottle of champagne, the cold wind stung my steadily balding head. My hair started thinning at fifteen. By the time I got to college, the shower drain was always clogged, and the bristles of my brush had disappeared under loose clumps. Another reason to be jealous of Colin and Biggie, who had hair thick as horsetails. This was the late Eighties, and hair was so integral to rock and roll, it had its own genre. I wanted to look like Tom Petersson on the Cheap Trick *In Color* album cover: all hair and aviator glasses on a Fatboy chopper. But locked in the bathroom, armed with two mirrors so I could measure the full 360-degrees of my male-pattern baldness, I looked like Phil fucking Collins, who looked like one of my political science professors. Worse, whenever I talked to girls, their gaze would start at eye level, then drift up my forehead. So I started widening my eyes and raising my eyebrows, trying to reduce the distance to my hairline. This made me look like Gene Wilder in *Young Frankenstein*—buggy eyes, street beggar hair, and wrinkles in my brow, parallel as swimming pool lanes.

Back inside, I stepped through pizza boxes and Old Milwaukee cans into the dining room, where a pack of high school kids was playing quarters. A senior named Tommy had just double-faulted, so the beer was his to finish. The table chanting "*drink-drink-drink*," he dipped his head back and chugged. Tommy bussed tables with Biggie at Bill Knapp's, and I guess we should have been pissed at the kid for inviting twenty high schoolers to our house, but we weren't pissed. We weren't pissed at all. Because Tommy always brought girls with him. Cute girls. By the carload.

He was passing the quarter to one of those girls right now. She had big, black hair and perfect white teeth—an orthodontist's "after" picture. Her bracelets clinked like wind chimes as she fingernailed the coin off the tabletop. Holding the quarter between her thumb and index finger like a robin's egg, she closed one eye and said to Tommy, "You better be thirsty, asshole." Then she shot and missed. Badly. The quarter didn't bounce; it just skidded to the base of the mug. A worm-burner. "Dammit," she said, and she slid the coin to her blonde friend.

I poured champagne into three plastic cups and pushed one toward Tommy and another toward this girl. "Happy New Year," I said. I wondered if they were dating each other.

She smiled thanks. Those full lips, those stunning teeth. I knew it wasn't okay to use a word like *stunning* when thinking about girls who still had homerooms and curfews, but Christ, stunning is what she was.

"Hey," I said, nodding over my shoulder. In the front room the lights were out, and "She Sells Sanctuary" by The Cult was playing. "Do you wanna dance?"

She stood up and said, "Yeah. I do."

I led her into the living room, where high school girls were go-going on the coffee table and drunk guys in baseball caps were stomping the cigarette-burned couches. "I'm Joe, by the way," I said.

She looked me right in the eyes. "I'm Kate."

Our last few gigs as The Wire had been at Bernie's Bagels, a basement deli that reeked of sewage and pastrami. Sometimes, even with the stage lights in my eyes, I could see the skinny dreadlocked man sipping coffee in the back booth, and I'd get shaky at the thought of playing for him. For years, I'd been reading his name on telephone poles, on marquees, on record covers: Willie Phoenix.

Willie's skin was the color of Baker's Chocolate. He sang like Wilson Pickett, wore his Telecaster upside down like Hendrix, and had Elvis Costello's gift for cutting a pop gem. And Willie didn't play second to James Brown or anybody else when it came to putting on a show. Singing, guitar playing, songwriting, showmanship: In every category Willie was as good as we'd ever seen, and as a master of all four, well, who else is there? Prince? Springsteen? There just aren't many stools at that bar.

Years earlier Willie had signed with A&M Records, a surefire Next Big Thing. But it's damn near impossible to shed *Next* and *Thing* and become simply big. Against his wishes, A&M trumpeted him as the "Black Bruce Springsteen," hoping to catch the wave of blue-jeaned barroom rock that had almost made stars of John Cafferty, Michael Stanley, and Joe Grushecky. But the public didn't buy it (or enough of it), and the label dropped him after one record.

So Willie had slunk back to High Street. And if he was bitter, he didn't show it. He'd play his Tele with his teeth, behind his head, between his legs. He'd toss the guitar to the floor and hump it like it was a cheating wife. Then he'd leap into the crowd and solo from tabletop to tabletop, with Ricki C., his roadie, scrambling behind. Whatever chemistry is required to simultaneously absorb and illuminate light in that way that says watch-me-now, this guy had it. Even squeezed into Bernie's Bagels, Willie Phoenix was a rock star.

Willie did all his business at Bernie's, like The Fonz at Arnold's, and one night, after we finished a set, he called Colin and me over to his personal booth. "Your songs are getting better, man," he said. He wore black tights, Beatle boots, and a paisley vest. His hands were calloused smooth, like varnished wood. "More hooks. More pop."

"Wow, thanks," Colin said, but all night he'd been distracted by a group of guys playing pool in the corner. "How do you get *those* dicks to pay attention?" he asked Willie.

"Fuck 'em," Willie said. He pretended to chalk a pool cue. "The Rolling Stones could be on stage and those pool-playin' dudes would still stand back there going, 'Sing it, Mick.'" He blew invisible chalk from the tip of his invisible stick. "Crack!"

Our laughter was interrupted by the bubbly sound of two drunk girls stumbling down the stairs into the bar. They held their arms around each other, and with each step their hips bumped.

"See that?" Willie said. "That's the most important thing to know about rock and roll." He stood up and walked toward the phone behind the bagel counter. Being the Black Bruce Springsteen had earned him unlimited local calls. "Get the girls, man. Nothing else matters."

He eventually asked us to open for him at Bernie's and Ruby Tuesday, and, later, at the Newport Music Hall. The fact that Willie deigned to appear on flyers with us made us feel like we'd been knighted. He wasn't around for load-in or soundcheck, and we never saw him before or after the show. Instead he materialized from the cigarette smoke just in time to sing the first line of the opening song. He'd bring his sweaty sets to a close with a fifteen-minute version of Van Morrison's "Gloria." As the band hammered out a mighty E-chord, he'd hold his Telecaster up to the lights and yell, "Now that's rock and roll, people!" Then he'd disappear from the club, Elvis-style.

One day he stopped by our Patterson Avenue duplex, wrapped in an Army trench coat, his dreadlocks poking out from under a knit cap. Colin, Herb, Biggie, and I had become so cool that local celebrities like Willie just, you know, swung on by.

"So here's the deal, man," he said. "You guys need to get your songs on tape, and I want to produce you."

We said, wow, no way, that's awesome. But we had no idea what a producer did.

He booked us into Musicol Recording Studios, a small, wood-shingled ranch on a block of small, wood-shingled ranches. The studio, like the surrounding neighborhood, was past its prime, but at least it was heated. We'd been rehearsing in a storage unit out by the National Guard Armory. From a single wall outlet we powered our amps, the PA system, and two space heaters, and every time we fired up, we half-expected to overload the city grid, crippling the Ohio National Guard. Even with the heaters running, it was cold as a meat locker in there. We'd practice in winter coats, stocking caps, and long johns. Some nights I worried my tongue would freeze to the microphone the way Ralphie's tongue had stuck to that metal pole in *A Christmas Story*.

At Musicol, Biggie duct-taped headphones to Herb's head, I strapped on my bass, and Colin hit a few power chords. We stood like we always did, with our backs to Herb, facing an imaginary audience.

Mic'd up and ready to go, Colin suggested we try "It Takes Time," one of his heart-on-the-sleeve love songs. My songs back then were bad Rush knock-offs,[16] all head and no heart.

Herb counted four, but before we got to the first verse, Willie gave us the slit-throat sign. "Okay, fellas. Hold on a minute."

We let our guitars drop to our sides. Herb set his sticks on his snare drum.

"A couple things," Willie said. "First of all. Colin and Joe. Why are you facing the control room?"

"We're looking into the crowd," Colin said. "Like when we're on stage."

"You're not on stage, and there is no crowd. So turn and face your drummer." He positioned us so that we were all looking at each other.

"Now, do me a favor," he said. "Play this for me." He showed us the chords for a song he'd written called "Kill the Telephone." He blocked the arrangement on a sheet of notebook paper. *Verse-Chorus-Verse-Chorus-Solo-Chorus-End.* Two and a half minutes tops. After a few passes we made it all the way through without messing up.

Willie clapped his hands together and said, "Now play it twice as fast." This song was already faster than anything we'd ever written. "Like The Ramones," he said. "One Two Three Four."

It took us three count-offs to even get started. On the third try we got halfway through the first chorus before the cars went off the track: me pulling ahead, Colin lagging behind, Herb stopping altogether. Each of us falling apart in our own special way. The classic train wreck.

Herb yelled, "Fuck!" and chucked his sticks to the ground. Our fingers, Herb's arms and legs, weren't built for speed.

Willie laughed and said, "Try it again." And again. And again.

A half hour later we had it nailed.

Willie shook his head. "Nope. This time do it as slow as you can."

"Are you serious?" said Colin. Herb was turning white, he was so pissed.

But we did it. At a tempo that made Air Supply sound like Motörhead.

Willie spread his arms as if he were a lion-tamer with a stool and a whip. "Perfect," he said. "Now go back to the fast version."

Herb played the drums like he was punching somebody.

"Now do it with two verses before the chorus."

"Now do it with a double chorus at the end."

"Now extend the intro with a guitar solo, then I'll teach you the bridge."

"Play it just like that, except with a disco beat. Four on the floor."

"Lose the bridge."

"Bring the bridge back."

"Nope, lose the bridge. But play it fast again. With the disco beat."

We'd been in the studio for seven and a half hours. My fingers were blistered, and my brain felt like sausage gravy. "Kill the Telephone" was no longer a song; it was a Rubik's Cube.

Herb stretched out on the floor, eyes closed.

"Hey, Willie," Colin said. "Some of these versions, like, uh, the disco one? I'm not sure I get it. What's the *best* way to play this song?"

Willie patted Colin on the back. "The original way."

"The eight-hour-ago way?" I said.

"Yep."

"What the fuck," Herb said from the floor, too tired to be mad.

"Now we know for sure," Willie said. He walked over and beat his index finger against Herb's ride cymbal. "What? Seven, eight hours? That's nothing." He snapped his fingers. "A record needs to be good enough to last forever."

We had never before second- or third- or fiftieth-guessed our songs. The tunes went from our heads, to our fingers, and into the frigid storage garage with no modification. This realization that a single song contained a million other songs was like looking into a microscope for the first time.

Willie picked his Army coat off the floor. "You guys have done great today, man. Let's go home."

"Shouldn't we at least work on one Watershed song?" I said. Herb was sitting on his stool, with a stick in each hand, coiled and ready to spring. Colin's guitar was feeding back in something like anticipation. "Shouldn't we record *some*thing?"

"When you guys write a song as good as 'Kill the Telephone,' we'll work on it." Then Willie Phoenix buttoned himself to the clavicle bone and walked out the door.

Colin and I eventually wrote a few songs Willie liked, but the recording process dragged on and on. We were lucky if we finished the basic tracks for one song in a single session. Even after we got the hang of an arrangement, we'd still have to run through twenty takes before Willie was happy. Herb took his frustration out on his drums, and work would often stop while we waited for Biggie to change a snare or kick-drum head.

"Look, Willie," Colin said. "I know we want this tape to be as good as it can be, but it is just a *demo* after all. It doesn't have to be perfect. It's more important that we keep things loose and rock and roll, you know?"

"No," Willie said. "I don't know. Where I come from, people make *records,* not demos." He paced the control room. "You can't expect an A&R

guy to hear a weak-sounding track and imagine what it'll sound like on the radio." He pointed to Biggie, who was sitting on the couch, reading *Billboard.* "If you want to end up in *there,* your songs have to be radio-ready."

The two most important things, he said, were the vocals and the drums. Vocals were what people heard, and drums were what they felt. If those two elements weren't spot-on, there was no saving the song.

A few weeks later, Willie pulled Biggie aside to tell him we should hold auditions for a new singer. He said my voice was too brittle, and Colin's was too thick. We both had pitch problems. We'd just changed the name of the band anyway, so the timing made sense. New name, new singer. But Biggie never ran the idea by Colin and me. He told Willie no. No way. Colin and I might not be the best singers in the world, Biggie said, but we were the best singers for Watershed.

After changing to the new name, an all-too-common response was "Watershed? Is that like an outhouse or something?" Biggie silenced the dipshits by designing a logo that spelled out the meaning, straight from *Webster's: wa-ter-shed. fig. An occurrence or time after which a significant change, as in public opinion, is noticeable.* None of us knew our way around a computer, so Biggie worked up the logo using a pair of scissors and a copy machine. He went with the only colors available: white for the *wa-ter* side and black for the *shed* side, with a ripped-paper effect down the middle to suggest a literal watershed. Two of Tommy's little buddies then painted a banner of the logo for an art class project, and when their school was looking for a band to perform at a lunchtime assembly, they lobbied hard for Watershed. A month later, Biggie was hanging that banner on the cinder block wall of the high school cafeteria: Olentangy High School, Kate's high school.

Taking advice from Willie, we'd recently updated our stage look. The Wire had played in T-shirts, jeans, and tennis shoes, as if we'd just stepped out of an Anthro 101 lecture and onto the stage. But as Watershed, we coordinated in all black and white. That afternoon in the lunch room I was dressed in black jeans, black boots, and a crow-black cowboy hat that concealed my baldness. Two songs into the set Herb pulled his shirt over his head, and teenage girl-screams shot through the school. Colin's stage banter—commanding and self-deprecating—brought the room to their feet. There were a hundred girls in the cafeteria, and it looked to me like Colin had convinced every one of them that he was singing to her and only her. From under my hat, I scanned the tables for Kate, wondering how to perform this trick not on one hundred girls, but on one.

A few hours after the four o'clock bell, Kate and her friends knocked on the door of the Patterson duplex. I drew two cups of beer from the kegerator, and Kate and I settled onto the porch swing. My thigh touched hers. On her jeans she'd written THE SUGARCUBES in ballpoint pen. "You guys were good today," she said.

In the living room Colin was dancing with two of Kate's friends to The Royal Crescent Mob's "Big Show." I tugged my hat to my eyebrows and said, "You want to go for a walk?"

By the time we got to Tuttle Park, the sun had set and the streetlights had come on. It was a warm night for early spring, and dew glistened in the grass. We walked past the swing sets and basketball court until we found a set of stairs, semi-hidden by a row of bushes. I stood against the rail, and Kate leaned into me, putting her hand on the small of my back. Her hair smelled like shampoo and cigarette smoke. It was the best thing I'd ever smelled. Better than cut grass, pine needles, a lumberyard. Better than anything.

We kissed, and I hoped I was doing it right, but it was tough to find a good lip-angle because the brim of my cowboy hat kept knocking against her forehead. Kate moved in closer, encouraging me, so I worked my hand under her sweater and felt the soft skin of her stomach. My hand slid up to her bra. The fabric was both silky and rough. This wasn't plain, white cotton; it had to be lace or satin or some exotic combination of the two. I knew that if she took off her sweater I'd be face-to-cups with a bra unlike any I'd seen outside the Victoria's Secret catalogue. I brought my hands to her waist, and slid them up her sides. This time, as my fingers traveled north, they took her sweater with them. I stopped just before I got to the underwire. I leaned backwards over the rail, trying to move my shadow out of the way. It was now as dark as this night was going to get, but if I turned her just slightly toward the nearest streetlight, I could see—

Purple. The bra was purple. And lacy. And Jesus.

"I should get going," Kate said. She brushed her hair from her face and glanced up at the streetlamp, which was haloed in the moist air. And then we kissed more.

That week I dialed her number. We talked about her classes and my classes. About the collapse of the USSR, the freeing of Nelson Mandela, the Mapplethorpe Exhibit in Cincinnati. We talked about how Buster Douglas's thumping of Mike Tyson had finally brought the heavyweight belt home to Columbus (Joe: *Did you see how Buster flat-out kicked his ass?* Kate: *Who's Buster Douglas?*). Then we agreed to go out Friday night.

I woke up at noon on Friday to find Tommy asleep on our couch. He was using his jacket for a blanket and a Taco Bell sack stuffed with burrito wrappers for a pillow.

I kicked a few empty beer cans to wake him up. "Tommy, man," I said. "I hope you're not too pissed at me, but Kate and I—"

"Don't worry about it." He sat up and reached for his glasses. "We're not dating." He started looking around for his shoes.

I dropped down next to him on the couch. The afternoon sun lit up the front window, but the house smelled like a bar at closing time. "You graduate in what? A month? What are you gonna do?"

"Probably stay at Bill Knapp's a while." He laced one high-top, glasses sliding down his nose. "Then, I don't know. Figure something out."

"What about Kate?"

"What about her?" He stood up to look for his other shoe.

"What's she doing next year?"

"Next year?" He was limping around the room in one shoe and one sock. "You know. School."

I hoped this didn't mean some college far away. "Ohio State, probably. Right?"

He gave up on the shoe and turned toward me. "Kate's not graduating this year."

"What does that mean?"

"She's not a senior."

I remembered her purple bra. My hands going under that purple bra. "She is eighteen, though."

Tommy's eyes went wide.

"What is she," I said, blood pumping faster. "Seventeen?" Seventeen was safe. Only three years younger than me.

Tommy shook his head and laughed.

My heart was beating from somewhere behind my forehead. The implication of what I'd done in Tuttle Park came over me like a fifty-foot wave. I rubbed circles into my temples. "So, she's like, I mean, what you're telling me is that she's fucking *sixteen?*"

Tommy laughed so hard he almost popped a hernia.

"Bullshit," I said, and I stood and circled the room. There was his shoe, in the ornamental fireplace. I chucked it at him. "No way she's sixteen."

But Tommy was laughing too hard for this to be a joke.

"All right already. I get it, funnyman." Kate was sixteen. And I was twenty. So what did that make me? A creep who skulked the playgrounds with his hands in his pockets? A pedophile? Or just a loser. *Sweet Sixteen.* That quaint expression wasn't cute and pink and cuddly. It was criminal.

"Six*teen.*" I said it out loud, hoping to disarm the word by taking it out of my panicky imagination and putting it back into the world where age was, as they said, just a number.

"Sixteen isn't what's so funny," Tommy said.

"Then what the hell is?"

He took off his glasses and rubbed his eyes. "She's fifteen."

The math was easy but I had to count it on my fingers anyway. By the time I got to my thumb, Tommy was limping upstairs toward the bathroom, still minus his right shoe.

I'd felt up a fifteen-year-old in the shadowy corner of a city park. I thought of Humbert Humbert and his nymphet; Jerry Lee Lewis and his teenage cousin-wife; Chuck Berry, locked up under the Mann Act. I stared at the couch dust floating in the sunlight, following one particle up and down as it rode the air in the room, passing from dark to light and back.

As the recording sessions wound down, we sent out press releases announcing that Willie Phoenix was our producer. A few writers took the bait, and feature stories appeared in the *Lantern* ("Watershed Going For It All") and in a local rag called *Stage Magazine* ("Watershed: Coming Into Their Own"). In those articles Colin boasted that Watershed would stay together for the rest of our lives. I said, "We're either going to be the most successful band ever or the most annoying band ever . . . we're never going to go away."

One night, we sat in the Musicol control room, listening to the final mix of Colin's newest song, "Freedom." While he and I slapped five about how great it had turned out, Biggie was nose deep in Sun Tzu's *The Art of War*. The book was a gift from The Toll, who'd recently hired him on as a roadie. On long drives and in hotel bars, the Toll guys told him that they'd played twenty-two states before signing with Geffen. In those days they were so broke, they ate nothing but peaches and peanut butter sandwiches. "You want your Watershed guys to get good?" they said to Biggie. "Drive them five hundred miles to play for no-fucking-body."

The Toll convinced Biggie that the only way for us to get signed was to quit school and start touring. Immediately. Now Biggie was trying to convince Colin and me. "It's too cozy playing in Columbus every weekend," he'd say. "We need to get out there and play for people that want to *hate* us."

Biggie and Herb had already flunked out of Ohio State. Herb didn't have the focused concentration you need for college, and Biggie concentrated *too* hard. In his math classes, instead of memorizing formulas and then plugging and chugging like everyone else, he tried to discover his own formulas. He might only answer one question on a midterm, but he'd prove it, perfectly, from scratch. Now that they'd failed out, there was nothing keeping Biggie and Herb in Columbus but their restaurant jobs and their girlfriends, both hurdles easily cleared.

Leaving school would be tougher for Colin and me. This was partly because, for all our talk about wanting to be rock stars, we hadn't quite wrenched ourselves from the idea that young adulthood is a scavenger hunt: *Pick up High School diploma.* Check. *Apply to College.* Check. *Frame college diploma.* Check. *Look for job. Make money. Get married.* Check. Check. Check. Then there was the blockade our parents would surely put up. So far they had encouraged the band thing, but they would never, ever let us quit school—even though they'd all made their share of less-than-sure bets when they were our age. Colin's mom, a distant cousin of the Kennedys, was a socialite from Champaign who'd rebelled against her family by marrying Mr. Gawel, a go-with-the-gut guy who took ten years to graduate from Western Michigan. Shortly after he married Mrs. Gawel, he liquefied her savings account to start his business. And God knows my parents had traveled an unorthodox route to the suburbs. The fact that they had to renounce their vows to the church in order to get married hadn't stopped them from doing it.

Here in the control room, "Freedom" rang though the studio monitors. On tape Colin was singing: *My parents couldn't see just where I was going. I beg 'em for my life and for a chance to show 'em.*

Biggie looked up from *The Art of War.* "If you guys want freedom, you've got to take it." He said we could make all the champagne toasts we wanted, but unless we were willing to break free from our hometown, our parents, our girlfriends, and our dead end jobs, we'd always be empty talking ballot-stuffers. "If being in a band is what you want to do for the rest of your life, then why the hell are you wasting your time with anything else?"

I said that yes, I'd absolutely hit the road—next year, after I graduated.

Biggie smacked his fist on *The Art of War.* "There is no fucking next year." He shot up from the couch. "If it's the right thing to do, then it's the right thing to do *now*." He shoved *The Art of War* into Colin's gut. "What about all that *no retreat, no surrender* crap?"

Colin glared at him. "I meant what I said."

"People say lots of stuff," Biggie said, jabbing a finger at him. "But what are you *doing* about it?"

Then Willie walked into the control room and took Biggie outside. Colin and I could hear them. "You're not ready," Willie said.

"We'll get ready," Biggie said. "The road will make us ready."

"Look, man. I'm almost forty years old. Everywhere you guys want to go, I've already been. Right now you're too young to understand the odds."

On the recording, Colin sang the second verse of "Freedom." *I never dreamed about a Mercedes Benz, just a record or two and a tour that never ends.*

Out in the hall, Willie said, "Do you know how many better singers there are than Colin and Joe? How many better songwriters? Better musicians?"

I looked toward Colin. One of the lines to "Freedom" was *I just wanna play just like Willie Phoenix,* and here was Willie Phoenix, telling Biggie that we were nowhere near his league.

"There aren't many better bands," Biggie said.

"Just do me a favor," Willie said. "Let these guys graduate first. Get a degree to fall back on. Then, sure, go out there and try to make it." As they walked back into the studio, Willie gave Biggie a big-brotherish whack on the head. "Be as smart as you are, man."

I knew I should cancel my date with the fifteen-year-old Kate, but thirty years of rock history were telling me to go through with it. Since rock and roll's earliest days, when Pompadoured greasers sang to the bobby-soxers and the sock-hoppers and the poodle-skirted, fuzzy-sweatered dolls of the dance floor, songs have been written for and about teenage girls. Rock's forefathers went after the daughters of America's newly expanding middle class who, thanks to their parents' post-war discretionary income, had money to spend. And rock music gave teenage girls something of their own to spend it on. While parents and teachers told these girls that they were too young to matter, boys with guitars—like Johnny Burnette ("You're Sixteen"), Neil Sedaka ("Happy Birthday Sweet Sixteen"), and Chuck Berry ("Sweet Little Sixteen")—were taking the teeny-boppers heart-attack serious.

Still there was a canyon of difference between singing about young girls and actually touching them. And the cut-off between what was mildly rebellious and what was sick and predatory was a firm sixteen.

Limbo under that sixteen barrier, and you seemed penitentiary bound. I'd never heard a song called "She's Foxy and 15" or lyrics that crooned, *You're fifteen, you've just stepped out of a training bra, and you're mine.* Jerry Lee Lewis's career-threatening cousin was thirteen. Chuck Berry went to jail for a fourteen-year-old. Was I living the lyrics to some song—"Fast Little Fifteen," maybe—that I'd have to finish from the slammer?

On Friday night Colin, Biggie, Herb, and I were drinking beer in the living room when through the window I saw Kate's blonde friend cruise past our house. The car pulled over just long enough to let Kate out.

Her hair was done up just so. She looked nineteen easy.

As we watched her climb the porch stairs, Herb punched me on the shoulder and said, "You're lovin' it."

"She's even hotter at fifteen than she was at eighteen," Colin said.

Biggie stood up and aimed for the kitchen. "The Olentangy PTA is gonna bust down the door any minute."

Kate and I slid into a booth at an Italian restaurant, and while we waited for our drinks, I said that Tommy had told me her age.

She ran her finger down the menu, all business. "Three years' difference is a lot," she said, "but I don't know. It's not *so* many."

Wait a second. Three years? "But Tommy told me you were—" I looked around. It was still light outside, and the place was mostly empty. Still I lowered my voice. "Tommy told me you were fifteen."

"But I turn sixteen next month, so the difference is really like two years."

"Hang on." I leaned away from her. "How old do you think I am?"

"Eighteen, right?"

"But I—" And the waiter showed up with our drinks. I sat on my hands and ordered a pizza. When he left I said to Kate, "But I'm in college."

"I know. A freshman."

I slid my Coke to the side. "Did Tommy tell you that?"

"No." She sipped hers through a straw. "I don't know. I guess I just assumed. Since you're friends with him."

I leaned in closer, to kissing distance. "Kate," I said. "I'm a junior. I'm twenty."

She shut the menu and leaned back from the table. "You look younger than that."

I pulled my cowboy hat down tight. When I was a freshman at OSU, she was in the eighth grade. When I was in the eighth grade, she was eight. When I was eight, she'd barely graduated from Pampers. Each snapshot of the age difference was more alarming than the last. I was scared that five years would be insurmountable, and scared that it wouldn't be. Because if I called Kate tomorrow and the next day and the one after, and if we made a date for next Friday, and if we found another shadowy spot in another park, but went even *farther* this time, maybe as far as two people can go, then what did that make me? Jokes about jailbait and cradle robbing aside, I was pretty sure the state of Ohio had an exact name for twenty-year-olds that had sex with fifteen-year-olds. And here I smashed into the word that I hadn't until now allowed myself to form. Because if Kate and I did have sex—and God knows I wanted to, from the first time I saw her, I wanted to—then would I . . . would I be a *rapist?*

But Kate was counting into the safe, narrowing future. "If you were thirty and I was twenty-five," she said, laughing, "this wouldn't be weird at all."

The waiter dropped off the pizza, and I fumbled with the spatula cheese, sneaking looks at Kate's chest, wondering what her bra felt like, imagining a moment when there'd be nothing separating her skin from mine.

"I don't see anything wrong with us dating," she said. Then she sipped the last of her Coke. "But I'll never be your groupie."

That spring I walked a little taller down High Street. I had the Willie-produced tape in my Walkman, I had a girlfriend in the suburbs, and I knew that my junior year at Ohio State would be my last. Watershed was dropping out and hitting the road, flying the Columbus nest.

Colin and Biggie had come home from spring break with the decision already made. As we sat in the living room, they told me the story of how Colin had finally come around to Biggie's side. They'd left Panama City

Beach in Colin's Pinto, they said, aiming for spring training in Tampa. As Route 98 became US 19, Biggie fired a beer can out the window, where it bounced along the pavement. He looked out to the Florida dusk, listened to the hum of the tires. The wind whipped his hair and made his unworn seat belt thwack like an angry stepdad's leather strap. "Anything easy ain't worth a damn," he said.

Colin pinched a dip of Biggie's Copenhagen. Biggie wasn't quoting Sun Tzu or The Toll; he was quoting Woody Hayes. And Colin was listening. Since the eleventh grade, he and Biggie had been the closest friends of any of us. In high school they used to stay up late, just the two of them, sipping stolen beers and weighing the entry-level existentialism of post-adolescence.

"The point is," Biggie said, "lots of people graduate from college."

Colin nodded, tongue-ing the tobacco into his bottom lip. "I know one thing. We weren't put here to do what lots of people do." He reached into the glove box for Springsteen's *Darkness on the Edge of Town*. As the sun disappeared from the passenger window, he gassed the Pinto through scrubby, one-story dots-on-the-map—the landscape of Tom Petty songs. But this wasn't Florida. Not anymore. Not with "Badlands" and "Adam Raised a Cain" and "Something in the Night" pouring from the car stereo. This was the swamps of Jersey. The Dakota hills. This was the American night, and Colin was inside it, the way you are when you're behind the wheel, on a dark highway, running away from one thing and toward something else.

"Candy's Room" ended with Springsteen whispering, *tonight*. Now it was just Colin, Bruce, and a lonely piano.

I got a sixty-nine Chevy with 396 / Feulie heads and a Hurst on the floor.

The words were about drag racing, about shuttin' 'em up and shuttin' 'em down. But Colin understood what Bruce was really singing about, and it wasn't cars.

Springsteen was telling Colin to reach for the wheel that steers you through your days and wrestle it from your parents and your job and your own preconceived notions of what a lived life is supposed to look like. Crank that wheel back and forth until you know you're driving that motherfucker. Because this is a blues song, and you're at a crossroads, baby.

Make a right turn and all is straight and well lit, a thick, AAA-approved line on the map.

Turn left and there's no road at all. You have to plan it and pave it and fill the dang potholes yourself.

As Bruce sang to him, Colin knew which direction he was going to turn the wheel. Because in this life, like in the Springsteen song, *some guys they just give up living and start dying little by little, piece by piece.* But some guys, the ones with the balls to take the hard left, well, those guys *come home from work and wash up. And go racing in the street.*

The Second Leg

5

Going Mobile
Cleveland, Ohio

"LET'S HIT IT," BIGGIE SAYS, AND HE LIFTS THE DRUM HARDWARE INTO the Econoline.

Hands in my coat pockets, I'm standing at the back bumper, watching him shove the hundred pound case into its regular slot in the pack. Six p.m. and it's already dark, Columbus-in-January dark. Over on Fifth Avenue, drivers are hustling toward happy hour, but here at the warehouse where we practice, nobody but Biggie is in a Friday rush. Could be the weather. Wet snow sticks to the parking lot in cottony flakes. A wintry mix, the weathermen call it. With the muffler blowing warm exhaust through my Levi's, I'm in no hurry to move from this spot, even though soundcheck starts in two hours and it's two and a half from Columbus to Cleveland on a sunny day.

The van's two rear seat benches are splayed on the blacktop next to me. Wonder what the boys at Hertz would say if they could see their baby now—seats pulled and askew, as if the van had coughed them up and spit them out. With a power drill and lug wrench, Biggie torqued the mounting bolts loose and wrestled the benches to the ground, freeing up more cargo space, which he filled with half-stacks and guitar cases, tight as a Tetris game. You couldn't pour a pint of water into this pack, but somehow Biggie squeezes my duffel bag between the kick drum and the basses, saying, "Wouldn't want you to break a nail, sweetheart." He slams the doors shut and whacks the side panel with his open palm. A love tap. "Done and done," he says. Then he pulls his orange hunting mask from the top of his head and uses it to wipe the sweat and snow from his face.

I help Biggie carry one of the seat benches inside the cinder block warehouse and into the practice room. We share the space with Mike Landolt, a recording engineer who has worked on a bunch of hit records, but the one that hit hardest was Maroon 5's Grammy-winning, ten-times-platinum *Songs about Jane*. I know the album went ten times platinum because Maroon 5's ten-times-platinum record hangs on the practice room wall, framed and shiny.[17] Colin, Dave, and Pooch are standing in the platinum glare now, laughing, catching up on how everybody spent the five days since the Chicago show.

Dave cracks a Bud Light, saying he worked ten-hour shifts at the country club. "But it wasn't all bad," he says. "I crushed the overtime, and the beer girls are smoking hot."

"How much you think those chicks make?" Pooch says.

"Let me guess, Pooch," Colin says. "College girls in short-shorts working drunk, middle-aged golfers for tips?"

"Solid business model," Pooch says.

Dave laughs. "They clean up."

"And I bet they love it that you're in a band," Colin says. "You're out there. Playing cool cities."

Dave nods. "They always want to hear about New York."

"Of course they do," Colin says. "You're ten times hipper than those corporate knobs that hit on 'em all day."

"I don't know," Pooch says. "Corporate knobs tip big."

Dave takes a slug of beer. "All I know is those girls are way more interested in the band than my wife is." He tells us he spent the week soft-shoeing around Sarah, who was pissed that he'd been gone playing shows and pissed that, now home, he was *still* gone, pulling double shifts and drinking too much. He sloshes down a Percocet. "I gotta hit the road just to sober up."

Biggie lumbers back inside, bear-hugging the second bench by himself. He's surely wishing that Ricki C. were here to help, but Ricki is roadying for Hamell On Trial this week, so Biggie's in for a workout. He fires his Maglite around the room, doing the idiot check, making sure he didn't forget to pack something. "No idiots here but the guys in the band," he says.

If you're like me, you want to believe that bandmates are always as close as brothers. You want Strummer and Jones to have been best mates. You want Townshend to be first in line to give Daltrey a kidney. But the fact is, a lot of bands barely tolerate each other. Take the band Train, for instance. Our manager, Thomas O'Keefe, is their tour manager, and he told us that once, when they were shuffling onto their bus after a few days off, one dude said matter-of-factly, "Hey, I got married last week." The other guys came back with "No shit?" and "Well, then. Congrats." Here's what this means: (a) The groom not only didn't invite his bandmates to the wedding, he hadn't even told them he was *planning* a wedding; (b) Not one of them was offended at the snub; and (c) Nobody but O'Keefe thought any of this was the slightest bit odd.

I remember once—after a show at Small's when Colin and I were drinking at the bar, cracking each other up—I caught the drummer from Detroit's The Fags staring at us like we were exotic birds. "I can't believe it," he said. "You guys actually *like* each other." But that was Colin's plan all along. Be friends first, then form a band. You can't just wish a bond into being. For the last five days I've been sleeping in Biggie's attic, eating his bananas and using his wife's body wash. When he went to the bathroom I knew about it. That's a bond.

Now he claps his hands and says, "Let's bolt. We can talk at eighty miles an hour."

Before we shut out the lights and set the alarm, I look up at Maroon 5's ten gleaming, platinum discs. I know that the Watershed friendships are priceless and immeasurable, but goddamn. I might have traded a little of that friendship for a few more records sold.

Eighteen years since we first started touring, and I still feel an adrenaline spike when I climb into the van: the rich stink of the exhaust and the dusty smell of the heater, the squeak of the wiper blades and thrum of the engine, the sensory experience of driving toward an unknown future, one made solely of possibility.

Leaving to go on tour is the breaking of inertia, hurtling into motion bodies that have been at rest. The rocket on the launch pad. The slingshot stretched tight as a violin string. It takes tremendous energy to switch from stasis to action, but that moment is beautiful in its destruction. The rocket shattering the grip of gravity. The rock shot free of the sling. Once you're moving, inertia insists that you keep moving. You are mass. Velocity. Momentum.

That's what dropping out of school felt like, like being shot from a cannon. In that fall of 1990, when everybody else on Patterson Avenue was shuffling back to class, Biggie stuck his old cherry-wood desk in the corner of our dining room, and on the wall above it he tacked a four-month dry-erase calendar. September to December. One hundred and twenty-two dates waiting to be booked.

Colin and I hunched over the desk, reading an old tour itinerary Biggie had swiped from The Toll. On every page was a new club in a new city. The project was to convince a few of these places to give us a gig. It seemed simple enough. We'd divide the list by three, send out promo packs, then make follow-up calls. In the first round of our rock club draft, Biggie selected CBGB in New York. Colin took the Blind Pig in Champaign. I nabbed Uncle Pleasant's in Louisville. Then we went around again, until every venue The Toll had played was somebody's responsibility.

To fatten our promo kit, we had a friend write a biography that described our sound as guitar-fueled, Midwestern power pop. We slid this new bio, a few newspaper articles, and the Willie Phoenix–produced cassette into Kraft paper envelopes, licking shut package after package until our tongues tasted the way Gary, Indiana, smells. The post office workers knew us by name. We were bursting with the determination of Mormons on mountain bikes.

As with all cold calling, the most important trick was to get the decision-maker on the phone. But to get to that person, you first had to negotiate with whoever picked up—a bartender or door guy or janitor.

Hello, Uncle Pleasant's.
Yeah, um, I play with a band called Watershed, and we're interested in booking a show?
[silence]
Hello?
Yeah. Uncle Pleasant's.
I'm from Watershed? I'm looking for a show.
You're from where?
Watershed. From Columbus, Ohio.
Look. You're gonna have to call back later. It's too noisy in here.
Click.

The next day I called two hours earlier, before the bands started soundchecking and the bar got too loud.

Hello, Uncle Pleasant's.
I called yesterday? I'm from Watershed? I'm wondering if I could book a show?
From Water-what?
Watershed. We're from—
And you say you wanna play here?
Exactly.
You're gonna have to talk to Mark. He books the bands.
Cool. Is he there?
Nah.
Do you know when he'll be in?
Maybe tomorrow. Or the next day. I'm not sure. Try back then.
Click.

By mid-September the calendar was still blank.

But there was another problem. Let's say one of these clubs finally did pencil us in. How would we get to the gig? In Colin's Pinto? We'd be laughed back to Columbus. No, we needed a van, which meant we needed money.

"Money trouble is no trouble," my dad said one day that fall, when the two of us were out to lunch. Like The Wolf, Harvey Keitel's fixer in *Pulp Fiction*, he has a way of stripping an issue down to manageable parts. "Disease. War. Crime," he said. "That's trouble. Money's an easy fix." He took a sip from his Arnold Palmer. "How much do you need?"

I winced. "Two thousand, maybe?"

For my dad that was probably two weeks' pay, but he set his fork on his plate, reached under the table for his briefcase, and said, "Who do I make the check out to?"

The first van we looked at was a scarlet and gray '82 Chevy with seventy-seven thousand miles on it. Biggie and Dave Cook—the mechanic friend we'd brought along to make sure we didn't get sold a lemon—poked under the hood. "See that engine, Biggie?" Cook said. "That's the best motor ever made. A Chevy Straight Six. Keep the oil changed, man, and it'll run forever."

Because my dad had fronted the cash, I got to drive the new van home. Curbed among Patterson Avenue's Jettas and Civics, it looked heavyweight and strong, a work boot on wheels. We named it Rocco, in honor of Rocky Balboa, underdog supreme. And we'd found Rocco just in time. Because on the calendar, one date was no longer blank.

Biggie had drawn a fat star on Monday, October 1. The Patio in Indianapolis. Monday was New Band Night. We'd be the first band of three. No guarantee, just a split of the door and a promise that if things went well, they'd slide us a Tuesday. We slapped fives. Hell yeah.

Soon Colin confirmed the Blind Pig, and I nailed down Uncle Pleasant's. Uncapping the marker and drawing that star on the calendar was more satisfying than any A I'd earned in school. A few days later there was a star for Frankie's in Toledo, and one for O'Cayz Corral in

Madison. November was taking shape too. Detroit. Charleston, West Virginia. On the dry-erase board I saw enough stars to make a minor constellation.

Now Biggie steers the van up Route 315, past Ohio Stadium and through Worthington. Banking along the outerbelt, we pass the Anheuser-Busch mega-brewery. Colin cracks the window and yells, "Keep 'em coming, boys!"

It didn't always seem like it, but touring in the early Nineties was relatively easy because there was an established network of clubs that booked unsigned and indie-label bands. The Metro in Chicago and the Decade in Pittsburgh. Chapel Hill's Cat's Cradle and Athens's 40-Watt Club. The Bottleneck in Lawrence and the 9:30 Club in D.C. These bars packed 'em in for bands like Fugazi, Black Flag, Minutemen, The Dead Milkmen—bands who'd built the template for touring: get in the van, play the punk club, sell the merch, crash on the floor, drive to the next town, repeat. Fanzines hyped the shows; indie record stores stocked the vinyl; college radio stations invited the bands to play live on the air. Repeat, repeat, repeat.

We came of age on this grassroots model, so we romanticize it even now, eighteen years later. But as we merge onto I-71, aiming for Cleveland, I'm thinking about how inefficient touring is. Back then, we'd drive for eight hours to play for eight people, and if we sold five tapes, we'd call it a stunning success. The Internet, however, makes touring seem as quaint and outmoded as the Pony Express. Bands today don't need to squeeze into a van. They can just post a song to MySpace and upload the video to YouTube. Bam. Listen for free then download with a mouse click and a credit card. Why drive from town to town, when you can drive Internet traffic instead?

Here's why. Computers ease commerce, but they can't replicate the power of seeing a band in person. Watching a band in a bar is a visceral experience (the crowd, the volume, the spilt beer). Listening to an mp3 through one-inch speakers, well, it just isn't. Bands are better in the flesh for the same reason that fucking Angelina Jolie is better than jerking off to a jpeg of her.[18]

Why is Watershed still touring now, in the age of the Internet? Could it be the sensory experience of playing *with* people *in front of* people? The fun of drinking a lot and sleeping late and wallowing in the kind of behavior that's frowned upon in everyday life? Because we're like an old battleship that's doesn't easily change course? Yes, yes, and yes.

We set out on the indie club circuit that fall, but we didn't see ourselves as an indie band. We weren't going to be the alternative to anything. We were going to be *the* thing, a major label act. If even three people were in the crowd, we played like those three were A&R reps. Maybe that chubby girl playing pinball had an uncle in the music biz, or maybe that loner nursing a beer was talent scout. In his day planner, Biggie took detailed set notes, keeping track of which songs were working and which weren't. The day an A&R man finally appeared in the audience, we'd be ready.

But what were the odds of a record exec showing up at a pizza shop in Oxford, Ohio, or at a laundro-bar in Cincinnati? We figured the quickest way to get signed was to score a date at the mecca of rock clubs, CBGB. Back in the Seventies, label scouts had discovered the Ramones, Television, Talking Heads, Blondie, and even Tom Petty on CBs' cockeyed stage. The Toll had sealed their Geffen deal there. From what we assumed, the average A&R guy spent so many nights at CBs, he probably kept a toothbrush behind the bar. But every time Biggie got Louise, the talent buyer, on the phone, she'd say, "Can't talk now. Try me next week." Biggie always answered, "Sure, Louise. Thanks. Have a good day."

Frustrated, we asked Willie Phoenix what to do. He smiled and said, "You want to play CBs? No problem. Some chick that works there likes to suck my cock."

But it was Biggie's Midwestern manners that finally won Louise over. One day, instead of curtly dispatching him, she said, "God, you are so fucking polite." Biggie could hear pages rustling. "I think I've got a date for you."

Biggie raised his fist toward the ceiling.

"Fuck yeah!" Colin said, climbing onto his back.

Biggie piggybacked Colin around the dining room. Herb and I piled on, and we all collapsed to the floor.

"And get this," Biggie said, pulling Herb's elbow from his eye socket. "It's a Saturday night. And we go on last."

Sweet, sweet validation. Only two months out of school, and already we were headlining a Saturday fucking night at CB fucking GBs. Start spreading the news.

A few weeks later I maneuvered Rocco into the line for the George Washington Bridge. When I leaned out the window to hand four dollars to the toll collector, it felt like we were paying for admission into a giant amusement park. I imagined that the collector was a tout with a top hat and a cane, giving me an exaggerated bow. He'd tap his cane on the hood, wink, and point us over the shimmering Hudson. Welcome to Manhattan, chappy.

From the bridge we could see the sun hitting the Chrysler Building. And there was the Empire State, rocketing skyward. Further south, the Trade Center towers stood firm and strong, like America's two front teeth.

Down the West Side Highway, across 14th to Broadway, left on Bleecker. And there it was. Straight through the windshield. CBGB. Sharing the block with a street mission, CBs might have lacked the grandeur of the buildings that cut Manhattan's skyline, but it towered in our imagination. To four guys from the Buckeye State, this bar, with its brick façade and dirty-white awning, boasted a Wizard of Ozian mystique.

I followed Biggie inside. The only light in the place came from the door we'd just opened and the neon behind the bar. We walked slowly, absorbing every smoky molecule. Then Biggie scrunched his nose, inspected the sole of his boot.

He'd stepped in a pile of dog shit.

With a short bark, the dog in question came moping around a corner. Gray and mottled, it seemed to consider nosing our crotches, before huffing something that sounded like, *Fuck it,* and dropping to the floor.

A man with a gray beard followed behind the dog, firsthand evidence that pets and pet-owners could look alike. "Yeah, guys," he said.

"Are you . . ." Biggie said. "Are you Hilly?" Hilly Krystal owned the place. It was Hilly that had first opened the doors to the Ramones.

"Which band are you?"

"Watershed? We're playing last."

He headed toward the bar. "Load straight onto the stage. Soundguy'll be here any minute."

Biggie hustled back to the van, and I bent down to pet the dog, who snorted and rolled over as if he were doing me a favor.

There may have been shit on the floor, but CBs was a tightly run ship. With six bands per night, it had to be. The soundguy told us where to drop our gear and where to stash our cases, then we ran through a quick version of "Rise," the lead track from the Willie-produced cassette. The splintered monitors looked like they'd been dropped from a DC-10. The microphones tasted like smoke, rust, and beer. Singing into them was like licking the screen door at a VFW hall. But from my spot on that weirdly angled stage, we'd never sounded better.

The soundguy cut us off halfway through the song. "Make sure you're back by 1:00 a.m.," he said. "I'll try to get you on by 1:30."

Nine hours 'til showtime. Let the waiting game begin.

I walked down the basement stairs and into the men's room, where the walls were spray-painted, and the toilet was coppery with hard water stains. But rock wasn't supposed to be scrubbed and 409'd. Rock was the mildew, the slime, the dog shit. I unzipped, thumbed my pants to my knees, and sat, sanitation be damned. Then I noticed that there was no door. I was sitting on the pot, looking directly up the stairs. If anyone were to come down right now, he or she would be looking straight into my crotch. Crappus interruptus. I buttoned up and walked out.

The soundguy met me at the top of the stairs. "Dude," he said. "Go shit in the pizza shop next door."

Colin had wandered off on his own, so Herb and I walked Bleecker toward NYU. We people-watched through Washington Square, browsed the used record stores on Thompson Street, walked down Mulberry through Little Italy and into Chinatown, and made our way back up Bowery to the club.

We'd only killed two hours. So we went for pizza slices next door, watched the last two bands soundchecking, and played two-man euchre at a bar table.

But it was still only 8:00 p.m.

So I decided to take a nap in the van, where I found Colin stretched out inside. He told me that he *had* taken a shit in the CBs bathroom. Fucking guy was always one-upping me.

Far too wired to sleep, I went back to the pizza shop and read the *Village Voice* cover to cover, from the masthead in front to the escort services in back. Somewhere in the middle, I found the CBs ad, and I discovered that Watershed, although last to play, wasn't the headliner after all. Two other bands, The Brandos and Maria Ex Communikata, got the headliner-sized font.

Just before 2:00 a.m., The Brandos waved goodbye, and Maria Ex Communikata took the stage. The crowd pressed to the front. CBs was packed to fire-code capacity. With a flash of strobe lights, Maria Ex launched into their set. Two female lead singers, one white and one black, sang with operatic voices over gothic heavy metal. They wore vintage velvet dresses, and their tits were corseted to two inches of cleavage. They looked like naughty Victorian librarians, or like strippers drawn by Edward Gorey. The crowd went ape-shit. Maria Ex could have played until breakfast, and the audience would have been ecstatic. I felt like I'd been beamed fifty years into the future, to a time when the proliferation of human growth hormones and Madonna videos had left seven-foot, heaving-bosomed maidens to walk the earth. This was high-concept performance art, and I was too big a hayseed to understand it. But one thing was clear: We were about to get blown off the stage by opera-singing librarian strippers.

Maria Ex finished at 3:15, forty-five minutes until closing time. Biggie sprung into action, gathering amps and cymbal stands and trying to shove everything onto the stage as fast as he could, but Maria Ex was taking their sweet time getting out of the way. They were saying hi to the people in the front row and breaking down their backline lazily, as if the night was over. Their fans, 300 or so of them, were bending underneath tables for jackets, slogging toward the front door, and steadily becoming 280, 250, 200.

Biggie glared at the two Maria Ex strumpets. He kept the trains running on time, by God, and he didn't abide a band that dragged ass. "Fuck this," he said. "We're going anyway." He dropped my amp directly in front of Maria Ex's bass player's amp, and he backed Colin's amp into their guitar setup, blockading them in. They wouldn't be able to load out until after our set. The Maria Ex tarts hissed.

By the time Herb finished setting up the drums, there were fifty people in the bar. Forty. Thirty. Colin and I nodded that we were ready, and Herb counted us into the opener, "Hero of a Tragedy," an appropriate choice, because there were now fewer than ten people in the crowd, including the soundguy, the bartenders, and the dog.

Halfway through that first song, the staff started putting the chairs up on the tables. Then the houselights came on, and we could see bar-backs wiping down their stations and pushing trashcans across the floor. Biggie watched Maria Ex's white singer jam her fingers into her ears and walk out to the street. In his show notes, he wrote "Gut check."

The soundguy's voice came through the monitors like a vice principal calling a classroom from the office. "Thanks, guys. Might as well call it a night."

I felt sick to my stomach. We'd driven five hundred miles and waited for almost twelve hours to play one song.

Colin leaned into the mic. "If it's all the same to you, we'll keep going."

"Whatever," said the soundguy. He backed away from the board and headed for the bar.

Colin picked up his mic stand and moved it to the center of the stage, turning his back to the bar, facing Herb, studio-style, just like Willie had taught us. I turned my microphone around too, and the three of us stood in a circle, looking at each other. It didn't matter that nobody else was there.

I nodded *go ahead*, and Colin launched into the opening riff of "How Do You Feel," a brand new song we'd never played live. He started singing the first verse, and over my shoulder I saw a guy standing at the foot of the stage, pumping his fist and playing air-guitar. Colin and I turned toward him, opening the circle a slice. The guy was wearing a Maria Ex T-shirt. Biggie wrote in his show notes: "Some guy is loving it? Every cloud has a silver lining."

But by the time Biggie looked up from his notepad, the Maria Ex fan had disappeared. "He's gone," Biggie wrote. We muscled through two more songs and called it a night. The last line in the show notes reads, "Remember the Alamo."

Colin, Biggie, Herb, and I had been together for almost six years, and yet we were only twenty-one, just getting our shit together. The Toll, on the other hand, was grinding apart. Their second major-label effort was a commercial disaster, and Geffen dropped them. Being dropped is the end of the road for most bands. After playing every shitty gig in every shitty town trying to get signed, losing the deal is almost always the lethal blow. The Toll broke up immediately. For all their soapboxing and *Art of War*-ing, they were just as fragile as any other band. Watershed felt betrayed for about ten minutes, before saying, *Fuck 'em. It's our turn.*

Rocco's odometer rolled like a slot machine. In 1991 we played eighty-odd shows, from Minneapolis to Macon, without the help of a record label, a booking agent, or a manager not named Biggie. If we could route Toledo with Detroit or Madison with Chicago, fine. But if not, that was fine too. We'd play Cincinnati on Thursday, Charlotte on Friday, Detroit on Saturday. We'd drive all the way to Philly or Baltimore for one show, then turn-tail for home. Biggie stuck a framed photo of Ohio-born General William Tecumseh Sherman on the dashboard, and we'd roll down to Georgia[19] and South Carolina while joking about Watershed's march to the sea, about foraging liberally—then we'd flip the good general face down to keep from getting a brick through the windshield. Talent-buyers called us the hardest working band in America. Drunk bikers said we were the best band they'd seen since Black Oak Arkansas. Bartenders slid us free drinks saying, "Too bad nobody was here tonight. The place is usually packed."

This was the year Colin and I should have graduated from OSU. We should have spent a June morning in folding chairs on the stadium turf, swaying to "Carmen Ohio," tossing our caps into the air like Hail Mary passes. Then we'd have marched out of that stadium and into a job at Nationwide or Huntington: into a cubicle, into a minivan, into a thirty-year mortgage on a suburban split-level and two weeks a year at Sea Pines.

On long rides up and down the East Coast, we told ourselves we felt sorry for those capped-and-gowned suckers who'd have to work forty-five good years to earn one last decade of cart golf and gimpy tennis. Colin wrote a song called "Five for Two" that summed up the bad deal our classmates had made: *Five days a week you put your jacket on / Five days a week you take your jacket off / You're working your life for some other man / You're trading five days for two your whole life, my friend.* The Watershed plan was to live like John D. MacDonald's literary hero Travis McGee, the self-proclaimed "salvage expert" who works when he wants, thereby taking his retirement in installments. Our golden years were happening right then and there, lived a few hours at a time: a sunny off day in Charleston, a pre-soundcheck matinee in Milwaukee.

We put absolute faith in the future we were designing on those van rides, and for faith to be worth a damn, it must be oft-tested. Even when we played a string of crappy shows—for no crowd, no money, no industry attention—we were certain the next one would lead to something bigger. The Class of '91, however, would always be stuck in their square gigs. As Churchill might put it, Watershed might be drunk, but those poor stiffs—in their Men's Wearhouse blazers and pleated slacks—would always be ugly.

Our diploma—or something like it—came that fall, in the form of a review in *Alternative Press* magazine. I stood in the bookstore for twenty minutes, reading the blurb over and over:

Together since 1985, the members of Watershed seem determined to hang tough until the hands of fame point to Columbus. When it does, they'll be ready. With their insistent arena rhythms, sweet pop harmonies, heroic melodies, and relentless sincerity, Watershed could be the U2 of Ohio. Or the Tom Petty: y'know, the sort of big, mainstream rock act that can't possibly ever be cool, but which you sometimes like despite yourself.

I had to bite my tongue to keep from shrieking like a middle school girl at a New Kids on the Block concert. This was our first mention in a national publication. I skipped over the *can't be cool* part and focused instead on *arena rhythms, heroic melodies,* and *mainstream rock. Alternative Press* was proof that dropping out of school—even to play comic disasters like CBGB—had gotten us closer and closer to *big.*

We're still two hours from Cleveland, driving through the outer reaches of Metro Columbus—through the exurban ring that will have much to say in this year's presidential election. Because the city's demographics closely resemble those of the entire country, Columbus has for years been a test market. We got the Shamrock Shake and the McRib sandwich long before most everywhere else, and I can remember reps from M&M/Mars handing out free samples of the then-new Peanut Butter Twix on the statehouse lawn.[20] All kinds of products, from paint to politicians, test their mettle in Columbus before going national. The city's slogan ought to be, IF YOU CAN MAKE IT HERE, YOU CAN MAKE IT ANYWHERE, which is why it's so damn frustrating that these days Watershed is *only* big in Columbus. For most bands, a fifty-person following is huge, and yet, inside I-270, we've drawn a few hundred for the last fifteen years. Take us outside the outerbelt, however, and our audiences are tiny.

As we head north, Biggie's got the dial tuned to CD101, one of America's last great independent stations. Because CD101 isn't owned by a huge corporation, the program director, Andy "Andyman" Davis, has the freedom to play what's good, not simply what's been spoonfed to him by record promoters and programming consultants. The man's got bills to pay, of course, so he'll spin the usual alternative rock fare: U2, The White Stripes, Green Day, and so on. But now, as if programming the station specifically for us, Andyman follows The Clash's "Brand New Cadillac" with "Dancing with Mr. D" by The Stones. In this, the era of ClearChannel, CD101 is a throwback to the days when the DJ actually had some room to do a little jockeying.

Andyman also plays Watershed. A lot. In regular rotation, alongside The Hives and The Strokes and everybody else. Ten days ago, on New Year's Day, the station counted down their top two thousand songs of all time, and eight Watershed tracks made the cut. "Obvious," the lead single from our most recent studio album, clocked in at #160, a ridiculous thirteen slots better than "Should I Stay or Should I Go?" and three better than "Rock N Roll High School." Even I think #160 is way too high for Watershed, but I'm not about to look the CD101 gift-horse in the mouth. Andyman and his station are the fundamental reason we've held a Columbus following for so long.

Now, as we're slowly losing the CD101 signal, I'm still puzzled by our inability to extend the Columbus buzz to other towns. And this has me thinking of a different trip to Cleveland, in 1992, when Biggie and I sat in a hotel ballroom, listening to a panel of A&R reps talk about how becoming big at home was the best way for bands to get noticed *beyond* home.

"Look around," said an A&R guy with shoulder-length hair. "Look at the sheer number of you. And this is just one city. In one state."

There were maybe two hundred of us attending the Undercurrents Music Conference, Cleveland's answer to South By Southwest.

"And guess what?" Shoulder-length Hair said. "You all want the same thing." He shook his head to say, no, we weren't all going to get it. Because demo tapes littered his office. Tapes filled milk crates and wicker baskets. Tapes were stacked like Jenga on desks and end tables. And every day the guys from the mailroom (who were in bands themselves) tossed twenty-five new tapes on the pile.

When the A&R panel took questions from the floor, a fat indie-girl with bad skin and pigtails stood up. "So, we're all sitting here in Cleveland freaking Ohio, right?" she said. "What are the chances of anybody being discovered here? I mean this conference is nice, I guess." She looked from one panelist to the next, five people with the power to give any of us the record deal we so badly wanted. "But I don't see any of you hanging around Cleveland the other fifty-one weeks of the year."

Grunts of agreement from the crowd.

Shoulder-length Hair explained that, yes, some music scenes attracted more attention than others, and New York and L.A. were always going to be hot. But other scenes popped up all the time. "Right now, things are happening in Seattle," he said. "Before that it was Athens. Minneapolis. But leaving your hometown to try to cash in on the new scene can be a big mistake." He said that if any of us did move to, say, Seattle, we'd probably get there too late. The buzz would have died. And the bands and labels that had made the scene would see newcomers as party crashers. "Trust me," he said. "If you're the biggest band in Chicago or Buffalo or, yes, even Cleveland, we will find you. It's our *job* to find you." He flashed the smile of an Ivy League rowing captain. "Your job is to get so huge we can't miss you."

Biggie and I drove home that night determined to dominate Columbus. The first step was to start a mailing list. Most bands brought a notebook to shows, begging the crowd for signatures. We went through the phone book and signed up everyone we could think of: classmates and co-workers and ex–Worthington High cheerleaders. Kate dug up the addresses of Olentangy kids. My sister worked her all-girl dorm. Colin's sister recruited the girls in her sorority.

Once we had a base of three hundred (mostly female) names, we sent out monthly postcards. "Greetings from Columbus," these cards would say. "We're touring behind a new tape produced by the legendary Willie Phoenix. Please check us out in one of the following cities: January 4, CBGB in New York. January 5, The Avalon in Chicago. January 6, The Uptown in Minneapolis." We figured that if Columbusites, with their city penis envy, knew Watershed was playing in bigger, cooler towns and at famous clubs like CBGB, they'd show up at our hometown shows to see what the national fuss was about. Nobody needed to know that landing a gig at CBs was actually pretty easy[21] or that we usually played for small, uninterested crowds. By spreading word of our successes (be they successful or not), we got people to believe things were happening. This would then snowball into things *actually* happening. Such is the nature of buzz.

Colin guessed that we could amplify this buzz by making ourselves *less* available in Columbus. The hometown shows should feel like concerts, he said, not like any old night in a bar. So we started playing Ruby Tuesday the last Saturday of the month. That's it. If you wanted to see Watershed, but didn't want to travel to Detroit or Pittsburgh, you had to wait. The strategy worked. We established ourselves as a headlining act, routinely drawing two hundred or more. The Columbus shows would then bankroll money-losing jaunts to Atlanta and Madison and every other city where we played for almost nobody. But the important thing on those lonely nights was that we were someplace *other* than home, and that people in Columbus knew it. The next month there would be 220 at Ruby's. The next, 250. Soon we were Ruby's biggest drawing act. Surely it was only a matter of time before A&R reps noticed.

Even though Watershed had become a successful Columbus band, we weren't exactly part of the Columbus *scene*. Ruby's sat two blocks east of High Street, in the hinterlands. The epicenter of the scene was a bar called Stache's. The Replacements had played there, as had X, The Misfits, and Nirvana. If you were a national touring band in the Eighties and Nineties, you'd been there. The owner, Dan Dougan, printed up shirts that said as much: STACHE'S—YA BEEN THERE. We *had* been there, but mostly to watch other, more buzz-worthy bands.[22] Month after month, we called Dougan, and it was always, "I can give you a Wednesday." But one day, as we sat stuffing envelopes, he called us. "Hey, man," he told Biggie. "I heard you guys are packing 'em in at Ruby's. What are you drawing? Like 250?" Dougan offered us a Friday. A Saturday. Whatever we wanted. We started alternating our monthly shows between the loyal but off-the-map Ruby's and the music-scene-approved Stache's.

Still local critics either dismissed us as a frat-rock band or ignored us altogether. We got no love from the national press either. In the early Nineties it was common to read in *Spin* or *Entertainment Weekly* that Columbus was The Next Seattle.[23] As evidence, the articles would list bands like Scrawl, Thomas Jefferson Slave Apartments, The New Bomb

Turks, and Gaunt. None of those bands had a following as big as ours, but their following seemed to matter more. Our crowd was a bunch of people; their crowd was a scene.

It took me years to understand that the scene—a very loose web of record labels, rock critics, record store clerks, and the bands they signed or wrote about or played in—really only existed within the margins of the music rags and in the minds of those, like us, who felt *excluded* from it. But in those rags a history was written. Today almost every account of Columbus music in the late Eighties and early Nineties names Scrawl, TJSA, New Bomb Turks, and Gaunt as the defining groups of the era. Acts like Willie Phoenix, The Toll, and Ronald Koal have been written away. But by drawing so much critical attention back then, Scrawl and TJSA *did* define the era. They defined it for us, anyway. Because we didn't know how badly we wanted critical acclaim until we saw *them* getting it.

We were what music writers called "careerists." This was the dirtiest word of the day, and we kind of understood why, but not really. If being a careerist meant wanting to play music instead of having a real job, then Watershed was guilty-as-charged. But we also wanted to be liked by the cool kids, so we showed up at Scrawl shows, listened to New Bomb Turks CDs, and bought beers for Jerry Wick from Gaunt. Taking cues from these bands, we eventually learned to shut up about how badly we wanted to be rock stars.[24] In public, at least, we became humble and self-deprecating, which better fit our suburban earnestness anyway.

One afternoon at Bernie's Bagels, Colin found himself sitting next to Ron House, the main man in TJSA, as he'd been in the semi-legendary Great Plains before that. He also moonlighted as a rock critic. While House read a paperback, Colin wondered aloud about *credibility* and how music writers could create it and also fall under its spell. But it wasn't too late for Watershed to win over the press, was it, Ron? After all, power pop was the musical movement du jour. The critics had rediscovered Big Star. Teenage Fanclub, The Posies, Goo Goo Dolls, and Matthew Sweet had been showered with praise. If music writers dug these bands, surely they would embrace Watershed and our brand of guitar-fueled, Midwestern power pop. Right, Ron?

"Listen, Colin," House said, eying him over the top of his book. "You guys will never be a writers' band." He didn't explain why. He must have figured he didn't have to, that it was obvious.

Colin rode his bike home and told the rest of us what House had said.

"Who the fuck cares what Ron House thinks?" Biggie said.

"Fans are way more important than writers," I said. But I wasn't sure it was true. Maybe no bands were credible until critics bestowed credibility upon them. Maybe *Alternative Press* was right. Watershed could be big, but we couldn't ever be cool.

Between Mansfield and Ashland, Dave opens a beer and tells us his mom has pancreatic cancer. The doctors don't yet know her prognosis, how badly it has spread, or whether it's hit the lymph nodes. Dave is unsure how worried to be, how sad to be. He only knows that his mom will soon start radiation treatments.

We try to be supportive, but what do you say? *Wow, Dave. That sucks, Dave. How are you holding up, Dave?* I'm taking my cues from Colin. His mom died of lung cancer, so he knows a little about what Dave is or is not feeling.

Colin asks Dave a few questions, and he doesn't skirt the edges of the disease like the rest of us do. He uses words like *metastasis* and *malignancy*, loosening cancer's hold by speaking its tongue. Colin then talks about losing his mom, about what those last days in the hospital were like. You'd think deathbed stories would be the last ones you'd tell, but Colin's instincts are right: this talk is helping. Soon Dave is laughing. We all are.

"And there was this weird thing that happened," Colin says. "Just when things were at their worst, and we knew my mom was absolutely dying, that it was a done deal and all the treatments were over, no chemo, no surgeries, nothing—when that happened, it was like a giant cloud had broken up. There was nothing left to hope for, so we could concentrate on enjoying the time she had left. For those few weeks, everything was, you know, kind of great. We laughed a lot. We told stories. It's like we were celebrating the end of hope."

For a few seconds the van is quiet except for the whine of the tires. Then, because Watershed is never far from Colin's thoughts, he laughs and says, "I guess this is the *Celebrating the End of Hope Tour*."

"Perfect," I say. "Obama's got the hope market cornered. Let's go the other way."

Dave laughs and says, "Watershed: Celebrating the End of Hope. Print up the T-shirts, Biggie."

But we're an hour late for soundcheck, and Biggie's getting edgy. He's driving herky-jerky—gunning us from lane to lane on wintry-slick I-71, accelerating too fast, stomping the brakes too hard—all of which is making Colin nervous as an astronaut's wife. I know he's itching to say something to Biggie, to tell him to slow the fuck down, but Colin's justifiably scared of making the driver more irritable than he already is, so he directs his comments to the van as a whole. "Has it ever once *mattered* whether we made soundcheck on time or not?" Colin says. "Has the gig *ever* suffered because we were late?"

Biggie doesn't take the bait. He operates with the single-mindedness of a military man. His job is to get us there.

When we finally do land in front of the Beachland Ballroom, with its glass-block and vintage neon, we can hear that the opening band has already started their set. No soundcheck for us. Biggie goes into drill sergeant mode: "Joe, go inside and get the load-in door opened. Colin and Dave, we'll move straight into the kitchen and set up there. Pooch, break out the guitars and start tuning."

A former Croatian social club, The Beachland is two bars: the velvet-draped Ballroom and the smaller, wood-paneled Tavern. Tonight we're booked in the Tavern, with a capacity of maybe one hundred. The last time Watershed played here was opening for Hamell On Trial[25], but I was here more recently on an assignment for *Esquire* magazine. For a couple years now I've been contributing to their "Best Bars in America" series. The work is as plum as you'd guess. I go to bars, drink, then pitch the most interesting ones to the magazine. According to *Esquire* and me, the Beachland Ballroom is one of America's best. But if Watershed had never played here, I never would have pitched it, and it wouldn't have been featured in the magazine. That *happenstance* can be so important is a little disheartening. The Beachland was a great bar long before I wrote about it; all I did was enter it into the record.

There's already a decent crowd in the Tavern. The tables are full, and a few people are perched at the bar. The opening band features a familiar face: Bill Stone, who used to be the singer-guitarist for Cleveland's Paranoid Lovesick. They were power pop guys about our age, funny, with catchy songs, and we became friends immediately. In the early Nineties they were kicking ass in Cleveland; they had buzz, and the A&R sharks took notice. They appeared on a bill with Weezer and opened for Oasis on the British band's first-ever US date. Drew Carey came to one of their shows. But PL never got signed. The record reps moved on to the next Next Big Thing, and Paranoid Lovesick became just another band, slugging it out in the trenches. Now, looking at Bill on stage with his new group, I'm happy he hasn't stopped playing. But damn. They look old up there under the lights with their skinny arms and thick middles.

After our set, I catch up with Bill at the bar. He's pushing forty, with a new baby at home, and he makes his living inspecting houses. I buy him a beer and tell him it's great to see him. Great to know he hasn't quit.

"Aw, shit. Thanks," he says. "But you guys are the ones still carrying the torch. You're carrying it for bands like us, bands who dropped it." He clinks his beer against mine. "So don't stop." Then he hands me a copy of the *Cleveland Free Times,* one of those top-of-the-cigarette-machine papers. "You got a little press," he says, pointing to the article.

Back in the '90s, when exuberant pop-rock acts such as the Gin Blossoms and Matthew Sweet roamed the land, Columbus, Ohio's

Watershed seemed to be performing at the Grog Shop every other month, joining such local ensembles as The Waynes, World in a Room, and Fifth Wheel on the list of favorites of area fans who liked clear, singable melodies and smart, searching lyrics . . . But Watershed never got its big breakthrough, and one might be forgiven for thinking the band had vanished off the face of the earth along with those aforementioned acts.

I don't remember once playing with The Waynes, World in a Room, or Fifth Wheel, but I remember every show we ever played with Paranoid Lovesick. And yet there's no mention of them here. I hand the paper back to Bill. Tell him again it's great to see him. Then I walk away, thinking about how hard it is to get written into the record and how easy it is to be written out.

6

Rock and Roll Professionals
Toledo, Ohio

I'LL SAY IT LOUD AND PROUD: I LIKE TOLEDO. HAVE SINCE 1987, WHEN I saw my first KISS concert at the now-razed Sports Arena.[26] Toledoans are scrappy, and they've got civic pride. Toledo reminds me of Tacoma in that way—in a lot of ways, really. Both are port cities, glass cities. Both sit in the shadow of a much bigger town. But Tacoma's lucky: We're linked to Seattle and the rising tide of prosperity that computers and coffee beans brought. Toledo's anchored to Detroit.

Frankie's, the club we're playing, sits across the Maumee River from downtown, in East Toledo, a neighborhood perennially on the verge of gentrification. Ten years ago, when Watershed last played here, East Toledo seemed finally to be making the turn from slummy to arty. But driving along Main Street tonight, nothing much looks improved. Biggie parks across from the bar, near a bleak strip mall that holds an uninspiring grocery and at least two beauty supply shops.

A string of vans and SUVs lines the street in front of the club. Teenage boys with angular hair and skinny jeans spill from open doors. Girls with striped tops and pierced lips bounce from van to van.

Pooch's laughter fogs our windows. "Looks like a Hot Topic store exploded," he says, which is funnier when you know he buys his stage clothes at Kohl's.

Biggie reminds us that Frankie's has scheduled an early, all-ages show. We'll load in after the youngsters are done.

Colin perks up at the sight of the hot emo chicks. "Heeeeyyyy," he says through the closed window, in the leery-eyed accent of an old creeper. "You ladies like rock and roll? Wanna party with Uncle Watershed?"

"We've got beer!" Dave says, reaching into the cooler for a few.

"Shit, let's sell 'em for three bucks apiece," I say. "Like the ice-cream man, but with Budweiser instead of Bomb Pops."

"These kids don't drink," Biggie says. "Look at 'em. They're too bright-eyed. Got too much energy."

"They're rocking for God, right?" I say. I'm searching for Jesus fish on the backs of the vans. "Gotta be."

"Fuck yeah," Biggie says. "Anytime you see punks with money, you know God's in the mix."

One of the boys jumps from a jeep and chases a girl into Main Street. When he catches her, he musses her hair, which was pretty mussed to begin with.

Pooch presses his nose to the glass. "I think he's gonna pork her."

"Kid's a virgin," Biggie says. "He's not porking anything."

"Then let me take a shot at her," Pooch says. "At least I know what I'm doing."

"And you've got a baby daughter to prove it," Colin says. He reaches into the cooler. "Want one, Biggie?"

"I think I do," Biggie says.

We sip our beers and keep tabs on the young bucks across the street.

Tonight marks our forty-first gig at Frankie's. In the early Nineties we played here about once a month. Rob, the owner, has renovated the club since then. There's more chrome, higher-tech lights, and on the far wall, he's hung a Wall of Fame. I elbow through the underage crowd to get a closer look. Tacked behind a sheet of Plexiglas are old posters, publicity photos, and newspaper articles for bands like The White Stripes, The Verve Pipe, and Hole. And sandwiched between the Royal Crescent Mob and the Smashing Pumpkins, there's an early press photo of Colin, Herb, and me. Herb's hairline has receded a little in the fifteen years since then, but Colin and I look pretty much the same. I check over my shoulder to make sure none of the kids has caught me staring at a picture of myself, then I tap the glass twice and head for the restroom. The Frankie's Wall of Fame is a low-watt affair, but it feels good to have made it. Not making it would have felt infinitely worse.

When that photo was taken, my day job was at Vision Center Industries, a sheltered shop run by my dad, where disabled folks did packaging and light manufacturing work for local companies. Fifty or so employees, many of them blind, boxed truck parts for Volvo and screwed together heat-sink assemblies for Toledo Scale. They collated and bagged and shrink-wrapped, and because they were paid piece-rate, they did it over and over, day after day, for years. I was a floor supervisor, in charge of material handling and quality control.

I wasn't allowed to see the employee files, but my guess was that one longtime worker, Chris Clarkson, was autistic. He was blessed with an acute memory and a deep well of obscure facts. "Joseph Oestreich," he'd say as I filled his table with taillights to box up, "do you know the president of Atlantic Records?"

"Not personally," I'd say. He'd been asking me this for a year, ever since I let it slip that I was a musician.

"It's Ahmet Ertegun. He's Turkish."

"You don't say."

Chris's disorder, autism or whatever it was, was characterized by rigidity, a need to maintain daily patterns. He clung robotically to them. "Joseph," he'd say, "who do you like better, the Stylistics or the Impressions?"

I hadn't heard of either of them. I was twenty-one, and I didn't know Philadelphia Soul from Chicago Soul from Soul Train.

"Joseph, whatever happened to Ray Parker Junior?"

I'd try to break his rhythm by mentioning that Watershed played Louisville or Detroit the night before.

"Joseph, did you know that Interstate 64 goes through Louisville? And Lexington. And Charleston. And Richmond. And . . ."

I'd climb onto my forklift and gas the engine. But before I could pull away he'd ask me his favorite question, the one he asked every single day without fail. "Joseph," he'd say, "when is Watershed going to get a recording contract?"

"One of these days, Chris," I'd say, rolling the lift forward. "One of these days."

We'd recently moved our gear into a utility room in the corner of the Vision Center warehouse. No more puffy coats in the storage garage cum walk-in freezer. The new practice spot was huge, heated, and once the employees clocked out, we had the run of the place. We'd sit at the receptionist's desk and make long distance calls to clubs. We'd stuff envelopes in the conference room, make flyers on the copy machine. When it was time to load out, we'd open the overhead doors and pull the van right up to the practice room. No rain. No snow. We were climate-controlled, baby. Like a frickin' Holidome.

My supervisor was a fan of the band, and he'd called me into his office one day to say he was offering the room as a fringe benefit—100 percent rent-free. I knew that technically my dad was my boss's boss, but if the rock and roll gods deign to bestow upon you a sweet rehearsal spot for the low, low price of nothing, you don't worry about whose idea it was. You just scrape and bow and say thankyou-thankyou-thankyou. Then you move your stuff in before somebody gets wise.

We practiced three nights a week, writing the songs that would become our first, full-length record. Herb was now sous-chef at the four-star Worthington Inn, and his shift didn't end until 11:00 p.m., so we rehearsed from midnight to 2:00, which made getting up for work at 6:45 problematic. But as I dragged myself out of bed those mornings, I counted my baggy eyes as more evidence that Watershed was paying the dues that would, oh yes, lead to a recording contract. Dig *that*, Chris Clarkson.

Driving to and from work, I listened to the good-time-oldies station, singing along to songs like "Palisades Park," "Red Rubber Ball," and "Up on the Roof." One day, as I was motoring around on the forklift, I found myself humming a tune that sounded vaguely familiar: *Are you coming over tonight? Take my hand, it'll be all right.* I must have heard it on the radio, but I couldn't place it. Sometime after lunch it hit me: Maybe *I'd* written this song. I sure hoped it was mine, because the melody seemed just as catchy as "High on a Mountain of Love" or any other feel-good-oldie, but I was afraid that if I didn't get it on tape, I'd forget the melody and the song would be lost forever. I sped the lift toward the practice room, past Chris Clarkson, who was tangled in two hundred feet of radiator hose.

"Joseph, when are you going to get a recording contract?"

I waved him off and hopped down from the lift as it was still moving. Inside the room, I picked up Colin's Telecaster and hunted for a chord progression that would fit the tune that was streaming through my head. *Are you coming over tonight.* D to E. *Take my hand it'll be all right.* A to F-sharp minor. In a hushed voice I sang what I'd just written, but it wasn't like I'd written it at all. It seemed to have always existed. I just happened to be the one to pluck it from the sky.

But a melody this catchy deserved better lyrics. *Who* would be coming over? *Why?* Was I singing to Kate? She was my girlfriend, after all. For two years. I was no longer the balding wallflower I'd been in high school.

Wallflower . . . that was it. The word sounded just right, shy but determined. I had to find a way to make the wallflower idea work in the song. By the time I got home that afternoon, I'd written the chorus—the words and melody lining up like tumblers of a safe I'd unlocked. *I'm a wallflower child, singing out of tune up in my room. I'm a wallflower child in full bloom.*

When I played it for the guys at practice that night, Colin said, "It's good. Really good. But you know Willie would want us to take it up to Ramones speed."

I barked out 1-2-3-4 like Dee Dee Ramone, knowing that I'd finally written the kind of song I wanted to write. No more complicated Rush rip-offs. This tune was straightforward and simple, melodic and fast. I'd grabbed that wallflower that I used to be, booted him to the middle of the gym floor, and said, *Dance, motherfucker. Dance.*

That winter we went into the studio to record a batch of new tunes, including "Wallflower Child" and "How Do You Feel," the song we'd first played at CBGB. This time we wanted to succeed or fail on our own, so instead of working with Willie, we booked time with an engineer who didn't worry about nailing every part to perfection. The sessions were loose and rock and roll. Colin decided to title the resulting album *The*

Carpet Cliff, a metaphor for our leap from the suburbs into the rocky canyon of nightclubs and truck stops. We knew that compared to people with real troubles (like the workers I saw every day at the Vision Center) we'd stepped from one cushy life to another, from an Oriental rug to renter's-grade Berber, but still, the change felt real enough to us.

If Columbus was carpet, Detroit was busted glass and rusty nails. We'd been playing there regularly, ever since we'd befriended a Motor City band called The Generals. We first met them in Toledo, at Frankie's, on a night they opened for us. They had greaser-slick hair and blue jeans rolled up rockabilly style, but the song they played for soundcheck was a Stonesy blues number. The rhythm guitarist moved like a young Keith Richards, and the lead player looked like Ronnie Wood. The singer just stood there in his Red Wings jersey and rocked.

Most nights, bands spend soundcheck sniffing each other, like dogs thrown into a pen. They communicate via cocky silence or a ridiculous indie-cred pissing contest. But that night the Keith-esque guitar player bellied up to the bar natural as a cowboy, introduced himself as Kevin, and offered to buy me a shot. I said I was fine with the Coke I was sipping. Soon both bands convened around one table. We talked Columbus: The Toll, The Mob, Willie Phoenix. We talked Detroit: The Motown Museum, The MC5, Iggy and the Stooges. I asked Kevin about the slumping auto industry and the Michigan economy. He recommended *Rivethead,* Ben Hamper's assembly line memoir. I told him to read Raymond Carver, John Irving.

Eventually the soundguy sent The Generals to the stage. Their songs weren't as catchy as ours, but they were grittier, with titles like, "Somewhere Your Mother Is Down on Her Knees." Their new CD was called *You'll Eat What We're Cookin',* and we did.

After their set, I went up to Flip, the bass player, and said, "You guys wrecked this place."

Flip looked like a man who packed brass knuckles, but he thanked me sincerely, as if I'd done something nice for his grandma.

The Generals became our brother band. They'd open for us at Ruby's, and we'd play with them in Detroit at Paychecks and Lili's 21. They'd stay with us on Patterson Avenue; we'd crash at their house on Eight Mile. One day, after returning from a four-day swing through the South, we got a message saying that one of The Generals had died. It was Flip. He'd wrecked on the drive home from a gig in Flint. For the next ten years, almost every person I'd meet in Detroit would have FLIP tattooed on his arm.

Shortly after the ink dried on their FLIP tattoos, The Generals plugged in a new bass player and replaced the Ronnie Wood guy with John Speck, a nineteen-year-old skater-punk/tattoo artist who was the best guitar player I'd seen since Willie Phoenix. With Speck in the band, The Generals got even better. They routinely blew us off the stage.

Kevin eventually slid *The Carpet Cliff* to Detroit's Chaos Records, and the label decided to include "How Do You Feel" on *Fist Full of Chaos*, a compilation of Motor City bands. The CD release show was at Detroit's St. Andrews Hall. After our set, I stood at the bar with Kevin, and every time someone walked up to him, he'd say, "Did you see Watershed? These guys are going to be fucking huge, man."

Then John Speck, the new General, tapped me on the shoulder. Speck had reddish-blond hair and freckles, but he was no Howdy Doody. His was the face of an IRA man. His forearms were thick as five-pound pork tenderloins, and he'd tattooed F-A-I-T-H across his knuckles. Of all the Generals, I would become best friends with him. And when Speck's your friend, he's your best friend, boyo. But he can go from wanting to fight for you to wanting to fight you without you knowing he's flipped the switch. Earlier that night Kevin told me that Speck had once broken a guy's nose with one lightning-fast head butt. "Don't stand too close to him," Kevin said. "You'll end up collateral damage."

But now Speck was smiling. "Hey, Joe," he said. A vein pulsed above the bridge of his nose as he shouted over the band. "I've been listening to *The Carpet Cliff.*"

"And what do you think?" I wasn't sure I wanted to know. Once your new album has been out a while, your friends stop sugarcoating their opinion. They'll tell you things like, *Hmm . . . it's not my favorite* or *I liked the demos better.*

"I think your songs are better than Colin's," Speck said.

"Wow, man. Thanks." If one person was saying my songs were better than Colin's, then surely someone else was telling Colin that his songs were better than mine. Still, I'd never been singled out before, and it felt great. I smiled big and open.

Speck ordered us two beers. He wasn't yet twenty-one, but that didn't matter here. "'How Do You Feel' is an awesome song," he said, "but Colin does that whole ballady Springsteen thing. Your songs are more my speed." We clinked beers and he said, "You know what my favorite song of yours is?"

I shook my head.

Speck raised his F-A-I-T-H fist and started singing, "I'm a wallflower child . . ."

The next morning I sat on a folding chair in the basement of The Generals' house. The sun streamed through the glass block windows, making kaleidoscopic streaks on the concrete floor.

"How bad is this going to hurt?" I said to Speck. The St. Andrews after-party had raged till daylight, and upstairs, everyone else was sleeping off his hangover.

"The meat on your shoulder dampens the pain," he said, unpacking tattoo supplies from a leather case. "Head tats are the worst. And knees and elbows. Shoulder's no big deal."

I'd wanted him to tattoo me last night, but he said I was too drunk. I'd bleed like a hemophiliac. So now I was hungover in a basement on Eight Mile, where a nineteen-year-old was loading a tattoo gun. With a Bic pen he drew the design on a piece of wax paper, printing the letters backwards. Then he popped the top on a stick of Old Spice and rubbed the deodorant on my left shoulder. "The alcohol will transfer the image. Then I'll trace it with the needle." He peeled the paper away, and there was the mock-up in Bic ink, upside down and backwards. WALLFLOWER arcing across the ball of my shoulder. CHILD spelled out underneath.

Speck flipped on the gun, which buzzed like a yellow jacket. His eyebrows pinched together in concentration. That vein above the bridge of his nose was back. "You ready?"

I clenched my jaw, anticipating the pain. This was my chance to back out. Head up to the kitchen and wash the ink down the drain. Wouldn't I regret this when I was eighty and my skin was loose and leathery? Nope, I decided, this part of my life needed to be documented. Like a concert T-shirt that proves you were at the show, the tattoo would be a souvenir brought home from the days when I played in dingy bars and slept on stained carpets. Someday, when I was old, I'd stand at the mirror and turn my knobby shoulder to the glass, and in that fading ink I'd read the story of a kid who took his guitar from the edge of his bed into America's rock clubs. A kid who formed one of the biggest bands in his hometown. A kid who, when those letters were sewn into his skin, knew that he and his best friends were on the verge of everything they wanted.

Now, in the Frankie's bathroom, I do turn my shoulder to the mirror. The tattoo has faded in the sixteen years since Speck inked it, and the letters have gone blurry. It looks like it says CAULIFLOWER CHILI.

As part of the recent remodeling, the bathroom walls are now covered with chalkboard. Over the sink someone has written WATERSHED ROCKS! Underneath, somebody else—surely one of the emo kids—has responded with, WHAT IS ROCK?

The club is loaded with tortured-looking suburban brats, thumbs in their pockets, legs drawn together. They look like sensitive types who worship The Smiths or Joy Division. But tonight they're nodding along to a nü metal outfit slumped on stage—a guttural mix of shouting and rapping over a bed of hyper-compressed guitars. This is screamo music, I guess. Yuck. I'd rather listen to The Carpenters or Seals and Crofts. Even Bread, in their infinite softness, rocks harder than this. Too much of this band's sound is digitized— from the computer-generated drum loop to the Line 6 guitar amps—so they're oddly quiet. For all their moaning and barking, the music is nutless.

I cut through the screamo sea and out to the sidewalk, wishing that Speck was on the bill tonight. These God-rocking youngsters could learn something from an honest-to-God rocker. After The Generals broke up,

Speck's new band, Hoarse, signed with RCA. The label gave them a nice push at radio, and for a while in 1996 Hoarse seemed primed to hit big. They set out on a national tour opening for Seven-Mary-Three, who were riding high on their radio mainstay "Cumbersome." But one night, when Speck was supposed to be driving the van from St. Louis to Denver, his bandmates woke to find themselves in Detroit. Something had put a burr in Speck's ass, and he'd said *Fuck Denver* and steered for home. Tour over. I don't know the cause and effect of what happened next, but either RCA dropped the band, so they broke up—or the band broke up, so RCA dropped them.

Here on the sidewalk, several of the musician kids and their girlfriends are cuddling and playing footsie. This is cute and all, but it's a breach of etiquette. You don't hang around with your girlfriend at the gig. You just don't. Rock isn't cuddly, rock is *Fuck Denver*. These kids are fifteen years too young to have seen Hoarse, but some of them might have seen Speck. Last fall his newest band, HiFi Handgrenades, landed the opening slot on a string of Foo Fighters arena dates, and now word is that more Foos shows are in the offing. I'm thrilled for Speck. I'm also feeling a tinge of professional jealousy. I hope he doesn't go *Fuck Denver* on the Foo Fighters, but I know he probably will. That's the vexing thing about the guy. His timebomb-like volatility is what makes him the real rocking deal—until it inevitably explodes in his hands.

All the emo-canoodling reminds me that I need to call Kate.[27] It's been nine days since she flew back to Tacoma, and she now seems to be weathering my absence well. Whenever Watershed goes on tour her sadness takes a semi-predictable arc. The first few days are the worst, but then she gets used to me being gone. She starts to like having the house to herself—likes it so much, in fact, that the point of greatest tension is usually when I come home, and suddenly there are twice as many dishes in the sink and the bathroom towels are no longer hung the right way. Then it's the having-me-around that takes getting used to.

I'm expecting some additional flak this tour because Kate and I had planned to hang out together for these two weeks. School doesn't start again until February, so we'd talked about camping in the San Juans or booking a B&B in Victoria. This was the first time in three years Kate and I had agreed to set aside a break in the school year for a romantic getaway; I'd filled all the other breaks with Watershed dates. This time she made me promise.

But, alas, rock and roll is built on broken promises. And instead of hiking on Orcas Island or sipping high tea at the Fairmont Empress, Kate has spent the last nine days with her dissertation. When she gets burnt on Victorian Lit, she walks the neighborhood or drops in on a yoga class. One night she went out for Vietnamese with friends from the university. Tonight she's drunk. It's 8:30 here in the east, which makes it 5:30 for Kate, but she tells me she's already polished off a bottle of cabernet.

"Awesome," I say, "You deserve it."

"It's been great," she says. "I'm lying on the couch; I've got the back massager plugged in; and I'm watching a *Project Runway* marathon."

"Who's been booted?"

"I've lost track. I've been painting my nails and talking on the phone most of the time."

This is good. She's been calling her friends back home, being proactive against loneliness. She tells me that last night she drove up to Seattle for a haircut in Ballard and shopping in Belltown.

"That sounds fun," I say.

"You could have been here with me," she says, "but you've made your choice."

I try to steer the conversation back to drunken happiness. "So what did you buy?"

"I don't have many minutes left on the cell," she says. "Let's talk after nine. Or e-mail."

I say I'll call her back after the show.

"I'll be passed out by then," she says, laughing. "I'm not living on rock star time."

"Bottle of wine before dinner? That's pretty damn rock star, I gotta say."

It's great to hear Kate laugh.

In the spring of 1992, Kate was seventeen, a senior, shopping for a prom dress. I was her twenty-two-year-old boyfriend, sneaking her into Ruby Tuesday through the emergency exit. By now fifty fans would regularly show up for Watershed's soundchecks. By 10:00 a line would stretch out the door. By 11:00 the crowd would be backed four deep at the bar, and three hundred drunken college kids would press toward stage, yelling "Wa-ter-shed!"

One night, as The Generals blew through their opening set, Kate and I stood near the bar. She cupped her hand to her mouth and yelled into my ear that she loved me. She tried to hold my hand, but I let hers drop. So she slid behind me, reached her arms around my waist, and joined them at my belt buckle. Her hips moved against me. She was dancing. But I broke away, with more force than I'd intended.

"What's wrong?" Kate mouthed the words over the band. She brushed a strand of hair from her face. She looked her age. Exactly. Not a day older.

There was no way to explain over the volume. I waved for her to follow me downstairs to the dressing room.

"Are you mad at me or something?" she said. On the wall behind her, graffiti read, THE ROADIE'S CREED: 1. GET THE MONEY 2. GET THE MONEY 3. GET IN THE VAN.

"I've told you this," I said. "About how Willie says we have to get the girls."

"I know, but—" The fluorescent lights made her freckles stand out. I could see each one individually.

"And part of the reason the girls come," I said, "is because they think they have a shot with the guys in the band."

"A *shot?*"

"It's nothing personal."

"How can it not be personal?" Her face had taken a sharp edge. "You're asking me, personally, to stay away from you, right? That's what you're asking?" She dropped to the chintz couch and busied herself picking something from her shoe. "This system works out really well for you guys, doesn't it?"

Soon Kate would have to drive back to the suburbs and her midnight curfew, climbing into bed before her mom could ask too many questions. But I'd grown up. I was about to take the stage to a sold out crowd. I'd played CBGB five times. I'd walked alone on a dark Detroit street to a Taco Bell where the cashier stood behind an inch of bulletproof glass. What was I doing dating a high school kid? Her mom. The prom. Sneaking her through the side door. One big hassle.

"Are you saying you want to fuck one of these girls?" she said.

"No. No-no." I slid next to her. "But they have to think I might."

She stood up. "I told you I'd never be your groupie."

"Come on, Kate," I said. And I reached over for a hug. "You're my girlfriend."

She smacked my hand away. "Not tonight I'm not." And she stormed upstairs where she watched the last three Generals songs from the front row.

Still the line snaked around the building, and the doorman switched to one-out/one-in to keep the fire marshal happy. Getting a drink or taking a piss was now a fight-provoking half hour wait. Some kid stumbled out the front door with a bloody nose, and the line cheered: somebody else was let in.

When Watershed took the stage, the roar hit like a mule kick. The audience sang and shouted out requests. "Wallflower Child! How Do You Feel!" Colin had long stopped writing set lists. Instead, between songs, he and I would meet at Herb's kick drum, and like an audible-izing quarterback, Colin would call out the songs on the fly, based on whatever "defense" the crowd was showing us. His head would swivel between Herb and me: "Go-go-go!"

That night between songs I heard "Joe-Joe-Joe!" as people fought to the front of the stage to get closer to me. But none of these voices was Kate's. She was gone.

I hang up with Kate and immediately smell The Superfan's perfume, sweet and strong. A Georgia schoolteacher, she has travelled all the way to Toledo just to see us. Somehow she finds the time and money to hop planes and rent cars, and no Watershed show is out of range. No day of the week is insurmountable, during the school year or otherwise. A Friday in Marquette, Michigan? No problem. Thursday in Chicago? Done. It doesn't surprise me at all that I smell The Superfan's perfume tonight at Frankie's.

"I knew it," says Dave.

"Like a cat in heat," says Pooch.

We met The Superfan a few years ago at Atlanta's Dark Horse Tavern. It was her first Watershed show, and she'd come as the date of a longtime fan from Michigan. Mid-song, a thunderstorm knocked out the power, and the club went dark. We finished a capella, with the ten or so people in the crowd holding up their cell phones like lighters. Soon it became clear that the power wasn't coming back on, so we said goodnight and packed up in the dark. Then I headed to the bathroom, where I ran into the Michigan guy. He was standing on the tile, his smiling face lit up by candles that had been placed on the sink.

"Hey, man," I said.

Then I looked down and saw The Superfan kneeling on the piss-wet floor, her mouth at his crotch. And I saw another guy, standing behind Michigan fan, aiming his camera phone at the action.

"Whoa. Sorry," I said, and I backed out of there.

The next time we came through Atlanta, The Superfan showed up alone. She'd broken up with Michigan guy. "And I got Watershed in the divorce," she said.

That night she trained her laser-like libido on Dave and Pooch. I'm sure they were flattered. Hell, I'm sure they encouraged her. But neither one was going to take her up on it, so she settled for the bass player from the opening band. She fucked the guy in his car in the Dark Horse parking lot. Later she told us, laughing, "I made that kid listen to Watershed the whole time."[28]

Now The Superfan sees me and waves. "So good to see y'all!" she says, and she gives me a big hug. I hug back. She's a good woman. Like Watershed, she's finding a way to stay in the game.

The all-ages show over, the emo contingent clears out fire-drill fast. They probably have to be at church in eight hours. So what's left is twenty-five loyal Watershed followers plus The Superfan and Superfan II, a woman who has driven from Connecticut to be here. She's like The Superfan minus the bathroom blow jobs. Median age of the crowd: roughly thirty-nine.

As we wait at the bar to go on, one exceedingly nice couple asks if I'll sign a CD for their son. A few more fans ask for autographs. It feels like we're making progress on this tour, however minute the increments.

Rob, the owner, walks up and says he's buying shots for the band. Whatever we want.

"Tequila," Dave says.

Rob slaps Dave on the back. "Tequila it is, new guy."

"I'm the new guy," says Pooch.

"Sorry, man," says Rob. "I thought you were a fan."

"That's 'cause I'm so much younger than these grizzly bastards," Pooch says, pointing to Dave and me.

The bartender delivers the shots. "To Watershed," Rob says, raising his glass. "You never called it quits."

"I've been trying to quit since I joined," Dave says. "They won't let me."

"You can quit tonight, Dave," Colin says. "Just as long as we reunite tomorrow."

Dave smacks the bar with a flat palm. "Sold."

We knock back the tequila.

"Wait," Pooch says. "Can I quit too?"

Colin pokes him in the chest and says, "Anytime you want, Pooch."

"I don't get it," Rob says, collecting the glasses. "I thought for sure you guys would make it big."

"We did too, Rob." I give him a slap on the back. "We did too."

That spring one thing was certain: We'd outgrown Ruby's. It was time for a jump in weight class. While Biggie and I were brainstorming venues that held four or five hundred, Colin decided, fuck it—we should book the Newport Music Hall, a 1,700-seat club that had hosted every rock act that mattered. Not only had The Toll and the Royal Crescent Mob regularly packed the place, but U2, The Police, Bruce Springsteen, and KISS had all played the Newport (or its previous incarnation, The Agora) on their way to selling out arenas. We'd never heard of an unsigned band topping a Newport bill, but once Colin made the call, there we were, up on the marquee for all of High Street to see—which was scary as hell. Three hundred was a sellout at Ruby's, but it would barely register at the Newport. Every step we'd made since high school had been a step forward; it would suck to slouch back to Ruby's in embarrassment. So we faxed press releases and gave tickets to radio stations and sent two rounds of postcards to the mailing list. We printed flyers by the ream.[29]

Still, by the night of the show, ticket sales were *slow*. When the opening band started, the club was mostly empty. We were witnesses at our own wake.

"It's not *that* bad out there," Biggie said.

"Maybe our fans are too used to Ruby's," I said. "They don't know to look for us here."

Colin rubbed his temples. "We should have done a better job telling people this is a *concert*. Everybody expects us to go on at midnight, not ten."

"Enough with the loser-talk, ladies," Biggie said. "It's still early."

Then the Newport's manager walked up to the dressing room. "Guys? It's kind of light out there. If you want to pull the plug, I understand. It's not too late to cancel."

Just when it looked like we were doomed, fans started filing through the Newport doors. As the reporter for the *Lantern* wrote in his review of the show, it was as if six hundred people had been dropped off by a giant school bus. Standing on the side of the stage, peeking into the crowd, I saw an undulating field of heads, arms waving like wheat. My God. This *was* a concert. Suddenly I was twelve again, and Cheap Trick was about to go on. But wait a second. All these people had come to see *us*.

That's when I knew we wouldn't be slouching back to Ruby's any time soon. This was numeric proof. Watershed was the biggest band in Columbus.

Buoyed by that night, we pressed 45s of "How Do You Feel," with my song, "Give It Away," on the B-side, and we sent them to every college station east of the Mississippi. A few weeks later Biggie raced to Borders to check out the radio airplay charts in the *College Music Journal.* "How Do You Feel" was number thirteen in Pittsburgh. Number fifteen in Berea. Thirty in Bowling Green. Two in Toledo. In Mount Pleasant, Michigan, we were charting higher than Nirvana and U2. The station in Quincy, Illinois, had flipped the disc to the B-side, and our "Give It Away" was out-charting the Red Hot Chili Peppers' "Give It Away."

We added the *CMJ* chart listings to our press kit and sent copies of *The Carpet Cliff* to magazines. Only one reviewed the album, but that one was a big one: *Billboard.*

Columbus, Ohio–based band shows a nice flair for simple pop rockers that reflect influences from virtually every American band through the ages—most evident are Cheap Trick and Georgia Satellites. While not every song is a winner, there are little gems that embed in the listener's memory.

Little gems! We were on fire in concert, at radio, and in the press. A record deal was next. Had to be. We sent packages to every major label, knowing it was just a matter of time. And sure enough, our p.o. box was soon stuffed with company stationery.

After careful consideration of Watershed, I have elected to pass on them.
—EMI

I do not feel it is suitable for the current needs of our label.
—BMG

While the material overall is good, this is not a project for us.
—Polydor

I am sorry to inform you that I must pass on your project.

—IMAGO

The A&R staff has decided to pass on this product.

—ATLANTIC

The songs were interesting and there is obviously talent in the band; however, I am going to pass on this project at this time.

—MERCURY

The material is not in keeping with our musical direction at this time.

—ELEKTRA

I don't feel the material is appropriate for us at this time.

—ISLAND

I feel that we must pass at this time.

—CHRYSALIS

And every day at work, Chris Clarkson would ask me, "When are you going to get a recording contract?"

As loyal as we were to Biggie, the rejection letters told Colin and me that we needed a real manager, somebody with the juice to get us out of the unsolicited pile. In early 1993 we sent a package to Jim Ford, a New Orleans–based manager who'd helped the R.C. Mob land their Sire deal. Ford said he was impressed. If we ever played a gig in New Orleans, he'd come check us out. So we asked our New Orleans buddies Dash Rip Rock for an opening slot. The gig was during Mardi Gras, and the Dash guys knew Jim Ford well. They'd make sure he showed up.

Typical of Watershed's darts-on-a-map routing, we booked a gig at Frankie's—one thousand miles north of New Orleans—for the night before the Mardi Gras show. If we got out of Toledo by 3:00 a.m. and drove nonstop, we could make the 7:00 p.m. soundcheck in the Crescent City. Crossing into Central Time would give us a cushion hour. This could be done.

We left Frankie's in a February blizzard. Too tired to worry about the slick roads, I took to the floor, letting the squeak of the wipers and the sound of tires-on-slush lull me to sleep. When I awoke, the sun was breaking over the Kentucky hills, and we were parked in a truck stop. Biggie was bent under the hood.

"Want me to drive?" I said.

A bandanna in his mouth, he grunted something that sounded bad.

"What?" I said. "We burning oil?"

"Overheating." He let the hood drop shut, and he wiped his hands on the bandanna. "Lemme drive so I can keep an eye on the gauge."

The van had already blown through two radiators, so I knew the drill: antifreeze, Stop Leak, and a sign of the cross. I took a piss and crawled back to the floor.

By noon we were stopped at an auto parts store north of Nashville. The temperature gauge had been pinned to the red for the last hundred miles, but Biggie's bet was that the gauge was broken. Sweat ran down his face as he installed a new one right there in the parking lot. I checked my watch. As long as everything ran fine from here, we'd still make soundcheck.

We lost power just after Birmingham. Couldn't get the van over 50. By Tuscaloosa, we'd dropped to 40. South of Meridian, she wouldn't crack 30, and the whole van reeked of gasoline. It was already 6:00 p.m. Central. Soundcheck was lost. I was dividing *distance* by *speed,* calculating the impossibility of making our date with Jim Ford, when from underneath the hood came a horrible *clack-clack-clack.* Metal on metal. Loud as a shotgun and fast as the baseball cards in my Huffy spokes as a kid. Biggie sputtered to a gas station on the wrong side of Hattiesburg.

Colin and Herb, looking worn as dust bowl Okies, leaned against the smoking van, while Biggie and I found a payphone to call our mechanic friend Dave Cook.

"What color's the smoke coming from the tailpipe?" Cook said. In the three years since he had found the van for us, he'd kept it roadworthy by installing radiators, brakes, and alternators. Once, while we were on stage, Cook and Biggie rebuilt the carburetor in the bar kitchen.

"The smoke from under the *hood* is blue," Biggie said. "But what's it mean when *water* is leaking from the tailpipe?"

"It means you're fucked, dude."

First we'd cracked a head gasket. Then we'd thrown a rod. One of the cylinders had broken rank and gone solo. That awful *clack-clack-clack* was the sound of the getaway rod slapping against its metal housing. It was the sound of a Chevy Straight-Six, greatest motor ever made, taking a shit, the sound of a gig going up in blue smoke and tailpipe water. We'd played 215 shows since changing from The Wire to Watershed. And we'd never canceled a gig. Never.

"Good news is you can't fuck it up any worse," Cook said. "Drive it 'til she dies on you."

"How far do we have?" Biggie asked me.

"A hundred miles, maybe." But it was now almost 8:00. Even if the van ran a steady 30, we'd never make the gig by 10:30.

"I can't fucking believe it," Biggie said, wiping an oily bandanna across his face. His hands, face, and jeans were streaked with grease. "A hundred miles short."

Then I remembered the AAA Gold Card in my wallet. AAA would tow us for free—up to one hundred miles. The question was could they get a truck here fast enough.

At 8:30 the emergency lights crested over the highway, and the wrecker swung up next to us. While the driver hooked the van, Biggie called the club to say we'd be late. He double-checked that Jim Ford's name was on the guest list.

"Might be we got a little problem," the driver said as he set the winch that raised the nose of the van. "I can get the vehicle down to New Orleans, but how are all y'all gonna get there?"

"Can't we just ride in the van?" Colin said. We'd done this on previous tow jobs.

The driver took off his ball cap and rubbed his ruddy cheeks. "Well, if I was driving my flat-bed, that'd be fine. I'd just put the van up there with y'all inside it. But it's dangerous having you boys down on the ground. Especially going into that Mardi Gras monkeyfuck." Then he looked around at us, at our sloping posture and frazzled hair. "Y'all a band or something?"

Colin told him the story. How we'd come all the way from Toledo. How in New Orleans we were going to play for the bigwig who could get us a record deal.

The driver pulled his hat back on. "Keep your heads low so nobody can see you through the windows. And if we get pulled over, I'm sayin' I didn't know all y'all were back there."

Biggie and I sat in the truck. Colin and Herb were ducked back in the van. With the yellow lights pinwheeling, we slid through Slidell and crossed Lake Pontchartrain. The driver was right. Mardi Gras was a monkeyfuck, but his party-lights cleared traffic. We pulled in front of the Rendon Inn at 10:25. Five minutes to spare. There was no time to load-out. Biggie grabbed two guitars and ran inside to ask Dash if we could borrow their amps and drums.

The driver dropped the van in a loading zone. Colin, Herb, and I shook his hand and gave him a thirty dollar tip, a T-shirt, and a copy of *The Carpet Cliff.* He asked us to sign the CD for his kid. "For when you boys get famous."

I stood on the street breathing the rich Delta night. Spanish moss and show-us-your-tits beads hung from the trees. We were stuck in New Orleans with no idea how we'd get home, but we'd made it. We'd *made* it.

Jim Ford never showed. He called later to say, sorry, something came up. But by then it didn't matter. If the four of us could get through blinding snow, highway heat, and a jacked-up van and still make the gig, we could do anything.

Now Biggie tells us it's about that time. I empty my pockets, plug in my bass, and check the stability of my mic stand. If the base is uneven and I step on it during the show, I'll get a microphone in the teeth—the rock equivalent of stepping on a rake. Colin, Pooch, and Dave are all smiles, doing mini-rituals of their own.

The crowd is light, but only compared to how packed the bar was two hours ago. Actually I'm a little surprised at how many *have* waited it out. Aren't these people tired? Don't they have babysitters to relieve?[30] I'm wishing—and I know Colin, Dave, and Pooch are too—that a few of those hot emo chicks[31] would have stuck around. Shallow but true: A show is at least ten times more fun when you're playing for the subset of humans you are sexually attracted to. Tonight we'll have to make do with The Superfan and Superfan II. Would I prefer our groupies not be menopausal? Clearly. But I guess bands get the groupies they deserve.

From song one Watershed's Toledo fans cheer loud and rowdy, fired up to have us back on the North Coast. The Pabst and whiskey flow steadily from crowd to stage. Tonight we sound like a train bent on derailment, one that somehow, just barely, keeps all wheels on the tracks. Colin and I hit wrong notes. Dave drops a beat. Pooch flubs a few chords. And the show is better for these mistakes. This is rock, straight from fallible fingers.

During the closing song, "The Best Is Yet to Come," Colin sets his mic stand and mine on the floor. Then he, Pooch, and I jump into the audience, and we sing the last chorus from inside the crowd. We've stolen this bit from Springsteen, from Marah, from a hundred bar bands who each stole it from somebody else. The fifteen Watershed fans left in the bar have seen us pull this stunt many times, but still, their eyes go wide when we break the plane of the stage and step through the fourth wall. They rise to their feet, huddle around us, sing along.

Now that I'm down on the floor, and the lights aren't in my eyes, I can see two guys from the screamo band, sitting at the bar. One is nudging the other, yelling something through a cupped hand. I can't read lips, but it looks like they're digging this gimmick. They're pointing like kids at the zoo, laughing like an NBA bench when the scrub drains a meaningless three.

7

The Call Up
New York, New York

WHEN I WAS EIGHT, MY PARENTS TOOK MY SISTER AND ME TO MANHATTAN to visit my dad's brother Jim, who was a classical music critic living in Morningside Heights. His tiny apartment was stacked floor to ceiling with records, and the place smelled of cardboard and his neighbor's funky stir-fry. An ex–Division III pulling guard, Uncle Jim let me tackle him to the chintz sofa. He put my sister up on his shoulders and paraded her through his rent-controlled flat until he faked a buckling of his football-ravaged knees. He then promised to take us to the top of the tower at Riverside Church. "On a day like today you can see all of Harlem," he said. "You can see across the Hudson into New Jersey."

On a patch of wall still unclaimed by Jim's record collection was a print of Saul Steinberg's 1976 *New Yorker* cover, *A View of the World from Ninth Ave.* It's the one in which Steinberg draws the New York worldview as hyper-compressed and Manhattan-centric. Looking westward, a New Yorker sees Tenth Avenue, the West Side Highway, the Hudson River, and Jersey. Then the New York eye skims quickly over America's mostly unnamed, uninspiring mid-section, past Kansas City, Vegas, L.A., out to Asia on the horizon. The distance from Ninth to the Hudson is greater than from Jersey to Japan. The mighty Mississippi is erased. The Appalachian and Rocky Mountains are reduced to cow patties.

Even at eight I knew the difference between a cartoon sketch and a map, but still I was bothered by the geographical inaccuracies. Where was Columbus? Heck, where was Ohio? I wondered if this was what Uncle Jim saw when he looked west, back toward Watertown, Wisconsin, that hamlet of package stores and bowling leagues where he and my dad were raised, where their mom and dad and three sisters still lived.

"Is this what the view looks like from the top of that church?" I asked, pointing toward the Steinberg print.

Jim looked over at my dad, chuckled, and said, "Yeah, kind of."

For the next thirty years I'd sometimes feel like I was stuck inside that print, standing in unnamed Ohio, looking east toward a Manhattan that loomed comically large and out of scale. The Steinberg in reverse: A View of Ninth Ave. from the World. On clear mornings, as the sun rose over the midtown skyline, those buildings cast shadows that stretched all the way to Columbus.

Where were the record companies? In the spring of '93 that question pricked at all of us. We'd headlined the Newport three times and played 225 shows, from Albany to Tuscaloosa. But still no record company interest, no A&R men following our every move. They told us our job was to get so huge they couldn't miss us. We were huge. Where were they? Now it wasn't just Chris Clarkson, but our fans, friends, and people walking down the street—everybody in Columbus seemed to be asking, *When are you gonna get a recording contract?*

We sent package after package to the major labels. Nothing. We sent CDs to producers and managers, lawyers and agents. Nothing. If you were even remotely connected, we stuffed an envelope with your name on it. Still nothing. The worldview of the industry seemed to be like that of the New Yorkers in the Steinberg print. Watershed was stuck in invisible America. But we kept scattering packages like seeds, hoping one would eventually split open and take hold.

Sometimes the puniest seed, tossed into the driest, most unlikely patch of dirt—the afterthought seed, the throwaway seed—pushes through the soil, green and wanting. And sometimes you just get lucky.

It was nearing midnight. Colin and I had been stuffing envelopes for hours, and I was now cleaning up, gathering press clippings and copies of

The Carpet Cliff and stacking them in the filing cabinet. I told Colin we needed to hustle to band practice. If we left Herb waiting for too long, he'd get mad and go home.

"Hang on," Colin said, taking a slip of crumpled paper from his wallet. "I just remembered something." His tri-fold was so thick with receipts and business cards, a diagonal seam had formed, turning the wallet into a three-and-a-half fold. Colin was a scrap-paper millionaire. "We need to send a CD to Amy Yates. To give to her boyfriend."

Amy had graduated with us from Worthington, and she was living in New York, dating a guy who used to run sound for KISS. I wanted to tell Colin, screw it. Don't let KISS's ex-soundman compromise practice. The payoff wasn't worth the postage. But instead I did the collating and stuffing. Of course it was worth the postage. Licking a stamp is like scratching a lottery ticket. The odds are long, but at least it's a chance.

The call came in April. He said his name was Don Ketteler, and he was from a company called Crisis Management. His girlfriend Amy had slid him a CD by a band she knew from high school. He and his partners had listened to it. And loved it.

We were skeptical. After getting no-showed by a legitimate manager like Jim Ford, how much stock could we put in an ex-KISS soundman? And who were these partners he'd mentioned? Aging Blue Öyster Cult roadies?

Don said he wanted to see us live, so we told him we'd put together a CBGB show. But he wasn't asking us to come to New York. He and his guys would fly to Columbus.

"We have a show at the Newport in May," Colin said. "That's the one you wanna see."

And we kicked ass that night: no clams and no train wrecks. We played like our names were on the deed to the building. The crowd sang along to "How Do You Feel" as if they were auditioning for the part of "crowd" in a rock and roll movie. In the dressing room after the show, I hoped that Don and his partners had been there to see it, but if they hadn't—screw 'em.

The next day we met for lunch. Don was lanky, with a small head and a hawkish nose. Peering over his glasses at the menu, he looked more like a philosophy professor than a soundman or a rock manager. He was easily twenty years older than Amy, an age difference that made Kate and mine look trivial. Sitting next to Don was Danny Lawson, a bearded guy with baggy chinos and an untucked dress shirt. He wore a Yankees cap and a perpetual smile.

We asked Don about KISS. He told us that one of his jobs had been to pop in the cassette of the "Beth" backing track for Peter Criss to sing over. One time he accidentally inserted the *White Album* instead, and Criss was left to stand on stage for an embarrassing minute—with "Back in the USSR" blasting through the PA—while Don fumbled for the stop button. After the show he expected to be fired, but all Gene Simmons wanted to know was how the lights and makeup looked. Nobody in KISS cared about the sound.

Danny, it turned out, also had a soundman's pedigree. He'd been behind the board in '75 when Springsteen did a week's residency at the Bottom Line. The E Street Band was so loud in the tiny club, they turned their amps backwards.

We pressed for more stories, but Don closed his menu, saying it was time to talk about Watershed. "I was blown away by your energy," he said. He loved how Colin commanded the crowd, how Herb turned on the girls.

"And Joe, man," Danny said. "You sing in this sweet little voice, but you look like you might *eat* the audience."

Then Don pulled a document from somewhere and slid it across the table. "We flew here to offer you a management contract."

The papers sat in the middle of the table, splendid as a Thanksgiving turkey.

Biggie opened his day planner and started taking notes. "Management contract. What exactly does that mean?"

Don said that every artist fields a team. The band records the CD. The record company sells it. The publicist hypes it. The agent books the tour. "And the manager," he said, "oversees the whole shooting match."

"We help you build a career," Danny said. "We work for you."

"Who is *we?*" Biggie said. "You two guys?"

"Our third partner wanted to make the trip with us," Don said.

Danny looked at him and chuckled. His whole body shook with good humor. "But, you know, *two out of three ain't bad.*"

We didn't get the joke until Don said, "Are you guys familiar with Jim Steinman?"

Colin and I looked at each other and smiled. Jim Steinman had written all the songs on Meat Loaf's multi, multi-platinum *Bat Out of Hell,* including "Paradise by the Dashboard Light," "You Took the Words Right Out of My Mouth," and, yes, "Two Out of Three Ain't Bad." Bonnie Tyler's "Total Eclipse of the Heart" and "Holding Out for a Hero" were Steinman songs. So was Air Supply's "Making Love Out of Nothing at All." Steinman had also produced one of our favorite Billy Squier albums, *Signs of Life.* Coincidentally, months before, when we'd been trying to woo record producers, we'd sent Steinman a copy of *The Carpet Cliff.*

"Never got it," Don said. "But he sure loved the CD you sent to Amy."

Long separated from KISS, Don was now Steinman's personal attaché. A few weeks earlier, while riding a Town Car up to Steinman's Westchester County estate, Don had asked Jim's driver to slide *The Carpet Cliff* into the CD player. Halfway through "How Do You Feel," Steinman looked up from a copy of *Billboard* and said, "Sounds like the Gin Blossoms but with balls."

"Before we got to Jim's front gate," Don said to us now, "we'd decided to manage you."

"And if we do our job," Danny said, "you'll be bigger than the Gin Blossoms."

Don tapped his finger on the contract. "What do you say?"

What would *you* say? What would you say to ex-soundmen for KISS and Springsteen and their partner, the guy who'd written Meat Loaf's seven-times-platinum debut? What would you say if they made getting a record deal seem like a formality, as if the only question was whether your advance would be six or seven figures? What would you say if in the fine print of that contract you read the implicit promise to deliver everything you'd worked so hard for, everything you'd paid for in long drives and dank bars, everything you wanted and everything you didn't dare to want?

This is what I *wanted* to say: *Yes! Yes! Yes! I don't care about* X percentage of the gross *or* sunset clauses *or* points *or* in perpetuity. *I just want this to happen. Now.* But instead I looked blank-faced at the document. "We'll have to run this by our attorney," I said, though we didn't have an attorney. "Can you give us a week or two?" I was trying to contain my excitement. We'd been at it long enough to know the music business slapped you five with one hand and broke your nose with the other.

Don stirred his iced tea. "Take all the time you need."

We called a Columbus lawyer who'd worked with the R.C. Mob and Scrawl. His office was on a high floor of a downtown skyscraper, all windows and wood. We sat at a sparkling glass table, sipping the Cokes his secretary had brought us.

"You guys are fucking insane if you sign this," he said. Then he laughed out loud. "I'll give 'em this: They've got balls. First of all they're asking for 20 percent of your gross. Remember, that's *everything:* your record contract, music publishing, performance royalties, T-shirt sales. If you decide to sell, I don't know, Watershed beer cozies, they get 20 percent. Right off the top."

Biggie tapped his pen on his day planner. "Can we get 'em down to fifteen?"

"You bet your ass we're gonna try," the lawyer said, shaking his head at the contract in something like admiration. "But that's just one example of how aggressive they're being." He then took us through every clause that would leave us exposed to managerial chicanery. But ultimately, he said, all music business contracts were unfair. The fact that we were going to get screwed was inevitable. All we could negotiate was how hard and for how long.

"They don't make money unless we do, right?" Colin said. "So wouldn't a higher commission give them incentive to work *harder?*" If Watershed made a hit record, Colin said, there'd be money enough for all of us. We could waste months haggling over a percentage point here and there, or we could just sign the damn thing and get to work. As we drove home from the lawyer's office, he said to Biggie and me, "Are we musicians or are we bean counters?"

If Colin was ready to sign the contract right there in the car, Biggie was ready to litter the freeway with it. He argued that Don and Danny had never gotten a band signed. They had no track record. And how involved would Steinman be if he couldn't be bothered to fly out for the Columbus show?

I took the diplomatic middle. Don and Danny's terms were a place to negotiate from. We'd try to win a few points, and once we'd reached an impasse, we'd sign.

Then Biggie came clean with the real source of his hesitation. *He* wanted to manage Watershed. After all the years, all the gigs, the books he'd read, the flyers he'd made, the amps he'd set up and drums he'd torn down, after all the time he'd spent driving the van when he could have been working a real job, making good money—after all that, hadn't he earned the right to manage us? To *really* manage us? Into the big-time? This was the prize he'd been working so loyally for. This was what kept his eyes open on those overnight hauls. This was why he fixed whatever needed fixing, strung whatever needed stringing, and placed call after call after call. Not for a record deal. But for this.

"That's ridiculous, Biggie," Colin said. "You're not qualified to manage us."

At practice that night, Colin, Herb, and I signed the Crisis Management contract as is. And we quickly learned that nothing makes you feel as important as making and taking calls to and from the 212 area code. We were always put straight through. Nobody was ever in a meeting. Our phone was finally ringing, and it felt like every ding of the bell would bring more good news.

One day we got a call from another New York manager. Colin answered from the kitchen, and I picked up on the bedroom extension. His name was David Sonenberg, and he ran a company called DAS Communications.

"D-A-S. Those your initials?" I asked.

"Good, kid," he said. "You're bright." He told us that Steinman had passed *The Carpet Cliff* to him. It was great, he said. Especially that one song.

"How Do You Feel?" asked Colin.

"That's the one. A smash out of the box." He gave us his bonafides: ex-musician, Harvard Law. He currently managed the Spin Doctors, whose album *Pocket Full of Kryptonite* had just gone triple-platinum. "And then there's my new band, The Fugees."

We'd never heard of them.

"You will," Sonenberg said. "And everybody will know Watershed too if you let me guide your career."

We told him we'd already signed with Don, Danny, and Steinman.

"Yeah, I know," he said. "I'm Steinman's manager. I've guided *his* career. And I'm going to be completely honest here, guys. Jim is . . . well, Jim is an *artist*. I mean that in a good way. But Don and Danny are a couple of *nudniks*. Don't get me wrong. I love those schmucks. But they're not equipped to handle you."

Sonenberg told us that he was the one who had encouraged Steinman to get into artist management in the first place, but Jim didn't have the experience to work a baby band by himself. And Don and Danny? Forget it. "Colin. Joe. Listen. In four months Steinman and Meat Loaf will be releasing the sequel to *Bat Out of Hell*. Do you guess Jim is going to have any time to look after you? Or might he be a little wrapped up?"

"A sequel," I said. "Really." Nobody I knew was clamoring for more Meat Loaf. This was just two years after Nirvana's *Nevermind*. The whole Meat Loaf, *Bat Out of Hell* thing just seemed so, well, bloated.

"I've talked to Jim. I've talked to Don and Danny. And here's how it's going to play out: We're going to co-manage you. Crisis and DAS."

"You want us to give up *40* percent of our gross?" I blurted, thinking of crooked contracts signed by bluesmen and boy-bands.

"No-no-no. Still twenty," he said, laughing. "Ten percent to Steinman and the nudniks, and 10 percent to me. And you get the best of both worlds. Daily attention from Don and Danny and all the resources of a somebody like me who knows what it means to piss in the tall grass."

"You *split* the twenty," Colin said.

"Trust me, guys," Sonenberg said. "This is a no-brainer. Now, if you'll excuse me, I'm late for a *bris*."

There were more meetings with the lawyer and arguments with Biggie, but ultimately we ripped up the old contract and signed the new one. Now Watershed was a band with more managers than members. Top heavy, sure. But in the same stable as Jim Steinman, the Spin Doctors, and The Fugees. Pissing in the tall grass.

We leave Toledo early and drive a straight nine-hour shot on I-80 toward New York. Dave breaks out the beer as soon as we hit the Delaware Water Gap, and now, as we're approaching the George Washington Bridge, everyone is feeling good and buoyant. Biggie has a Budweiser in his crotch. We're telling stories, laughing, K-Factor on the rise. We can't afford to stay in Manhattan, of course. One night on the island would bankrupt the tour. Luckily Kate's sister scored us the employee discount at the Newark Airport Courtyard. We'll head there later, but now, we've got an off night[32], and we've got drinking to do. Should we drink in Newark or Manhattan? I know what David Sonenberg would say: *It's a no-brainer.*

I've driven this bridge maybe fifty times over the years, and still my stomach burns with excitement as we manipulate the tollbooths. I'm thirty-eight, and a January rain is falling, but from scrotum-to-guts I'm feeling the summer nights when Colin and I were in middle school, snuck out of the house, ding-dong ditching the neighbors and throwing crab-apples at cars. I'm feeling the moment when the driver slams the brakes, and you know the chase is on, so you tear-ass through backyards and over fences, giving your adrenaline work to do. I'm feeling that horrifyingly thrilling moment when somebody yells, "Cop!" and you run and you run—not because you might get caught, but because you know if you stop to catch your breath, your heart will pump out of your chest and onto the grass. You are a machine made of muscle and bone, doing what you were built to do, intention and execution aligning precisely. Crossing the GW I feel, always and finally, like I'm in the right place at the right time.

We're aiming for the Old Town Bar, on 18th Street. It's been open since 1892, but I found out about it just last year, when I met an *Esquire* editor there for cheeseburgers and Brooklyn Lager. As Biggie drives down 14th, toward Union Square, the guys are calling me writer-boy and hassling me about my hipster New York friends. Tonight at the Old Town we're meeting a Columbus friend, Christi. She used to be a barista at Colin's Coffee, but a few months ago she moved to Manhattan to launch a singing career.

Biggie turns onto Union Square East, and I point across the square, toward the building where Don Ketteler still lives. "Back in the day, we spent a lot of nights on that guy's floor," I say to Dave and Pooch. Across 16th Street shines the neon of the Coffee Shop Bar. "And every waitress in that place was a Ukrainian supermodel."

"Then why is Biggie driving us to the writer bar?" Pooch says.

"Wait till you see Christi," I say.

We find a table in back, and when Christi walks in, she's emanating big-city confidence, from her knee-high boots on up. She's twenty-something and gorgeous. Pure, weapons-grade potential, wrapped in a thrift-store coat. Here in New York to make it.

Fifteen years ago, that was us.

It was springtime in Hell's Kitchen, and rain sluiced through the gutters on West 53rd, running over the leaves and mud that caught in the drain grates. Biggie pulled the van through Ninth Avenue and parked in front of a nondescript steel door. He hopped down and walked up to the building. There was no sign, nothing to indicate what went on at this address. Biggie knocked and waited.

To keep from getting too nervous, I tried to concentrate on the familiar: the rhythmic *click-squeak* of the wipers, the rain falling on the van's roof like a million marbles, the idle of our new engine. After the New Orleans breakdown, we'd laid out two thousand bucks for this motor, and now, like a jet engine just after takeoff, its steady growl was boldness mechanized.

Out the driver's side window, kids in windbreakers and rain slickers were lined up on the P.S. 111 playground, waiting for their teachers to lead them back to their desks, their pencil cases, their story problems. Watershed was waiting for a steel door to open. Behind that door was the Power Station, the famous recording studio. Crisis and DAS had booked us here to make a demo to shop to record companies. The building had once been an actual powerhouse, and even now, to the school kids across the street, it must have looked like an old factory. And it *was* a factory. Somewhere inside these walls Bruce Springsteen had made *The River.* The Rolling Stones had put together *Tattoo You.* David Bowie had laid down *Let's Dance.* John Lennon, Bob Dylan, and Madonna had all walked through the door that Biggie was now leaning against. So had Aerosmith and Dire Straits, Soul Asylum and AC/DC. The Power Station was owned by Jon Bon Jovi's uncle, Tony Bongiovi, and when New Jersey's second-favorite son was a teenager, he'd worked here, answering phones, making coffee, and asking Springsteen for songwriting tips.

Don and Danny buzzed us in and walked us through the lobby. I thought, *No fucking way can we afford this place.* Platinum records hung everywhere. Double Platinum. Triple Platinum. The main tracking room, Studio A, was polished and bright and symphony-sized. On its dome-shaped walls was more (and better) wood than an Aspen ski lodge. The control room glass was as thick and spotless as the windows at Tiffany's. The mixing board was long enough, complicated enough, and checkered with enough knobs to run NORAD.

"So, Don," I asked in the Studio A lounge, which had more (and better) appliances than Colin's mom's kitchen. "How can we afford this?" I was thinking of the run of shows we'd played the week before: Cleveland, Chicago, St. Louis. Like always, we'd lost money.

"You guys don't get it yet, do you?" he said. He leaned his long bones into the sparkling, eggshell Frigidaire. He didn't look the least bit worried. "You're in a new league now. Stop thinking small potatoes."

This might be a new league, but we were still the same broke dudes we'd been the day before, turning our pockets inside out to make the four dollar toll at the G.W. Bridge. Where would the money come from?

Danny explained that we wouldn't be paying for the demo up front. Steinman was one of the Power Station's best clients. He'd just spent hundreds of thousands recording the new Meat Loaf album, *Bat Out of Hell II,* here. As long as Watershed was with Jim, the studio would let us record *on spec,* which meant that instead of billing us hourly, the Power Station would take a point on our first major-label album. We'd record that album here, in Studio A. And when we did they'd back-charge us for the cost of the demo.

Biggie spoke up. "But we don't have a record deal—"

"Yet, Small Potatoes," Don said. He put his arm around Biggie. "You don't have a record deal *yet.*"

That night Danny walked us from Don's Union Square apartment to the Gotham Bar and Grill. To us *Bar and Grill* meant T-shirts and jean jackets, but as soon as we opened the door, it was clear that in Manhattan *Bar and Grill* meant something else entirely. The ceiling was draped with linen. The bar was long and polished. The tablecloths were white as a ream of paper.

Under his breath, Biggie said, "I feel like I just fell off the turnip truck."

While Danny checked in with the maître d', Herb strolled right up to the bar, smiling like he'd just parred the back nine at Brookside Country Club. He leaned between two forty-somethings—their jeweled fingers caging enormous wine glasses—and ordered Heinekens for all of us. As he reached for the bottles, one of the women nodded approvingly at his ass.

Then Don walked in with Jim Steinman, who looked more out of place than we did. His gray hair fell halfway down his coat, which was a varsity-style jacket, the leather sleeves sewn in the pattern of a soccer ball. He wore a spiked belt and gloves cut at the knuckles, exposing soft, pudgy fingers, piano-playing fingers that had clearly never done anything more laborious than hammering out Wagnerian harmonic suspensions. Steinman must have been creeping on fifty, but his face was unlined, and it held an expression of youthful wonder. He seemed both lost and perfectly at home, as if the whole world was the woods behind his house, a woods that hadn't yet shown him all its dark places.

Don had mentioned to us that Steinman had never learned to drive. Instead he relied on Charles, his full-time chauffeur, to steer the Town Car around Manhattan and up to Westchester County. He had also once taken out a half-page ad in the *Times* offering a reward in the thousands for the return of his lost cat. Don said Steinman was an eccentric in the mold of Phil Spector, the Sixties wunderkind producer who would later be convicted of murder. Both men were influenced by Wagner, taking the composer's sonic density and applying it to the pop song. Spector was famous for his "Wall of Sound." Steinman's production style—his guiding principle for life—was "Everything Louder than Everything Else."

Soon we were sipping fifty dollar *Côtes du Rhône,* and Steinman was telling the story of how, while recording *Bat Out of Hell II,* Meat Loaf had started hitting the gym and losing weight. This was bad news. Meat's gift was that he looked on the outside the way every awkward kid felt on the inside. In Steinman's songs, when Meat met the girl, lost the girl, and then won her back just to lose her again, those kids understood his pain with heartbreaking clarity. A thin Meat Loaf was a powerless Meat Loaf.

"Wha'd you do?" I asked.

"I left boxes of doughnuts in the Power Station lounges," Steinman said. "Tried to fatten him up."

The headwaiter raised his eyes to signal he was ready for the order. I was torn between the seared tuna and the filet mignon.

Steinman scanned the menu and said, "For starters, we'll have the entire left half."

"Very good, sir," the waiter said, unfazed that Jim had just ordered *half the menu.*

"Plus two each of the carpaccio, scallops, and foie gras."

"Excellent."

"And for the second course, I'll have the sea bass." Steinman pointed his menu toward us. "What looks good to you guys?"

He seemed to be trying to fatten us up too. Still I went with the filet.

"Well, since nobody ordered the tuna," Jim said to the waiter, "why don't you bring us one of those. And, heck, how about another order of the duck? And another filet. For everyone to share."

With Jim Steinman you got everything. Then you got everything else.

Later, as he forked through the last of his fish, he said, "What label do you guys want to be on?"

"We get to choose?" Colin said.

"Why not?" Steinman said. "I always have."

"Whatever label wants us the most," I said, swirling wine around my glass like I'd seen Herb do.

"But what will you do when *everyone* wants you?" Don said.

"You're the experts," Biggie said. "Tell us."

"Stop right there," Steinman said. "There are no experts." He leaned forward like he was telling us a secret. "Nobody knows anything. *Anything*. Not the record companies, not the radio stations. If they did, then every album would go gold."

I asked Steinman which label he thought was best.

"They're all good at different things," he said. "Take the Sony labels, Columbia and Epic, they can't break a new band. But they're the *best* at taking a band with a small hit and making it a smash. Tommy Mottola—"

"Head man at Sony," I said. I'd been doing my research.

Steinman nodded. "Mariah Carey's husband. He can't get you from zero to a million, but nobody's better getting you from one million to five." He motioned for Herb to pick out another bottle of wine.

"But didn't Epic just break Pearl Jam and the Spin Doctors?" I said. The seven-digit sales numbers, the wine, the food—I was drunk on all of it.

"Like I said. Nobody knows anything." Steinman scooted his chair back and stood up. "Especially me."

Once Jim was out of earshot, Don said, "What do you think of that soccer ball jacket? He's got three more in his closet at home. Once he decides he has to have something, he never wants *not* to have it."

When Steinman returned he said, "Richard Griffiths is the president at Epic. He A&R'd my first deal with Meat."

"And David Sonenberg is Epic's golden boy because of the Spin Doctors," Danny said. "He's in bed with everybody over there."

Sonenberg owned a brownstone around the corner from the restaurant. He'd bought it with Meat Loaf money. Steinman money. Spin Doctor money. "You guys sell enough records," Don said, "and he'll be able to put an addition on his house in the Hamptons."

"Do you really think we could have a hit?" Herb said.

Don smiled. "We wouldn't be here if we didn't."

Herb turned to Steinman. "How many do you think we can sell?"

I glared at Herb. This seemed like the kind of thing you just didn't talk about. But still, I wanted to hear Steinman's answer.

"Like I told Don on the day he played me 'How Do You Feel.' You guys are the Gin Blossoms but better. Ballsier. And their album is gold. Almost platinum." Steinman flagged the waiter and gave him the universal sign for *check please*. Then he looked at each of us, one at a time, and said, "If Watershed doesn't sell two million, we should all quit the business."

"Hey, guys!" Christi says, and it's hugs all around. She's got a thirty-two-tooth smile. Cheekbones round like walnuts in the shell. "It's *so* good to see you."

Biggie orders three pitchers and goes about the business of filling everyone's mugs.

"So, Christi," I say. "Tell me again how long you've been in the city?"

"About three months." She uncoils her scarf, drapes her coat over the back of her chair. Her sweater fits just right.

"And how's everything going?" Colin says. His face takes an expectant expression that doesn't look quite right on him. He's usually not much of a listener, but he's all ears now.

"Great," she says. Sounds like she means it.

Biggie looks lovestruck. "Starting to feel like home?"

She sips her beer and nods. "Now that I've got my roommate situation sorted out, and oh—" she looks at Colin, "did I tell you?"

"What?"

"I got a job."

"You've already got a singing gig?" I say.

"Still working on that," she says. "I'm talking about a job-job. At Electric Lady Studios."

A collective "wow" from the table. Electric Lady has been around since 1969. Jimi Hendrix built it, and pretty much every musician you can name has recorded there. It's in the same league as the Power Station.

We all clink glasses. Dave and Pooch are conspicuously quiet, ceding the conversation to Colin, Biggie, and me—the senior members of Watershed.

"I'm just the receptionist," she says.

"Not for long," I say. "You're gonna meet *every*body there."

"Really?"

"You'll have more gigs than you can handle," Colin says.

"You think?"

I want to say, *Are you kidding me? Don't you own a mirror? Haven't you seen your cheekbones?* She's not fishing for compliments here, and that makes her even more attractive. "What a badass you are, Christi," I say. "Twenty-what? Three? Four?"

"Four."

"Living in New York, sweet industry job . . ." I grab one of the pitchers and work my way around the glasses. "Is it cool if I live vicariously through you?"

Colin, Biggie, and Christi keep talking, while I smile and nod. The longer I sit here, the more I'm wondering if I'm attracted to *who* she is or *where* she is. Am I turned-on or jealous?

What if, later tonight, both of us drunk, I asked her to kiss me? What if she did? And what if it was *great*—better, even, than a drunken New York kiss could ever be? What if it turned out that the life I was supposed to live wasn't with Kate in Tacoma, but here with Christi, a continent away from grading papers and department meetings and the whole English professor dog and pony show? Maybe we'd put a little two-person act together, with Christi singing and me on guitar and harmonies. We'd play at Fez and Joe's Pub. We'd be critics' darlings, friends with Zooey Deschanel. We'd get a mini-profile in *New York* magazine. But we wouldn't care about that. We'd be too busy going for Tibetan food, attending poetry readings at the KGB Bar, and drinking the obscure vodka we bought from a Russian bodega in Brighton Beach. Of course there'd be sex, morning sex, afternoon sex, drunken sex, hot and cold running sex—

I slide my chair back and excuse myself to go call Kate.

"Hey, honey. It's me."

"Hi," she says. Nothing else.

I'm standing under scaffolding, protected from the sleet, but Kate's voice is colder than any Manhattan January. "What's wrong?" I say. She was having such a good time yesterday, drinking wine and watching TV. "Are you hungover?" This is not the right question.

"No," she says. Then nothing.

"Honey?"

Silence.

"You there?"

A long exhale, then, finally, "What are you doing." Flat. A statement.

How much fun do I admit to? The truth obviously won't work. *Oh man, I'm having a great time. Totally hammered in New York. Hanging out with a hot twenty-four-year-old singer. Wondering what my life would be like with her. Why? What are you doing?*

Kate loves New York. In fact, my fantasy future with Christi would be Kate's fantasy future with me. Shoot, Kate loves New York so much, she'd probably take the fantasy with Christi, leaving me out of it. The Kate/Christi act would sell more tickets.

A few years ago, when Kate and I were in New York, we stood staring at a Barney's window display. I'd never heard of the store, but the window sure was decked out. "Let's go inside," I said.

She shook her head. "We can't afford anything in there."

Shortly after we moved to Tacoma, I was in New York again, this time without her. Wanting to buy her something special, I walked up Madison Avenue to Barney's. Since we now lived in the chilly Northwest, I figured I'd buy her a scarf. Simple, nice. But the cheapest scarf in the place was $250. Plan B: a Barney's umbrella. Couldn't find one for less than $125. I rode up the escalators, floor stacked upon floor, amazed and even a little ashamed to find that Kate was right. We couldn't afford anything at Barney's.

Then I got to the top floor. Knickknacks. Gift sets. Salt and pepper shakers.

I found a date book, red leather embossed with BARNEY's, and I had it gift-wrapped. Kate cried when she opened it.

Now she's using that book to count the days I'm gone.

Seeing no path through the minefield, I plead ignorance. "Are you mad at me?"

Silence.

You don't need a psychology degree to know what that means.

In the summer of '93, Watershed had started recording the Power Station demos, and Kate had finished her freshman year at Ohio State. On the weekends, Colin, Biggie, Herb, and I would leave New York and head west across the Hudson to play a run of shows in the same bars as always. Whenever we could get back to Columbus, I'd work a shift at the Vision Center and spend time with Kate. Same day job, same girlfriend. On the surface not much had changed since Watershed had signed with Crisis and Sonenberg, but the world was starting to look entirely different to me. I'd sat at a dinner table with Jim Steinman. I'd laid down tracks in the same studio as the Rolling Stones. Watershed was, as Don and Danny kept reminding us, playing in a different league. Now when we walked into those same old clubs, it was with the knowledge that we'd soon be leaving them behind. We were being groomed for the majors.

At that time a friend of ours from high school was playing center field for the Cubs' Triple A affiliate. One night I asked him if minor leaguers really called Major League Baseball "The Show," like the characters in *Bull Durham* do. He said, "Everybody I know calls it 'The Pros.'"

That summer I was discovering that when you're *this close* to being called up to The Pros, everything in the bush leagues—everything you've tolerated, even some of the things you've loved—starts to feel intolerable, unlovable.

Watershed spent most nights that summer sprawled on the floor of Don's Union Square apartment. He and Amy were nice enough to let us live on the sunny side, with its tall windows and view of the Greenmarket. At night I'd fall asleep to men jackhammering on Union Square West, to cabs driving over manhole covers, to horns—so many horns. Then I'd wake to the smell of Don's strong Café Bustelo. The sun would pour through the windows and land on Colin and me, tucked into our sleeping bags. Herb, with his achy drummer's back, would be stretched across the couch, reading a Keith Richards biography. Biggie would be folding the ratty van blankets he slept on, saying, "Rise and shine, ladies. Gotta be at the studio in a half hour."

We'd walk the crowded sidewalks, and thanks to Herb and his Keith bio, I'd have The Stones stuck in my head. Past the hot dog vendors and leaflet men I heard "Monkey Man." Ducking in and out of Subway cars it was "Shattered." Drinking beer in Central Park it was "Doo Doo Doo Doo Doo (Heartbreaker)."

There's no better soundtrack for New York City than The Rolling Stones.

We learned that Keith Richards was in town that summer. "That's where he lives," one of the studio's production assistants told us. "On the top floor of that building. You can tell he's home 'cause the junkies are hanging out in front. The junkies always know first."

It turned out Keith wasn't just in town. He was recording at the Power Station with his side project, The X-pensive Winos. The production assistants—kids our age who'd come to New York to learn how to be record producers, but were mostly mopping floors and patching cables—snuck us into Studio C to get a look at Keith's gear. They unlocked the doors, and there everything was, shiny in the soft studio light, all set up and ready for the Winos to play it.

Herb sat at Steve Jordan's drum kit and tapped the circus-size ride cymbal. He plucked at Charlie Drayton's bass. Then he walked to an open guitar coffin and stood over Keith's guitars. Like Arthur and Excalibur, Herb slowly pulled out the white Silhouette, the one Keith had played at the Hollywood Palladium. I snatched it from him and slung it over my shoulder. Keith Richards's guitar plays just as good as you think it should.[33]

Back in Columbus, Kate was waiting tables to cover tuition, eating chicken pot pies and frozen burritos. College now seemed like kindergarten to me. I'd recently read that Dave Pirner from Soul Asylum had left his hometown girl for Winona Ryder. So predictable. So lame.

Guy gets a gold record and drops old Sally Faithful, the stand-by-her-man sweetheart, for a movie star. Then again, Winona was hot. And famous. And in his league.

I'd started to suspect that Kate's league was a notch below mine. But how could I know for sure? She was the only girlfriend I'd ever had; there was no one to compare her to.

But now I *did* have someone to compare her to: Winona Ryder. Or someone like Winona. A new girlfriend who was not only beautiful and famous, but breathed the rarefied air of The Pros. Okay, so Winona was taken. But Uma Thurman might be available. Don had once mentioned sitting at a Tibet House benefit with Meat Loaf's daughter, Pearl Aday, who was not only a knockout herself, but was friends with Uma Thurman. I knew people who knew Uma Thurman! What if Uma was the one? Tall, lovely Uma. Or Pearl Aday even? Precious Pearl, daughter of Meat. And I'd never know because I was stuck with the first and only girl I'd ever had sex with.

One day that fall Kate skipped work to go to her first boyfriend's funeral. The poor kid had wrapped his motorcycle around a tree. Instead of the funeral, I went to band practice. Kate was understandably hurt. After the proceedings she called me, too sad to be angry. I offered no consolation, only one-word answers. Finally she got fed up and told me to come over to her apartment. We needed to talk.

"What's your problem?" she said, her hair still tied in a funereal ponytail.

"I'm fine. Everything's fine."

"The band is going so well, and you're still not happy."

Actually everything was better than fine. And I was pretty damn happy, my relationship with Kate notwithstanding. Sonenberg and Steinman were shopping our new demo to the biggest wigs at the biggest labels. Meat Loaf had just released *Bat Out of Hell II*, and "I Would Do Anything for Love (But I Won't Do That)" was a number one smash. Watershed was now brought to you by the people who'd delivered the multiplatinum Spin Doctors and the number-one-with-a-bullet Meat Loaf.

"I miss you," Kate said.

"Here I am."

"Not really. Even when you're home, you're not home."

"I'm *right here*. I can't be any more here—than *here*." But here was not where I wanted to be. Even as we talked, my thoughts drifted back to Manhattan. I thought about how much I loved grabbing a coffee and a croissant at Dean and Deluca before our sessions, how much I looked forward to plunking down five bucks at the Coffee Shop Bar for a Heineken and an excuse to stare at the waitresses, how great it was to wake up on Don's floor with the sun and the city spilling though the windows and The Stones rolling around my head.

Kate backed away and said, "Why are you being such an asshole?"

I knew why. I'd known for months. But I'd just now worked up the guts to tell her. "It's not gonna work."

"You and me, you mean."

"It's just. Kate. We're not going anywhere."

"What are you saying?"

I looked into my lap. "I guess I'm saying I don't want a girlfriend."

"But—" she said. She must have seen it coming, but it still hit her like a hand grenade. Her face was suddenly wet with snot and tears. "You mean you don't want me."

"Listen." I wanted to hug Kate, kiss her, wipe her eyes. But I wasn't allowed to do that now. Tears ran down my face, each one of them an insult to her.

"What?" she said. "What?" She looked open, vulnerable, beautiful.

I wiped my eyes with the back of my hand. Then I turned toward her and said, "I don't love you anymore."

Back at the table it's three more pitchers from Biggie. He fills my mug, and then hands me the keys to the van. "You got it," he says, meaning: *you're driving, asshole.* That's fine; Kate's bad mood took the wind from my drinking sails anyway.

Biggie orders a double Jack-and-Coke and scoots his chair closer to Christi. I wonder if he knows he's cock-blocking my imagination. Still it's good to see him getting loose. I just wish he'd told me I was driving *before* I drank five beers.

Christi leans into the table. "So what about you guys?" she says. "Tell me about the big show tomorrow."

"Nothing to tell, really," Colin says. "We've got a few fans here, so we're going to play for 'em. Just like we would in any other town."

Colin's playing it cool, but I know it's killing him to say this. It's killing me to hear him say it. Our New York shows used to matter—because somebody important was coming out to see us. Or because we thought somebody important might come see us. Either way, there were stakes.

Last week, when we were off in Columbus, a lawyer-regular asked Colin, "So what's the deal with the New York show? What's the angle?"

Colin gave that guy the same answer he gave Christi. "We've got songs. We've got fans. Might as well play one for the other."

"Ahhhhhhh," the lawyer said. "Your angle is *no* angle. Shrewd."

The fact is everyone—even those unconnected with the industry—expects your New York shows to be important. Inconceivable that a band would play New York just, you know, *because*. And that's why Christi asked. Implicit in her question was: Is anybody coming out to see you?

Nobody's coming out to see us.

I sure hope somebody comes out to see us.

"Really, it's just like any other show," Don said. We were sitting in his apartment. Through the windows I could see the trees in Union Square. It was October and the leaves had started to turn. "The only difference is that this show could change your lives." He snapped his fingers. "Like *that*."

I'd lived long enough to know that life grows outward as slowly and subtly as those tree branches in the square. Every day each branch looks exactly as it did the day before, but from season to season the difference is obvious. Years earlier, while riding the COTA bus, Colin said to me,

"We have to start a band." A life-changing moment. But the changes that moment precipitated could only be seen with the long view of memory. Nothing had changed like *that*. Now Don was saying that the show we'd play tomorrow night could snap the branches of our lives. Like a lottery win. Or a heart attack.

"But it's not exactly a show," Danny said, rising from the couch. "It's a show*case*."

The gig was essentially an audition. Bands did this all the time for A&R men. Sometimes they played in private rehearsal studios, sometimes right in the carpet-and-chrome office of some honcho or another. Tomorrow, thankfully, we'd be playing in a bar, the environment where we were most at home. Still, Danny said, showcases were tricky beasts. Take the set time, for instance. We'd be starting at 7:30.

"Who goes to see a band when it's still daylight out?" Herb asked.

"Record companies," Danny said. A&R people worked in the city, but they usually lived commuter distance—in Port Washington, say, or Plainview—and they weren't going to take the Long Island Railroad all the way home, just to catch the train back to Penn Station. And they weren't going to kill six whole hours after work waiting around Manhattan either. The 7:30 start time gave A&R reps just enough time for drinks and sushi before cabbing over to the club.

Secondly, Danny said, we shouldn't expect the record companies to clap or cheer or even pay attention. "They'll probably hang out in the back and talk to each other. That's okay, and it doesn't mean that the set isn't going well. Even if you only get golf-applause between songs, just keep rocking."

Still, to combat the staleness of a jaded industry crowd, Don and Danny had told us to recruit as many Columbus ringers as possible. "If you only see one Watershed show this year," we'd told everybody back home. "This is the one." Don and Amy offered floor space to anyone who made the drive, and it looked like a dozen or so Worthington and college friends would be taking them up on it. We'd also heard that a pack of OSU grads who were now working at New York investment firms and brokerage houses were coming. Over the years I'd been jealous of their fat paychecks and high-rise apartments, but I sure as shit knew that nobody was driving five hundred miles to watch these bankers and market analysts do their jobs.

"There's one last difference between a show and a showcase." Danny looked directly at Colin. "The set list. We have to be very exact about what we play, when."

"I have a pretty good idea," Colin said. He was holding a spiral notebook. The pages were filled with song titles, grouped in different combinations. "But I can't say for sure until I read the mood in the room."

Danny dropped to the couch and rested his forehead on the heels of his hands. "We can't afford a mistake, Colin." If we played "How Do You Feel" too early, the A&R people that wandered in late would miss it. And if we played it too late, those who left early would miss it. Danny raised his eyes to Colin. "Play the wrong song at the wrong time and it could cost you $100,000."

"How about if we just play a really good set, and if they like us, fine. And if they don't, they can get bent?"

"A good set is exactly what we want," Don said, turning to me. "But we need a very specific kind of good set."

Danny let out a slow breath. "Just *humor* me and write this down." He told us to open with "You Need Me," a new Colin song that started with a big, Van Halen "Everybody Wants Some"–style drum intro. This would immediately establish us as an arena-rock act, not a bar band.

"But we are a bar band," Colin said. "And, correct me if I'm wrong, but the show tomorrow is in a *bar*."

Danny started to answer, but he rubbed his temples and moved to song number two, "Nightshade," a song of mine that would make it clear right off the bat that we had two singers. Then, once we had their attention, we'd smack them with "How Do You Feel." "See what I'm doing here?" he said. "Every song has a purpose."

"I guess," Colin said. He looked toward me, but he was still talking to Danny. "But how do we know the room'll be ready for 'You Need Me?' 7:30 is too early for arena rock."

Biggie nodded and spit a stream of tobacco juice into a beer bottle.

"We all know tomorrow is this huge deal," Colin said. "But that's why we need to play it like it's *no big deal*. Like it's just another night in Toledo."

Don looked to the ceiling. "But it *isn't* just another night."

I stood up. "Toledo. New York. Whatever. We still need a plan, Colin."

"I *do* have a plan. I always have a plan."

"Okay, okay." Danny shut his eyes. "Do me a favor, guys. Please. Just this once. Open with those three songs. 'You Need Me.' 'Nightshade.' 'How Do You Feel.' In that order." He took off his Yankee cap and smacked it on his knee. "After that, do whatever the hell you want."

The next night, Colin, Herb, and I sat in the van, in front of a bar called Downtime NYC, waiting for Biggie to come out and tell us he was set to pop. It was quiet on 30th Street, quiet for a night that might change our lives. Every few minutes someone would open the front door to the bar, and in that interval between door open and door shut, I'd try to gauge the size of the crowd.

"So, is anyone, you know, *important* going to be there?" I'd asked Don the night before, after Colin had agreed to Danny's set list.

"Don't worry about it," he said. "Just play your show."

I later found the guest list on Don's desk. I recognized many of the A&R reps who'd confirmed they'd be showing up. Not long ago I'd addressed envelopes to those names. I'd read those names on album credits and liner notes. How could I think of tonight as just any-old show when right now these record company men were inside that club, waiting to see if we would live up to whatever hype had brought them here?

I had no idea what Steinman and Sonenberg had been saying to industry folks about us, but whatever story they'd told, it had been compelling enough to convince Richard Griffiths, the president of Epic Records, to hop the Concorde from London this morning. Now Steinman, Sonenberg, and Griffiths were probably sitting in the back of the bar, talking about Colin, Herb, and me. Talking about our songs and our rock star potential. I hoped Steinman had ordered the good wine at dinner.

Then Kurt Loder from MTV opened the door and slid inside.

This was awesome. This was terrifying.

If Kurt Loder was here, then anybody could be here. The Spin Doctors, Meat Loaf. Hell, maybe Pearl Aday. Maybe she'd brought Uma.

What kind of show were these big shots expecting? What band could possibly be worth a transatlantic flight on the Concorde? We were about to play for faces I'd seen on TV, for suits with the power to sign us on the spot. But first we needed to impress them, which meant that in addition to actually being good, we needed to make them *perceive* us as good. My forehead went hot with the hopelessness of all this.

I knew we wouldn't choke. Not tonight. No, tonight we'd be great; I had limitless faith in Colin, Herb, and Biggie and in what the four of us could do together. But I had almost no faith in some record company guy's ability to *recognize* our greatness. Then I remembered something my dad told me on the day I interviewed for my job at the Vision Center. "There's no reason to be nervous," he said. "Because you can't hide who you are. They'll either hire you *because* you are you—or they won't. There's nothing you can do about it."

So this showcase was just a job interview. Or a first date. The bad news about dating is that you can't *make* someone love you. But that's the good news too. You don't have to.

I thought about Kate back in Columbus. I'd loved her once. What had changed? What had she done or not done? Nothing. There was nothing she could have said. Nobody she could have been. Nothing had changed but me and my expectations. I felt like I deserved better, more. Now I was about to get it.

Biggie knocked on the side of the van. "You feel like making some noise?"

My heart was beating from between my ears, but no longer with nervousness. With determination. We were ready.

"Good evening, ladies and gentlemen." Colin stood at the microphone, squinting into the lights. He played a few open notes with his right hand and raked his hair with his left.

With the lights in my eyes, I could only see the first two rows. There was Kurt Loder. A few Watershed fans in front were looking over their shoulders at him. I turned to Herb, who was already shirtless. He was focusing on Colin like a snake about to strike. As soon as Colin gave him the nod, he'd kick out the drums to "You Need Me."

"So this is a little earlier than we're used to playing," Colin said. "And everybody is a little more sober than usual." Scattered hoots. "My guess is that we all feel like strangers at a cocktail party. So let's get to know each other a bit." He extended his arm to include Herb and me. "We are Watershed. From Columbus, Ohio." Yelps from the Columbus faithful. Colin turned the microphone toward the audience and shouted into the air without the mic, "And you are?"

A few people laughed. A few actually shouted out their names. In my black jeans, black jacket, black baseball cap, I was waiting. Waiting for those booming "You Need Me" drums.

But Colin said, "Well, since it is so early, why don't we ease into things, huh? Nice and slow."

Nice and slow? Danny, wherever he was, was surely having an aneurysm.

"So this is a brand new song of ours, a song that kinda sums up the day for us. Maybe for some of you too. This is called 'Sad Drive.'"

Oh, no. "Sad Drive" is a slow-burning ballad with no real drums. Herb just plays *ticka-ticka-ticka-ticka* on the hi-hat. Like the seconds ticking away on Watershed's career.

Herb looked over to me. What do I do?

I'd figured that Colin might switch up the set list, just to show Danny who worked for whom. But "Sad *fucking* Drive"? Still, there was no time for an on-stage debate. And maybe Colin's stubbornness, his belief that he's always right, *was* Watershed. For better or worse we were about to showcase it. I nodded to Herb, *go ahead.*

Ticka-ticka-ticka-ticka.

Colin started to sing. *Now it's a sad, sad drive, on a sad, dark and lonely night. It's a sad, sad drive, when only one of us still has hope in his eyes.*

And in a blink, the show that could change our lives was over. I walked off the stage and handed my bass to Biggie, just like always. I carried guitar stands and drum hardware out to the sidewalk, just like always. If this showcase had been life-changing, shouldn't there be some obvious sign? All I saw was the traffic barreling down 30th Street.

"Good show," Biggie said, pushing the gear into the van.

"You think?" After "Sad Drive," Colin had called out the three songs Danny wanted, but I was afraid that maybe the damage had already been done.

"Yeah," Biggie said. "We nailed it."

I wanted so badly to go back inside and get definitive information from somebody, but if I did, I might find out that the verdict from the suits was *no.* As long as I stayed on the sidewalk, in my sweat-stained jacket and backwards ball cap, I still had a chance at *yes.* I wanted to hold on to *yes* for as long as I could.

The front door opened. It was Colin. "Sorry I didn't warn you about 'Sad Drive,'" he said. "But it just seemed so *dead* in there."

"No. It was good. It was the right call." I needed to believe this.

"So what do you think?" he said. Strands of his hair were stuck to the shoulders of his jacket.

"Like you said last night. 'If they don't like it, they can get bent.'" I needed to believe this too.

Colin's face brightened a bit. "But I'm pretty sure they did like it."

"What do you mean?"

"When I was coming off the stage, Sonenberg introduced me to some guy, I don't know, Richard Griffiths, maybe. And Steinman was there too. Anyway, this guy says, 'I can't wait to start working together.'"

"What. Wait. Holy shit."

Colin looked right at me. Grabbed me by the shoulders, which felt strange, for as close as Colin and I were, we rarely touched each other. "I think we fucking did it," he said.

Then Sonenberg slid through the door, wearing sunglasses that probably cost more than my bass. And every dime he'd ever spent on orthodontics was worth it, just so his smile could burn itself into my memory.

Then he said the best two sentences I'd ever heard. "Congratulations, you motherfuckers. You've got yourselves a record deal."

Our mouths must have hung open.

He nodded and gave us both hugs. Then he looked at his watch. "Get your asses back inside." That smile again. "There are some people I want you to meet."

Another band was setting up to play, but the energy in the room had shifted to the back of the bar, because that was where Watershed was hanging out. A blonde girl tapped me on the shoulder and offered me an Amstel. I was pretty sure I recognized her. She'd gone to Ohio State. Now she lived in New York and hung with the Wall Street crowd. I felt her fingertips drag lightly across the back of my hand. Her eyes never left mine. The look on her face was odd. Wide-eyed and flirtatious, sure. But something else. If she'd been looking at anyone other than me, I'd have said she was *starstruck*.

I said thanks and passed the beer straight to Herb, motioning for him to follow me to the men's room.

"It's done, Herb. We've got it," I said. "Epic Records."

"You're shitting me."

I smiled wide and shook my head.

"Wheeeeew!" And Herb jumped like Michael Jordan sinking a buzzer-beater. He was smacking the meat of his hands into the stall partition and laughing like a lunatic. Then two guys walked in. We nodded coolly and headed back out to the bar.

Don was playing host in a slick Italian suit, buying drinks for anyone standing nearby. In his oversized dress shirt and Yankees cap, Danny was giggling his way through a Springsteen story.

Sonenberg practically had Colin in a headlock. "You clutch mother*fucker*," he was saying. "That opening song, 'Sad Whateverthefuck,' was *perfect*. You should have seen the look on Richard Griffiths' face when you started singing."

Colin seemed to shrink under the praise, looking uncomfortable as Sonenberg continued. "Griffiths looked over at Steinman and me and said, 'Lovely song. Have I heard this?' Jim and I said, '*We've* never heard it. Must be new.'" Sonenberg gave Colin a noogie and said to nobody in particular, "I'm telling you. The kid's got *balls*."

Then Biggie walked in from the street. We looked at each other like Mobsters after a contract hit. I raised my eyebrows as if to say *It's done,* and he nodded and spit in his Coke can to say, *Good—that's good.*

"And *you,*" Sonenberg said, grabbing my shoulder. "You owned that stage. Griffiths said you were the coolest-looking bass player he's ever seen."

"Is he still here?" I wanted to see what a record company president looked like. Griffiths, wherever he was, answered only to Tommy Mottola, head of Sony Music. And Tommy Mottola answered to, I don't know, maybe the emperor of Japan.

"Steinman drove him home," Sonenberg said. "Jet-lag or something. But, listen. I want you to meet Frankie."

Leaning against the wall, standing near—but not too near—the other company brass was Frankie LaRocka. Musician-short and dressed in a black suit over a bright red T-shirt, Frankie was easily the coolest-looking guy in the bar. He was wearing dark sunglasses. At night. Indoors. Frankie was a drummer who had toured with David Johansen from the New York Dolls. As a session man, he'd played with Scandal, John Waite, and Bryan Adams. And he'd been Bon Jovi's drummer on "Runaway."

"But most importantly," Sonenberg said. "Frankie does A&R for the Spin Doctors. Which makes him the longest-swinging dick at Epic."

I was finally being introduced to an A&R man.

"Don't let him fool you," Frankie said in the curled-lipped way of a street tough. "Sonenberg's the biggest dick in this room."

"There are a *lot* of dicks in this room," Sonenberg said, looking toward a guy with an Ivy League haircut and another carrying a messenger bag. "And I'd better go suck some of them." He winked at Colin and me and walked over to the other two men, smile set, as per usual, on *stun.*

"Fucking weasels," Frankie said, shaking his head at the A&R competition. Then he turned to Colin and me. "You guys got a cool little band. We'll make a hit record together." His accent was pure Staten Island: hit "*rekkid.*" As in *rekkid* deal.

I looked at Colin. I'll be damned. We *had* done it. On Epic Records Watershed would be joining Pearl Jam and the Spin Doctors. Ozzy

Osbourne and Ted Nugent. Blondie and Boston and Social Distortion. We were now on the same label as Michael Jackson. We were now on the same label as Cheap freaking Trick.

"Where's the drummer," Frankie said, taking off his sunglasses. "I wanna meet that animal behind the skins." Behind the *skintz*.

I left Frankie to Colin and Herb. I walked past Sonenberg, who was talking to Ivy League Haircut and Messenger Bag. Past Don and Danny who were laughing with Biggie. Past our Patterson Avenue buddies. Past the OSU Wall Street alums and that blonde and her starstruck expression and—wait, look at that cute little mole on her cheek. But I was past her. Out the door and onto the sidewalk.

Standing on the 30th Street curb, I yelled "*Fuck, yes!*" to nobody and to the whole of Manhattan. The news was burning a hole in my pocket. I needed a payphone, a quarter, a calling card. I needed to tell someone. I needed to tell someone right now. I needed to tell someone that Watershed had a *rekkid* deal. Breathing that autumn air was like huffing aerated adrenaline. *Fuck, Yeeeeesssss!*

Later, Don shepherded us from the Downtime to another bar. The stools were filled with quick-pint-after-work types, their ties loosened and their shirts untucked. Yesterday, these corporate wankers and their happy hour girlfriends might have looked at us in our jean jackets and flannel shirts and thought, since when do the Future Farmers of America take field trips to New York? But tonight, moving en masse, we carried the momentum of the showcase with us—in our laughter, in our posture. And everybody in that bar looked at us like we were . . . well, they didn't know who we were. But they knew we were *somebody*. I waited at the bar for less than five seconds before the bartender dropped a cocktail napkin in front of me and said, "What can I get for you?"

8

The Majors
New York, New York

It's noon in the lobby of the Newark Airport Courtyard. Two pilots pull their roller boards out of the elevator and across the lacquered floor—blazers crisp, wings polished, stripes shining like pharaoh's gold. With high-and-tight haircuts and backs straight as engineered lumber, they slide their key cards to the cocoa-skinned desk clerk, whose tie is knotted in a perfect double Windsor. One pilot salutes. The other sights with his thumb and pointer finger. As the clerk goes about his clerkly business, they vaporize through the sliding doors.

A church group bunches around three tables. Some eat hamburgers from paper bags. Others play cards. The kids chase each other through the lobby, all arms and legs. The adults are layered with back fat, arm fat, and neck fat, and when they laugh they laugh with their whole bodies.

A man in chinos and steel toes sits across from a pantsuited woman. His dress shirt is so new you can still see the package folds squaring across his back. She's wearing a Bluetooth earpiece. He's filling out paperwork, lips pursed in concentration. She's telling him to sign there and there, her French-manicured nails clicking on the table there and there. When he's finished, she smiles. He wipes his palm on his pants before shaking her hand.

Last night Biggie tossed me the keys, which means this morning I'm not hungover. Maybe it's the three cups of coffee I've drunk while sitting here watching the hotel's Monday negotiations, but today I don't feel the way I usually do when Watershed's route intersects with the straight nine-to-five. I feel connected to my fellow guests, all of us swimming the same stream.

Maybe I'll go for a run on the treadmill, or take a few laps in the pool, then eat a nice salad. Sobriety rules. I should drive more often. Give Biggie a little relief. Speak of the devil, here he comes now: dirty jeans, workboots, delivery jacket.

"Whaddya say, Biggie."

He grumbles something unintelligible and walks past me and the dapper desk clerk, who says to him, "How's it going up there?" probably thinking that Biggie's a plumber, here to snake the drains.

A few minutes later, he circles the van out front. I put on my hat and gloves and head outside, where, with the van's side door wide open, Biggie's wetting a bandanna with bottled water and scrubbing the carpet under the second bench. We call this spot on the floor the Spider Hole, and we've all taken turns sleeping there, squeezing between one bench and the other, making Houdini-esque contortions so that our backs aren't jabbed by the seat brackets.

"Fucking Pooch," Biggie says. He holds up the bandanna, which is now caked with red chunks. "Puked up half a pizza."

The smell hits me before Biggie finishes the sentence. "What?" I say. "When?" An upchucking guitarist I should remember.

I do remember driving us (and Christi, her perfume an oasis of olfactory perfection) downtown, through the sleet, to the World Trade Center site. Colin's a disaster junkie: airline catastrophes, deadly tornados, vicious earthquakes, rogue waves, fallen bridges—they're like porn to him. But he'd never seen ground zero, so we curled our fingers into the fence and stared down at the construction pit. We read the memorials at Ladder Company Ten, and nobody said much. Then, because Poochie Trump wanted to make a more capitalistic kind of pilgrimage, I drove us to the Wall Street bull. From there we took Christi home. I remember the goodbye hug, the smell of her shampoo, the feeling of nostalgia for a future with her that would never come. On the way out of town we cruised by Original Ray's for a couple to-go pies, greasy and mouth-burning hot.

I can still feel a piece of charred skin dangling behind my front teeth. I remember holding a slice in one hand, the steering wheel in the other, circling the block trying to find the goddamn entrance to the goddamn Holland Tunnel. It was a minor miracle that I didn't wreck as I navigated the subtle differences between Route 1 and Route 9 and Route 1-9 and Route 1-9 Express and Route 1-9 Truck and the Turnpike Extension— before finally slipping us onto the Jersey Turnpike proper. I remember a drunk and happy Biggie dialing Springsteen's "Open All Night" into his iPod, and I remember thinking that New Jersey in the morning *does* look like a lunar landscape, just like Springsteen said it would. I remember Biggie turning to Colin and me, saying, "Why can't you retards write a line as good as that?" I remember a lot, but I don't remember Pooch throwing up.

Now a disembodied voice says, "I'll clean it up, Biggie," and for a second I think Pooch must have passed out in the van, spent the cold night here, buried under blankets. But he's standing behind me, still green around the gills. Getting a whiff of the stench, he pukes into his mouth a little, and I watch him choke it down. Thank God this is January, not August, but still, vomit is a smell that lingers. And you don't puke in the van, no matter what. That's one of rock's cardinal rules. You don't shit on the tour bus and you don't puke in the van. Once, after doing too many tequila shots with The Fags—the band John Speck formed between Hoarse and HiFi Handgrenades—I held vomit in my mouth for a half hour rather than puke in their van. When I finally couldn't stand it anymore, I spit the bile into my hat, which I cradled in my lap for fifteen miles. Their van still stunk for a month.

The smell of Pooch's vomit has corporate types wrinkling their noses as they hand their luggage off to airport cabbies. Having now compromised the Courtyard's business-friendly atmosphere, we're not in harmony with the straight and narrow after all.

Biggie wrings the wet bandanna into the van's trashcan. "This is where you should have aimed in the first place."

"I tried," Pooch says. "I just missed."

After Biggie gets most of the large bits wiped away, the business lady with the pantsuit and French manicure hurries up to the van dragging a suitcase behind her. "Excuse me!" she says, telescoping down the handle of her bag. "Excuse me!"

Biggie, on his hands and knees, his delivery jacket marking him as someone whose job it is to serve someone like her, doesn't bother acknowledging.

She checks her watch and then turns to me and says, "Is he the driver?" She's nodding toward Biggie.

"Most of the time," I say.

"Good then." She yanks the handle and rolls her suitcase toward the back of the van. "What time does this shuttle leave for the airport?"

In Watershed's first van, after the A&R showcase, after the smile from Sonenberg and the hit *rekkid* talk from Frankie, after the toasting and high-fiving and pats on the back, Biggie blew down Broadway. He ducked in and out of traffic, nearly catching air as he crested the rise in the intersections. West 27th, 26th, 25th Street. We sped past taillights and streetlights. Pink neon and pale halogen. Cops and cabbies. Looking out the window was like staring into a still photo of a moving train: all horizontal lines. There was the Flatiron Building, the MetLife clock tower, the sporting goods store that Paul Reiser's character owned on *Mad About You*. And there was Union Square, Don's building. Site of the Watershed after-party.

Biggie parked next to the carts and trailers from that day's Greenmarket, and we fell out one at a time, like from a clown car. I straightened my jacket and checked my backwards Detroit Tigers cap in the side view mirror. A bunch of the Ohio State Wall Streeters were smoking on the sidewalk, waiting to be buzzed upstairs. The blonde who'd bought me the Amstel was huddled with them.

Don's pad was crowded with Amy's New York friends and Euro-hot waitresses from the Coffee Shop Bar. I grabbed a beer from the bathtub and weaved into the living room, where Don was tapping a marijuana pipe on his coffee table, emptying the bowl onto that week's *New Yorker*. "This shit is like lawn clippings," he said, exhaling a smoke stream that could have been used to test aerodynamics. "Let's fire up the Steinman weed." Jim was a pot connoisseur, and his weed was broken down by country of origin, like gourmet coffee. Hawaiian. Thai. Sumatran.

While Don packed some green Cambodian, Herb stood at the door shaking a champagne bottle. "Water fucking shed, bitch!" he said, and he shot an arcing line into my face. Then he moved on to Colin and Biggie, cackling as he sprayed them down.

I wiped the champagne from my eyes and saw that Don had the pipe waiting for me. I took a few deep hits. There we were, in New York City, in a double-size apartment dense with waitresses who dreamed of becoming models and stockbrokers who dreamed of banging those waitresses. Everybody was beautiful, and everybody was there because of Watershed. And yet the four of us were sitting around Don's coffee table, talking to each other.

"Herb, man, I think this shit is laced," Colin said, more stoned than I'd ever seen him.

Herb couldn't answer. He was laughing too hard.

Colin passed the pipe to Biggie. "No. I'm serious. PCP or something."

"I'll take my chances," Biggie said, working the lighter.

Colin was lying flat on the love seat, hugging a pillow to his chest. "Biggie!" he whisper-shouted. "Biggie!"

Biggie exhaled. "What?"

"Don't let me slide off these cushions and out the window."

I leaned back and closed my eyes. It felt like I was floating, limbs draped over an inner tube, ass breaking the surface of a piss-warm lake, sweat droplets pooling in my belly button. What a rare and beautiful thing it is to live up to your own expectations.

In my head, Sonenberg was still saying, *You've got yourselves a record deal.*

And Frankie LaRocka was curling his lip and telling me, *We'll make a hit rekkid together.*

And Richard Griffiths was saying to Steinman in a lilting British accent, *That guy's the coolest-looking bass player I've ever seen.*

But suddenly, on the distant horizon of my mind, the sunny bliss of the Steinman weed was giving way to gathering thunderheads. This was the age of the bidding war. Nirvana's massive success had launched a signing free-for-all, and the major labels had started offering indie bands deals upwards of a million bucks. These indie upstarts had been courted with first class boarding passes and Knicks tickets and suites at the Four Seasons. For Watershed there'd been no feting, no bidding. One showcase and it was done. But then I remembered that we had something better than a hotel suite: We had the president of the company in our corner. Our deal had come from on high, from Richard Griffiths, and his presidential seal was what mattered. Everything else was stoner paranoia. The clouds parted and the bliss was back.

I opened my eyes and took in the scene: Herb and Biggie laughing, threatening to toss Colin out the window. Two impossibly gorgeous women shotgunning beers. And The Blonde, talking to some other guy, but looking straight at me. Now smiling and sending me a cocktail-party wave. Now excusing herself and walking my way. She said hi and dropped next to me on the couch. Don sent the pipe around, and she placed a hand on my thigh. She draped her other arm over my shoulders. She laughed at everything I said. *Wow,* I thought. *This girl wants me.* Because she'd been there tonight. She watched me on stage. She watched Kurt Loder watch me. She saw important people break out their Gold Cards and buy me drinks. If this party had happened yesterday, she wouldn't have looked at me twice. She would have eyed my ball cap and scuffed Doc Martens and thought, who does *he* know here? But tonight she watched me get a record deal. *And now she wants me.* This is what the big break looks like.

Two hours or ten minutes later The Blonde massaged the back of my neck and said, "I've got to work tomorrow." She reached for her jacket.

But I wasn't going to let her walk out of Don's alone. No sleeping bag and hardwood floor for me. Not on this night. "I'll flag you a cab," I said.

She took my hand and led me toward the elevators. Standing in front of Don's building, I saw a hundred more nights just like this laid out before me. Champagne and weed and neck massages from beautiful blondes. This was how it would be from now on. When the taxi pulled up, we both climbed in.

The next morning I walked out of her brownstone and onto the stoop, buttoning my flannel against the breeze that blew down the side streets of Hell's Kitchen. Graffiti-tagged panel vans clanged over potholes and steam grates. A garbage truck beeped backwards from a rusty Dumpster. I'd told The Blonde that I needed a cigarette, but that was a lie. I don't smoke, never have. It just seemed a good enough excuse to put some distance between her and me, so I could absorb all that had happened in the last fifteen hours. Yesterday I was regular-old Joe Oestreich, from regular-old Columbus, Ohio. Joe Oestreich, *Son of a Priest and a Nun*, who at fifteen bought a one hundred dollar bass from a strip mall music store. Joe Oestreich, *Bald Guy*, who started a band with his buddies. Joe Oestreich, *Dean's Lister*, who dropped out of Ohio State dreaming of a record contract. Today I was hungover in a city that smelled like piss and day-old fish.

As I ran my tongue along the sweaters of my teeth, a brunette in her twenties, pretty and put-together in a smart suit, leaned into the glass door. She held a stainless steel thermos in her hand and a copy of the *Times* under her arm. I pulled the door open for her and nodded good morning. She smiled and lifted her thermos to say thanks. Her heels clacked down the steps, and I stood there holding the door like I was waiting for her to come back for something she'd forgotten.

I watched her walk toward 10th Avenue, where she hailed the cab that would surely drop her off at Morgan Stanley or Condé Nast or a Big Six ad agency. Soon those heels would walk into the tastefully appointed lobby of a Park Avenue tower, or through the shadowy-even-at-noon streets downtown. She was probably not from New York originally. Maybe she was a Midwestern kid with a land-grant diploma. And like me and The Blonde and so many others from Provincial

America, she'd come to Manhattan wanting to wake up to find herself king of the hill.

And now more people my age appeared on the stoops and stairs of their apartment buildings. The men wore Brooks Brothers, and the women wore Ann Taylor. They straightened their ties, fixed their hair and lipstick, and admired their reflections in the lobby doors. Then they hustled off, the wind catching the tails of their suit jackets and the hems of their skirts as they ducked into the cabs that would take them to their high-rise jobs. They looked gym-built and sophisticated, catalog-worthy. They were young, and they were, as their hometown friends surely said when raising glasses to them, kicking ass. I was momentarily hit with the same jealousy that had spiked the last three years as Colin, Biggie, Herb, and I watched our friends graduate from college to adult-size paychecks. My insides tightened. My mental defenses stiffened, constricting to a layer of armor that shielded my ego from the sight of other peoples' successes. I wanted to fire back at those Brothers Brooks, at those Taylors Ann—to shout into the Manhattan morning, *Listen up, you Nouveau-Yorker yuppie fucks. You should all be jealous of me.*

I turned and caught my reflection in the glass. Still dressed in the black jeans and Tigers cap I'd worn on stage, I looked the same as I had last night and every night since I dropped out of school and into the van: suburban skinny and prematurely bald. But suddenly I felt different. I was strangely happy. But not just happy. Elated. Or something like the opposite of frustrated. *Heartened,* maybe. My chest seemed to expand with five boroughs worth of sweetness and light. My head funneled the swirling goodwill of the Eastern Seaboard into my brain. I wondered if this was how it felt to do a pile of cocaine: like a hundred-year flood of serotonin let loose in my veins. My jealousy no longer had teeth.

I sat on the top step and leaned back on my palms. Everything—the street, the city, everything—was exactly as it was supposed to be. There was a pattern to the world, a grand design. This must be how James Bond saw walking into a casino: every infinitesimal thing that was happening, from the croupier flicking the steel ball around the roulette wheel to the bombshell sucking a gin-soaked ice cube at the baccarat table, was happening for him alone. Manhattan, I now understood, was just waiting for me to tell it what to do.

Here in Hell's Kitchen, panel vans had always clanged, garbage trucks had always beeped. But on that morning, all that clanging and beeping was mine. Because somewhere in the Sony Building on Madison Avenue, attorneys were drafting the contract that would make me Joe Oestreich, *Epic Recording Artist.* And more immediately, in an apartment on the third floor of that brownstone, The Blonde was naked and wrapped in a sheet, waiting for me to come back upstairs.

As daylight broke between Midtown skyscrapers, we'd stumbled up to her flat. Soon my black jeans and Tigers cap were a pile in the corner. My Fruit of the Looms were lost in the bed sheets. A used condom was buried in the wastebasket. This had never before happened to me, this rock and roll coup. I'd never just met a girl at a Watershed show and then had sex with her. Until that morning the only person I'd ever had sex with was Kate. Now I was taking just the sort of Jaggerian bite of the Big Apple I'd envisioned when I broke up with her. The sun leaked through The Blonde's curtains, and she slid from the covers and called in sick to her job at Bear Stearns. I followed the sweep of her back, her ass, her StairMastered calves, feeling like a mailroom kid who'd shanghaied his way into the boardroom. Even my hangover felt like something I won.

Now I hit the call button for her apartment. I took the stairs two at a time, swearing I'd remember that day forever. Because that was the day when everything was perfect. The day before, I'd been regular-old Joe Oestreich, from regular-old Columbus, Ohio. But on that day, on that stoop, I was Joe *Motherfucking* Oestreich. Rock star.

Sonenberg had said the contract was a done deal, but November came without a written offer from Epic. I wanted to be patient, but I'd heard too many nightmare scenarios of signings falling apart. The worst involved

Uncle Mingo, a white funk band from South Carolina. One night, Colin found an article in Columbia's weekly newspaper announcing that Uncle Mingo had signed with Capricorn Records. *Good for them,* we said, though we were jealous. The next week, back in South Carolina, we saw the newest edition of the paper. CAPRICORN DEAL FALLS THROUGH, read the headline. According to the story, the band had been handed a contract, and they'd signed it. But Capricorn hadn't. And a few days later, the company pulled the offer. One week Uncle Mingo were rock stars; they next they were schmucks.

The Friday after Thanksgiving, Biggie and I drove to Toronto to see Meat Loaf at Maple Leaf Gardens. Steinman and Meat had now sold a million copies of the single, "I Would Do Anything for Love," and the full-length album, *Bat II*, had just been certified double platinum. The hockey arena was filled with Meat Loaf–loving Canadians. After the show Don took Biggie and me backstage. For years we'd watched hot groupies get escorted behind the curtain at Aerosmith and Cheap Trick concerts; now we were the ones with laminates. We were the VIPs. If the fifteen-year-old Biggie and Joe were there in our place, they would have pissed their pants, but to us twenty-four-year-olds, backstage was mostly boring. Cinder blocks and folding chairs. Nobody was blowing cocaine out of a stripper's ass. This was like a potluck in the church rec room. We didn't even get to meet Meat Loaf.

As we picked over the hard rolls and lunchmeat, I asked Don, "So how are the negotiations with Epic going?"

He dipped a broccoli floret into a tub of ranch. "I talked with Sonenberg this morning," he said. "We've got an offer."

I looked at Biggie. How had Don not mentioned this three hours ago?

"But the numbers aren't exactly where we'd like them to be," Don said.

"Why? Where are they?" I was crossing my fingers for six figures. Please. Six figures would mean Epic was serious about breaking us.

Don looked over the veggie plate and curled his nose at the desiccated carrots. "They've offered a quarter of a million dollars."

Holy shit! A quarter million. The number rang in my ears like a brick of m-80s going off all at once. I didn't hear anything else Don said.

A few days later, Sonenberg called to say he'd accepted the offer. "We could try to squeeze their nuts for more," he said, "but at the end of the day, a quarter million for a baby-band from Hickville, Ohio, is a generous deal. I'm happy."

We assured him that, yes, oh yes, Watershed was happy too.

"Go treat yourselves to a steak or something. You *nudniks* are on Epic Records."

At work the following Monday I beelined straight for Chris Clarkson. "Hey, Chris," I said. "Guess what?"

He looked up and grinned his grin.

"You asked for it, you got it, my man. Watershed just signed a recording contract. It's a done deal." I patted him on the back.

Not one facial muscle moved, not one tick of acknowledgment.

"A major label, Chris." I said. "Epic Records."

Looking at Chris's vacant expression, you'd have guessed I said something like, *Donuts sure are delicious.*

"Yep," I said. "Big ol' contract."

"Joseph Oestreich," he said, going back to his tape gun and cardboard boxes. "Will I ever get a job in data entry if I have to look at the keys when I type?"

The deal was for a quarter of a million dollars[34], but it wasn't like we'd be getting a check for $250,000 in the mail. This was the music business, not Publisher's Clearinghouse.

Today record contracts have changed to reflect the advent of digital music, but back before mp3s and iPods, they worked like this: Epic agreed to fund Watershed for $250,000, and they called this, cleverly, *The Fund.* In return, we'd deliver a finished album, which we would use The Fund to pay for. Once you added up studio time, tape costs, producers' fees, engineers' fees, and food and other living expenses, it was common for bands to spend $100,000 or more making a major label album. However, we had a huge incentive to keep costs down: Any money left over after making the record was ours to keep. So if we spent $100,000 on the recording, there would be $150,000 for us on the back end.

But we wouldn't be getting a check for that $150,000 either. By the terms of our management deal, 10 percent of our gross income went to Crisis and 10 percent went to Sonenberg, so that's $15,000 each. Also, $25,000 of the $250,000 fund was earmarked for tour support, so it could only be used to pay for road expenses. Still, as long as we kept the recording costs under control, there'd be a small fortune left over for Colin, Herb, Biggie, and me to split.

And here was the sweetest part of the deal: Even if Watershed never sold a single CD, we wouldn't have to pay Epic back. They'd take the quarter million on the chin; we'd walk with our share of the leftover money. The not-so-sweet part was that we wouldn't see any royalties on the sale of the CDs until we *had* paid Epic back their original $250,000. These royalties are called *points,* as in percentage points of the retail price of the CD. Our deal with Epic gave us fourteen points, so 14 percent of every $14.98 disc (or $2.10) would be ours. Except all fourteen points *wouldn't* be ours. Big name record producers typically take four points—four of the *artists'* points. So once Steinman took his four, that would drop us down to 10 percent. Plus the Power Station would collect a point as payment for the demo sessions. The guy who engineered the demos would take half a point. The engineer on the new record would take another half-point. This would reduce our royalty rate to 8 percent. Factor in the cut to Crisis and DAS, and we'd make more like 6 percent (or 90 cents) of each $14.98 CD we sold.

But again, we wouldn't see our 90 cents per disc until Epic had been paid back the original $250,000 fund—not out of the 86 percent of the retail price that was their share, *but out of the 6 percent that went to us.* This means that at 90 cents per CD, Watershed needed to sell 277,777 albums (over halfway to Gold) before we would have recouped our debt. At the point of recoupment Epic not only would have been paid back their original $250,000 investment, they would also have taken in $3,578,545 from the eighty-six points they kept.

Essentially the company had placed a quarter million dollar bet on a racehorse called Watershed. If we sold well, they stood to win the monster payout. But the odds were long, about 10-1, because only 10 percent of major label CDs sold enough copies to recoup. Bottom line: The labels didn't score often, but when they did, they scored big.[35]

The next time Sonenberg called, it was to tell us that he and Frankie LaRocka had decided that our first Epic release would not be a studio album, but a live EP. I wasn't sure anyone would care about a live album from a band they'd never heard of, but Sonenberg reminded us that the Spin Doctors had debuted with a live EP, and once that mini-release had primed the pump, the studio follow-up went triple platinum.

"Don't think of the EP as a regular release," Sonenberg said. "It's just an appetizer until the full record comes out. Something to tour behind."

I wanted to say that Watershed was entirely different from the Spin Doctors. They were a jam band, and in that hippified scene live recordings held more cache than studio albums. But in the rock scene, where Watershed would try to establish ourselves, fans were accustomed to hearing a band first on the radio and MTV, then they'd go see the band live. This much I thought I knew for sure. Then again, as Steinman said, *Nobody knows anything*. And I wasn't prepared to argue against Sonenberg and his triple platinum Spin Doctor strategy. So I said to him, "You're telling me it's a *promotional* tool?"

"Exactly."

"Epic won't expect it to sell?"

"Give 'em away for all Epic cares."

On January 14, 1994, we recorded *Three Chords and a Cloud of Dust— Live* at the Newport Music Hall. We'd been uncharacteristically quiet about getting signed, but in the weeks leading up to the show, we cranked the hype machine. Suddenly we were everywhere: the *Columbus Dispatch*, the *Columbus Guardian*, the *Lantern*, *The Other Paper*. All the local rags ran stories. And on a night when temperatures hit ten-below, a thousand people showed up for the Newport show—most of them Watershed fans, the others wanting to see what the fuss was about.

Colin and I now know how live records are made, but back then we were working under the foolish assumption that live meant *live*. Turns out that much of what constitutes a concert album is actually recorded in a studio. The producer usually starts with live tracks, but once the lead vocals are re-cut, the background vocals are added, the guitars are beefed up, the bass fixes are made, and the crowd noise is looped, double-tracked, or stolen outright from somebody else's "live" album, there might be nothing left from the night of the show but the drums.

Still the result is often truer to the memory of the show than the real warts-and-all deal would have been. A live album is a lie. But like all good fiction, it's a lie that tells a certain kind of truth.[36] The trouble was we didn't know that back then. So on the live *Three Chords* EP we fixed almost nothing except for a couple lead vocal takes and a guitar track or three, and we were left with a faithful rendition of how we played and sang that night: imperfectly live. We didn't know enough yet to be worried that nobody at Epic had insisted we fake the live album.

Fourteen years later, we're touring behind the sequel, *Three Chords and a Cloud of Dust II*. Like the original EP, this album was taped at the Newport, in front of a huge crowd, but this time Colin and I had the good sense to fix *all* the vocals. Then we wrote a blurb in the liner notes explaining how and why we didn't fix *anything*. Critics have praised the new album for its raucous authenticity. We're a little savvier now.

Tonight the *Three Chords II* tour takes us to Arlene's Grocery, a club on the Lower East Side. On our way down Third Avenue, my cell phone buzzes. Gotta be Kate. This is my chance to ease diplomatic relations before tonight's show. It sucks to take the stage with someone mad at you. Then again, from the day you start playing rock and roll, somebody is pretty much always mad at you.

But this isn't a call from Kate. It's a text from Ripps, an old college buddy who's now a lawyer in Westchester County. Back at school he used to date The Blonde.

Bringing 10 tonight! What time do u go on? Drinks before the show? Gimme a shout out from the stage!

Ripps is a good guy, but he's a Spotlighter of the highest order. Tonight he'll corner me in the bar like he always does, bragging about what he can do for us: the connections he can make, the deals he can seal. He's been known to tell people he's Watershed's attorney, to which I shake my head while surreptitiously giving the throat-cutting motion. The upside: He always brings a crowd, and he lets the band run up his tab. I like it when Ripps comes out.

I text back *8:00* then look up to see that we're driving past The Continental Club, the bar we played the last time we were in New York. The Continental was once Joey Ramone's hangout. Sonic Youth recorded a live album there. Now there's a banner out front advertising 5 SHOTS OF ANYTHING $10 (YES WE'RE SERIOUS). They no longer book bands.

Then Third Avenue becomes the Bowery, and we stop at the Bleecker Street light. To our left is number 315, where Biggie once stepped gloriously into dog shit. The CBGB/OMFUG awning is no longer there, but on the brick façade you can still see a shadow of the skeleton frame the awning used to hang from. Now there's a FOR LEASE banner hanging in its place, another rock club squeezed out by neighborhood gentrification.

Back in 1994, when we moved to Manhattan to start recording the full-length album, it felt dangerous to wander the Lower East Side. The blocks south of Katz's Deli were haunted by the ghosts of Johnny Thunders and a thousand nameless junkies. Delancey Street squeegee men sloshed pickle buckets from car to car coming off the Williamsburg Bridge. Cool-looking Puerto Ricans with slick hair and Juvie tattoos drank from paper sacks. So the Watersheds, pride of suburbia, roamed in a pack. Biggie carried his wallet in his front pocket, and he let his hair grow long and greasy. I threw away all my hats and shaved my head skin bald. We tried to make ourselves tougher marks.

Sonenberg's staff found us a studio sublet in Midtown, at 51st and 8th, around the corner from the Letterman show and a few blocks from the Power Station. It was a one-room apartment with a tiny balcony and a stove barely big enough to heat up a can of chicken noodle. Apparently, at $1,700 a month, the place was a bargain, but we were nervous about the price tag. Even with a fund of a quarter million, we still tried to scrimp wherever we could: (1) because we were raised with a Midwestern frugality and (2) because we knew that any cash we didn't spend would be ours to keep. In the Midtown sublet the four of us lived in a single room. Biggie and I slept in the bed, Herb bunked on the futon, and Colin crashed on the floor. There was just enough extra space to set up a card table, where we'd sip tallboys and play euchre, Herb and me versus Colin and Biggie, a buck a game. We passed the same crumbled bill back and forth. We'd never had so much fun.

The recording sessions, however, weren't so spartan. Jim Steinman was the executive producer[37], so the sessions were run his way: locking out Studio A at $2,500 per day; ordering-in sushi to the tune of $500; paying a guy $5,000 to play one piano chord over and over.

"I can play that chord," Colin said. "And I'll only charge us five bucks."

"No," Danny said. "It's gotta be Jeff Bova."

So Jeff Bova played the one chord, and we cut him a check for five thousand. When it came time to mix the song, we decided the part wasn't any good anyway. We left it buried. Five-large, way more than any of us had ever made in music—poof.

"You've got to stand up to Steinman," Sonenberg told Colin and me. "Danny and Don can't do it. They're a couple of nervous Hannahs."

It seemed to us like Danny was wilting under the pressure not to screw up "How Do You Feel," the single, the hit. One day he spent five hours trying to dial-in the rhythm guitar tone, until he finally surrendered and called in Artie Smith, a guru from nearby S.I.R. Rehearsal Studios.

Artie plugged Colin's guitar into the amp, hit a big A-chord, and smiled. "Listen closely," he said to Danny. "I'll tell you what to do."

Danny leaned forward, waiting for Artie to spill the secret.

"This is a Les Paul," Artie said. "And that is a hundred watt Marshall. You plug one into the other. You turn it up real loud. Then you press the *record* button."

We handed Artie a check for $250.

The quarter million may have been vanishing into the belly of the Power Station, but it was buying us experiences we never would have had at a cheaper studio. We drank coffee with Cyndi Lauper (not nearly as goofy as you'd expect), stood in the lobby next to AC/DC's Malcolm (tiny) and Angus (even tinier) Young, and rode the elevator with über-producer Rick Rubin (looks much younger in person). And our hearts dropped a beat when Steven Tyler (!) howled, "Owwww!" as he loped past us toward the receptionist's desk. Later we snuck into Aerosmith's studio and played Joe Perry's guitars, read from Tyler's lyric book, and staged impromptu puppet shows with his collection of stuffed animals. We still own a tall stack of drumheads autographed by the stars we were recording alongside, artifacts from the frontline of the dream.[38]

Blasting from the studio speakers, "How Do You Feel" and my latest tune, "If That's How You Want It," sounded like surefire hits. But within our team there were fundamental disagreements about the direction of the band.

Steinman was a pop guy. He wanted the record to be slick and Top 40, with lots of keyboards and space-age sonic effects—laser beam pulses, force field drones, and Dopplery pneumatic hisses.

Frankie saw Watershed 180 degrees differently. He wanted to keep us raw and punky. While Steinman was figuring ways to make us sound more like Billy Squier's "Rock Me Tonight,"[39] Frankie was lobbying us to cover "Pirate Love" by Johnny Thunders. Above all he wanted to make sure the record didn't end up sounding too Podunk and Springsteeny.

"But we're from Ohio," Colin would say. "How can we *not* be Podunk?"

David Sonenberg's number one concern was that "How Do You Feel" have a sleigh bell track. "Every hit song I've ever had has fucking sleigh bells in there somewhere," he'd say.

Meanwhile, Danny and Don were worried that Herb couldn't cut it behind the kit. They thought the drum tracks were stiff, so they wanted to start over with a session drummer—like Frankie.

But Frankie thought Herb was plenty good.

Sonenberg didn't care either way. His concern was with me. He *hated* my voice. Thought it was too high. Too wussy. He wanted Colin to sing *all* the songs.

But Danny thought Colin's voice was too gruff. Too earthy. He thought *I* should sing all the songs.

Steinman thought two singers was the key to the whole deal. McCartney and Lennon. Stanley and Simmons. Gawel and Oestreich.

But Sonenberg thought two singers would be impossible for Epic to market. They needed an Eddie Vedder, a Zack de la Rocha.

One day Frankie pulled Colin and me aside. "You know what Watershed's problem is?" he said. "You got too many chiefs and not enough Indians."

Colin wasn't worried. He thought the chiefs were *all* nervous Hannahs. I wasn't worried either. I had confidence in the songs.

When the sessions were finished for the night, we'd beat it to DJ Reynolds on West 57th. The place was just your standard-issue Irish pub, but we were discovering that everyone, wherever he's from, needs a bar in Manhattan where he can feel like a big shot. And the bartenders at DJs—like all good bartenders—made us feel important. As long as we slid through the door by 4:00 a.m., they'd lock us in and let us drink until *late* flipped over to *early*. Leaving the dark bar on those mornings was like opening movie theater doors to the blinding parking lot sun. We'd stumble squinting back to our apartment, while rise-and-shine Manhattan shuffled off to work.

On those walks Colin, drunken and introspective, would tell us that he was worried about his mom. For months she'd been unable to shake the flu, and now, he said, she was really, seriously sick. I suspected he was being his usual alarmist self. This was, after all, the same Colin who braces for the crash as soon as he climbs into the van. We all worry a little, but Colin worries louder than the rest of us. And that's what I thought he was doing with his mom: worrying loudly. Then she was diagnosed with stage four lung cancer. Colin started making regular trips home for chemo drips and hospital visits. Biggie and Herb would go with him.

I stayed in New York to continue work on the album. Most nights after recording, I'd walk back to our apartment, heat up a can of baked beans, and settle in to watch highlights of the Winter Olympics from Lillehammer. And there on the TV, clutching roses to her chest, waving to the crowds, would be Nancy Kerrigan. With her long dark hair, big white teeth, and great legs, Kerrigan looked like, and I mean *just* like, Kate. For two weeks, everywhere I went—the studio, the Irish bar, the window at Nobody Beats The Wiz, anywhere there was a TV—there was Kerrigan. She was Kate on skates.

On Valentine's Day, I sat in a coffee shop, staring at Kerrigan in a newspaper photo.

God, I missed Kate. I'd made a terrible mistake.

The next few nights, I lay awake in bed for hours. The apartment was on the twelfth floor and heated with a griddle-hot radiator, so even on the coldest nights, we slept with the window open. As sirens wailed and horns blew, I realized that I'd blown it. Somehow I'd thought that I couldn't (or shouldn't) love my first and only girlfriend. But my short time with The Blonde had made things clear. I'd met her for drinks a couple times, but once the thrill of the aftershow party fizzled, I wasn't interested. She was cute, smart, funny. She was all New York all the time. But she wasn't Kate. Lying there in bed, a few days after Valentine's, I knew for certain that I still loved Kate. And if I didn't win her back right that minute, 7:12 a.m. or whatever it was, I'd regret it forever.

I threw on jeans and a flannel, and I punched the elevator button. But I couldn't wait for the elevator to creep twelve floors, so I raced down the stairs. Standing on the corner of 51st and 8th, I looked in both directions, but I didn't see a payphone anywhere. I spun around and hoofed toward Broadway and the thousand lightbulbs that lit up the mammoth CATS! billboard. And there, cornered inside a parking garage, was a phone.

"Hello?" Her voice was still rough with sleep.

"Kate," I said, hoping to God it wasn't too late, that some other guy wasn't lying next to her. "It's Joe."

"I knew you'd call eventually."

"Is that a good thing or bad thing?"

"It's a true thing. All my ex-boyfriends called on Valentine's Day. You were the last holdout."

I leaned my head against the booth and watched the snow melt from my boots to the concrete. "How many of them asked you to get back together?"

"A few."

"How many did you say yes to?"

"None."

I looked up. "I've been such a prick."

"You sure have."

"It's just that—"

"Just what."

"That I've figured something out." I geared up for my big line, the line I'd been thinking about all night, tossing and turning. "The thing is, it seems like nothing counts unless I'm sharing it with you."

She laughed. "So you're feeling guilty and lonely and you want me to make you feel better."

"No-no."

"Then why did you call?"

"To tell you I love you."

There was a long pause.

"I love you," I said.

Still nothing from Kate.

I pulled the phone away from my face and yelled, "I love you I love you I love you!" The words echoed through the parking garage.

"I love you too," she said. Then she was laughing again. "You prick."

Through the entrance to the garage I could see a thin slice of sun hitting the side of a building. It looked just like a Hopper painting.

Two days later I rode the NJ Transit bus to Newark Airport and met her at the gate. We exchanged a movie hug, kissed through tears. Riding the bus back to Port Authority, she told me that a few weeks earlier, she'd been trying to cross High Street to get to class, when a car stopped to let her go in front. The driver rolled down the window, and Kate saw a look of shock on the woman's face. "Nancy! Nancy!" the driver yelled, "Oh my

God. It's Nancy!" Then another car stopped. Then another. A traffic jam on High Street.

"That's crazy," I said.

She waved it off. "I haven't bought myself a drink in a month."

That weekend I walked Kate past the Gotham Bar and Grill, gave her a tour of the Power Station, and stood with her on Madison Avenue, our necks craned, looking toward the top of the Sony Building.

One April morning, Colin, Biggie, Herb, and I teetered out of DJ Reynolds, onto 57th Street and down Eighth Avenue, laughing at the huge inflatable chicken that squatted on the McDonalds roof. The album was nearly finished, and spirits were soaring. A few days earlier, at the release party for the Spin Doctors' sophomore album, Epic's VP of Rock Radio Promotion told me that her staff was all fired up about "How Do You Feel." She whispered into my ear, "Get ready to be huge." We were ready. The Spin Doctors' manager was *our* manager. Their A&R guy was *our* A&R guy. Walking among Midtown's movers and shakers that morning, Watershed was The Next Big Thing From The People That Brought You The Multi-Platinum Spin Doctors.

We weren't in the apartment five minutes when the phone rang. It was Colin's dad, calling to say Mrs. Gawel had died overnight. Colin hopped a flight from LaGuardia, while the three of us tried to sober up for the ten-hour drive back to Columbus.

When Colin and I were kids, his mom and mine became unlikely friends. Thin and tan, Mary Ann Gawel took tennis lessons and wore bootie socks and white Reeboks. She drove a red Prelude with vanity plates. My mom, Mary Anne (same name, different spelling), was older and less athletic. She wore castaway jeans and sweatshirts, and she cut her own hair. My mom came from working class Milwaukee. Mrs. Gawel was born to kiss people on both cheeks. But both women were staunch Catholics in a way that ran deeper than just showing up for mass. On Sundays my mom, sister, and I would sit in the pew next to Colin and his mom and sister, and I could tell by the peaceful glow on my mom's face that taking the body of Christ meant something to her. I saw this same calmness in Mrs. Gawel. When she linked her fingers to pray, her face looked, well, *naked*.

When church let out, Colin and I would draw up plans for rockstardom while Mrs. Gawel and my mom talked about how great it was that we boys had found something we were so dedicated to. Colin and I would look at each other and roll our eyes. Parental support took some of the fun out of it.

Years later my mom gave me a copy of a letter that Mrs. Gawel sent to her when my mom was overseas, teaching in Kuwait City. I still keep it in my desk drawer.

Hi Mary Anne,

The last 1–2 months have been crazy for me. To make a long story short, I have a tumor on my lung. Could you remember me in your prayers from Kuwait? I have been through so many emotions with my family in the last week. I am wrenched.

Watershed is in N.Y. for quite a while to make some CDs (paid for by Epic records). This is it, Mary Anne—I'm pretty sure! Now it's up to them and God. Onward and upward, Watershed! They have worked so hard for so long. God bless them.

Hope everything is going alright with you, Mary Anne. Keep in touch, kiddo.

Love,
Mary Ann

At the funeral there was a bouquet of roses beside the casket. Tucked behind the baby's breath was a card that read, DEEPEST SYMPATHIES FROM FRANKIE LAROCKA AND YOUR EPIC RECORDS FAMILY.

Colin didn't have time to mourn. Three days after the funeral, he was back in New York, singing "Sad Drive," the song that had wowed everybody at the record company showcase, the song that would close the album we'd call *Twister*. I shut my eyes in the dark studio and listened as Colin put on his headphones, stood at the microphone and sang, *As soon as you went away, I remembered the things I forgot to say.*

On January 31, 1995, *Twister* landed in stores. The long wait for the release date would have been maddening had we not had the live EP to tour behind. *Three Chords* had given us an excuse to van around the country charming Sony's field promotions staff. Even though we were playing essentially the same clubs as always, touring with major label support made all the difference. At load-in there were Watershed posters already hanging in the bathrooms. There were blurbs in the local papers.[40] There was somebody from Sony armed with a Gold Card, waiting to buy us dinner and drinks. These promoters and marketing reps loved us because we were regular guys; they were sick of whiney prima donnas who treated them like the low-rungers they pretty much were. Many nights we'd let a record rep crash in our hotel room—we'd give him a bed, and two of us would take the floor.

Our everyman appeal played in the sticks, but back in Manhattan, inside the Sony Building, it was a liability. Steinman had warned us: "When you go visit Epic, make sure you act like rock stars." We smiled and shook hands and were Ritchie Cunningham–friendly. This confused everybody. Friendly doesn't sell.

Still, momentum was building. Sonenberg hired a well-known agency to book our shows, a rep from Mercury was talking up a six-figure publishing deal, and the sweetest of all: Frankie LaRocka landed us two gigs opening for Cheap Trick. The first was at Deer Creek Amphitheatre, Indianapolis's 24,000-seat outdoor behemoth. After we finished, Colin and I stood in the wings, and from spitting distance we watched the band that had inspired us to pick up guitars in the first place. The third best part was when Robin Zander came over, smiled at Colin and me, and said something we couldn't hear. The second best part was halfway through Cheap Trick's set, when I slipped into the crowd, wandered to the top of the general admission hill, and sat in the grass sipping a big-ass draft. I stared at the curvature of the seating area and the summer sky, and I tried to take in the vastness of the place. Had Colin, Herb, and I really just stood on that stage? The best part was when, sitting there on the lawn, I heard some guy yell, "Bring the opening band back on!" Yep, we were rolling.

But then the Spin Doctors released their second album, *Turn It Upside Down*. And it stiffed, monumentally. Measured in sales numbers (and what in the music industry isn't), this was one of the most severe drop-offs in history, and *Rolling Stone* made it the centerpiece of a feature on sophomore slumps. Shit was turned upside down, all right. Now Watershed was, um, the next thing from the people, ahem, who brought you the historically disappointing, cough-cough, Spin Doctors. Dark clouds tumbled west from Manhattan.

With *Twister* in stores, Frankie's A&R work was essentially done. He handed the project to the product manager, whose job was to make sure the Sony empire threw its almighty weight behind the record. She was our gal, the quarterback of the marketing campaign.

And she hated us.

We tried to win her over with a show at Brownie's in New York.

"Terrible," she told Don and Danny after the gig.

So we booked a second Brownie's show, determined to woo her into loosening the Sony purse strings. This time the heads-of-promotion for rock, alternative, and college radio were all in the crowd. We needed to crush. We *did* crush.

"Even worse than the first," the product manager said.

"Don't worry about her," Frankie told us. "She's the grim reaper." Still, he was worried that the *Twister* mixes were too thin, the production too slick.

Steinman, on the other hand, thought the production was too raw, and he blamed Frankie for it. Rumor was that Jim had gone directly to Richard Griffiths and flat-out demanded that Griffiths fire Frankie. Given the *Turn It Upside Down* disaster, Griffiths was probably considering it anyway. Somebody had to take Spin Doctor heat.

Meanwhile, everyone agreed that Watershed should be listed as co-producers of the record. "It's more your album than ours," Danny said to Colin and me. We thought getting the production credit was cool, but would we be the scapegoats if the album tanked? Were the chiefs empowering the Indians, or were they giving us just enough rope to hang ourselves?

That February, the hits kept coming. So and so isn't impressed. So and so doesn't get it.

"We're on our own out here, boys," Sonenberg said one day. It had taken us a week to get him on the phone. He was busy managing The Fugees, Joan Osborne, and Spacehog. He told us that Epic had decided to distance themselves from us, focusing instead on higher-profile projects like Pearl Jam's *Vitology*, Oasis's *Definitely Maybe*, and Michael Jackson's *HIStory*. Sony's promotion budget was tight, and floating a statue of the King of Pop down the Danube wasn't cheap. Before he hung up, Sonenberg said, "This is gonna be a tough nut to crack."

Tonight at Arlene's Grocery we opened for Heavy Metal Karaoke, which runs like regular karaoke, except that the aspiring frontmen and -women sing on a real stage with live musicians. HMK is essentially a cover act with an endless rotation of singers, and nobody takes it too seriously, which makes it hilarious and great.

Over the years we've noticed that New York bands—even the ones that don't pull karaoke singers from the crowd—are disproportionately shticky and ironic, often dressing in tennis outfits or matching Speedos or like Victorian strippers. My theory is that irony insulates these bands against failure. They want to be famous, but just in case it never happens, they can always take off their costumes, fall back on their Wesleyan diplomas, and say, *we were just kidding*.

Colin's theory is that New York acts have to rely on shtick because it's impossible to form a real band in the city. Real bands are built on *sum*, but NYC is populated with interchangeable *parts*, be they art school kids, aspiring actors, or those music school gunslingers who travel the subway with a gig bag slung over their shoulders. Even if these players can wrangle themselves into something that looks like a band, there's still no easy place to practice in New York. Real bands can have six-hour rehearsals if they want. Or they can drink beer, smoke weed, and just talk about practicing. This doesn't happen in New York, where bands often have to rent rehearsal space by the hour. Without a trust fund or a rich dad, how the hell can anybody *afford* to join a band in New York? It's hard enough just owning a van here. Last I checked, a parking spot in the city rented for roughly the same as a two-bedroom flat in most college towns.

Being in a band anywhere is expensive, but in New York you must have to work three jobs, which means you're too busy waiting tables to practice or play gigs. And even if you can get the night off to play a show, most bars only book forty-minute showcase slots, which, when you calculate the expense-per-minute, hardly seems worth the hassle. Then, with the added pressure that industry might be in the crowd, you play nervous and tight, and the audiences get stuck watching forty tense minutes of too-scripted showcase rock, which would never cut Midwestern mustard. Colin has long contended that if New York music fans could see the drunken, rollicking, two-hour sets that get played in Madison or Minneapolis, they'd shit their ironic thrift-store Toughskins.[41]

Whatever the case, Heavy Metal Karaoke sure is popular. During our set, the wannabe singers descended upon the HMK sign-up sheet like crows on carrion. Now, as I make for the bar, I've got no choice but to concede that Watershed is mere minutes away from getting blown off the stage by kara-*freaking*-oke. Which isn't to say our set was bad. In fact, this was maybe our best New York show ever, in spite of (or because of) there being almost nothing at stake.

Colin and I are drinking in the afterglow, such that it is, working the room like a wedding. At a back table sits our pal Will Allison, who's now a successful writer. His debut novel, *What You Have Left*, was released to an avalanche of press, including a feature in *Entertainment Weekly*. I ask him how the next book is going.

"Great," he says. "Shitty."

I know what he means. When people ask how this NYC show went—when they ask how Watershed's whole career is going—what will I say? Awesome. Terrible.

Will's with his friend Jeff, a fund manager who stands about four feet tall. Jeff says he's amazed that we've kept playing since high school.

I tell him I'm not sure if that's admirable or pathetic.

"Either way you've been aiming at something this whole time," he says. "That's the key. Having something to *aim* at. Whether or not you hit it is immaterial."

Jeff's a wise man. Generous too. Once, when we were standing in front of a bar in Chicago, a drunk blonde stumbled out, saw the three-foot Jeff, and said, "Oooooooh! You're so cute! I just want to hug you! Can I pick you up and hug you?" I wanted to smash her perfect teeth down her perfect throat. But Jeff, wise enough to know that this wasn't the time, place, or audience for a lecture on civility, clenched his jaw and let her hug him. Jesus, this man is big with patience and grace.

Now, a leggy HMK fan in fishnets and hotpants walks by. Jeff stops talking and stares. Her legs cut ribbons of air.

Gathered 'round the bar are Ripps, his brother, and the ten buddies they've brought. We've got clearance to run up Ripps's tab, so Dave and Pooch are drinking like it's their job. Again Ripps tells me he wants to be our lawyer.

"Watershed's got nothing to litigate," I say, giving Ripps a knock on the shoulder, "unless you want to defend Biggie on the DUI he's gonna get later."

I slide over to Kevin from The Generals, who now lives in Jersey. The last time we saw him was two years ago, when he booked us a show at a Manhattan Tiki Bar called Otto's Shrunken Head. We played in the closet-size back room for four people: Kate, a friend of hers, my Uncle Jim, who is now the classical music editor for the *New York Times,* and his wife, who's on the Brooklyn Museum Board of Trustees. The gig was especially dismal given that we'd played a packed CMJ showcase at the Continental Club the night before.[42]

Now Kevin's telling Colin that next time Watershed schedules an East Coast run, he'll book us into a Jersey strip club.

Colin says, "Can we get paid in ones?"

Then Don and Danny walk up. Frankie used to say that Crisis Management couldn't manage a lemonade stand; all they did was *create* crises. Maybe so, but I like them anyway. Watershed has enough ex-managers to field a baseball team, but Don and Danny are the only ones who showed up tonight.

Danny cracks a joke and gives Colin a hug. "Really good show, man," he says.

"And Joe!" Don says. "You look great." He puts a hand on my shoulder. "You look like a rock star."

I smile and say, "I always did, Don."

By mid-March it seemed that Watershed had chosen the perfect title for the record that would blow our major-label career to bits. *Twister* had been out for six weeks—and had sold 750 copies. We were eyeballs deep in shit.

But then, just when the album seemed dead on arrival, miracle of miracles, radio stations began to play "How Do You Feel." The program director at WRCX in Chicago made Watershed his pet project, spinning us sixteen times per week and booking us on *Mancow in the Morning* and on Lou Brutus's afternoon drive show. We stood in Sonenberg's office, so cluttered with gold records there wasn't a place to sit, and he said, "Gentlemen, if we can SoundScan fifty CDs in Chicago this week, we'll know the record is reacting. Epic will *have* to get back on board."

We didn't sell fifty CDs that week. We sold two *hundred* and fifty.

In April, armed with a suddenly hot single, we rolled out on a two-month tour opening for The Smithereens. The pay was $250 per night, so we traveled exactly as we always had: the same unairconditioned van, the band and crew in one hotel room. From our tour support money, we paid ourselves a fifteen dollar per diem. No salary, no benefits—just fifteen bucks a day and all the bologna we could steal from The Smithereens' deli tray.

And it was a fucking blast.

The tour opened in D.C. to a sold out crowd. Then Biggie followed The Smithereens' bus to Norfolk, where a new band called Ben Folds Five hopped on the bill. For two weeks Ben Folds opened for Watershed[43], and Watershed opened for The Smithereens, and the tour made its way through the Carolinas and Maryland and back up to the Northeast. Sometimes two of us would stowaway on The Smithereens' bus, drinking martinis and smoking cigars. Sometimes their drum roadie, Ira, would ride with us in the van, playing the demo his new band, Nada Surf, had just made.

In Charleston, The Smithereens' Jim Babjak tipped the hotel shuttle driver fifty bucks to be our designated driver for the night. In Baltimore, Pat DiNizio slid a bar owner a hundred to keep the joint open past last call, and we stayed there until daylight, passing an acoustic guitar back and forth in a drunken singalong.

Then a shift seemed to take place. At the Quinnipiac College show, The Smithereens looked old and out of shape, and most of the students disappeared long before the band played their big hit, "A Girl Like You." We blew them off the stage that night, and they knew it. Watershed had stolen the momentum. We were the up-and-comers.

The Metro in Chicago: Sold out. And half the crowd was there to see us. A Smithereens/Watershed double bill would have sold out two nights. Detroit: Same. From truck stop payphones Biggie would check in with Don, Danny, and Sonenberg. More good news: the secondary markets had followed Chicago's lead. "How Do You Feel" was added in Toledo, Springfield, Appleton. Twelve spins per week on Q-FM-96, *Ohio's Best Rock*. Ditto for CD101. Columbus's metal station, *The Blitz*, even added us. A booth over from Biggie, Colin and I would do phone interviews with writers from Cleveland, Pittsburgh, Milwaukee. Watershed now had a story to tell.

The tour dropped south toward Memphis, Little Rock, and on into Texas, with Sixpence None the Richer taking Ben Folds' spot third on the bill. In San Antonio, Biggie was backing the van up to the dock for load-out when he heard "How Do You Feel" coming from the stereo. He pushed the eject button on the cassette player, thinking, *Who's the dick that's been listening to his own song?* But no tape came out. The stereo was tuned to the radio. He rushed into the dressing room to tell us. "Guess what, ladies," he said. "Guess fucking what."

We must have celebrated extra loudly, because Ira, The Smithereens' roadie, walked by and asked if we could keep it down a little. When we asked why, he stepped inside, closed the door behind him, and told us that The Smithereens were meeting with their manager in the next room. The band had just gotten word that Capitol Records had dropped them.

Wow, we said, that sucks. But I was still thinking about Biggie's news. Radio play in San Antonio. Westward expansion, baby. Manifest destiny.

At a Flying J on the outskirts of Amarillo, Biggie walked back to the van smiling extra big. He looked stupid-drunk.

"What the fuck, Biggie," Colin said. "Did some guy stroke you off in the bathroom?"

Biggie kept smiling. "Better," he said. On June 3 *The Blitz* was doing their summer festival at Polaris Amphitheatre, the new twenty-thousand-seat venue in the Columbus suburbs. *Blitzapalooza* they were calling it. Biggie paused to let that sink in. Then he dropped the bomb. "And they want us to headline it."

Eyes bugged. Jaws dropped. Highs fived.

Meanwhile WRCX had pushed "How Do You Feel" into heavy rotation, which meant twenty-four spins per week in Chicago. Sonenberg told us to clear our summer schedule. Epic's promotion staff was suddenly all fired up about the scrappy Watershed. They'd lined up a whole string of radio shows for us. Blitzapalooza was just the beginning. We'd be playing amphitheaters all summer.

With that news, Steinman called Sony president Tommy Mottola to ask for a video budget and enough additional promotion money to give "How Do You Feel" a huge nationwide push. "If Watershed is a hit in one or two markets," Steinman said, "they should be a hit in *every* market." And even though Sonenberg still hated my voice, everyone was talking about my song "If That's How You Want It" as the follow-up single.

"We were the underdogs," Frankie said. "Now we're the comeback kids. The little band that could."

Off to El Paso, Phoenix, and Los Angeles, where we checked into the Riot Hyatt on the Sunset Strip. The gig was across the street at the House of Blues, so close we could have thrown a baseball through the HOB windows from the Hyatt balcony.

That night I saw Quentin Tarantino eating a burrito at Barney's Beanery. Then on Santa Monica Boulevard I was almost hit by a car in which Tommy Stinson from the Replacements was riding shotgun. Later I saw Dan Aykroyd walk a bag of trash to the House of Blues's Dumpster. He was wearing a tuxedo. This was L.A. like a *motherfucker*.

After the gig we threw a party at the Riot Hyatt. The Smithereens came. The House of Blues waitresses came. The Epic promotion reps came, wielding the Gold Cards that told us, yes, Watershed was back in the company's good graces. As the bash wound down, Herb and I filled condoms with beer and chucked them over the balcony, laughing as they burst on the pavement below. We stayed up to see the sunrise over Sunset.

A half hour's sleep and then we piled into an Epic rep's convertible for a breakfast meeting at Sony's Santa Monica offices. We shook the requisite hands and smiled the requisite smiles, and the very last person we met that morning took Colin, Herb, and me aside and said, "Are you guys drunk? It's 8:00 *freaking* a.m." Then he patted us on the back. Rock stars are supposed to be drunk at 8:00 a.m.

The tour ended in Las Vegas, where I lost two weeks' per diem trying to keep up with The Smithereens at the blackjack table. This left us seven days to make it back to Columbus for Blitzapalooza, the biggest show of our career.

Polaris Amphitheater was built on a patch of commercial-grade real estate that was once soybean and corn acreage. It pushed up from the land like a burial mound. On that misty June night—like all nights in all amphitheaters, or *sheds* as they're known in the industry—mosquitoes and Marlboro smoke floated through the headlights of the cars idling in the muddy lots. The DayGlo-clad parking attendants hovered, and kids palmed joints and hid cans of Milwaukee's Best in their crotches until the coast was clear. A quick pat-down, a ripped ticket, and everybody's inside, where it's like a state fair midway, down to the lemon shake-ups, hand cut fries, and the smell of sweat and grease and grilled meat. This is the American summer. Throw up an elephant ear stand and a beer truck, and they will come.

And come they did. Ten thousand people walked through the Polaris turnstiles that night. Ten thousand people came out to see the local boys who'd made it.

After the show we did the meet-and-greet with the contest winners. We did shots with the *Blitz* DJs. The Polaris staff interrupted to ask if we'd be willing to make impressions of our hands in plaster, for their Walk of Fame. With a paint-stirrer Herb spelled out WATERSHED '95 in the wet goo, trying to make permanent a fleeting moment.

Then we stood in a circle just the four of us, raising a toast—as we had in the Patterson kitchen five years before. Five years. And it *had* been a tough nut, but we'd fucking cracked it. All that was left was to dig our fingernails into the crevice and split that sonofabitch wide. By then I'd already put the Polaris show behind me. I was thinking ahead to everything that waited on the other side of that night: the summer tour, the radio shows, the next single. We stood in our circle and drank our drinks and told ourselves that after five years, this night marked a beginning.

It was a beginning, but not in the way we imagined.

Eleven days later Epic dropped us.

Central Park, 3:00 a.m. You expect throat-slashers and wilding. A gang scene straight out of *The Warriors. Watershed, come out to pla-ee-ay.* But there's nobody here. There are 1.6 million people living in Manhattan, but the park is ours.

With sixpacks dangling from our gloved fingers, we walk toward our usual spot, the Heckscher Ballfields. Ever since the Power Station days, night-drinking in the outfield has been our favorite New York pastime. We've dragged Puerto Rican girls from Yonkers off their bar stools and walked them through the dewy grass[44], and we've talked analysts from Accenture into cracking High Lifes out in center. "Are you guys insane?"

Danny would ask us. "You bumpkins'll get yourselves killed." We figured he'd watched too much local news. To us the odd thing was never that we were drinking in the park; it was that nobody else was.

Tonight after the Arlene's Grocery show, we shoved Ripps and his brother Ben into the van and disappeared them up to DJ Reynolds. PJ, the Irishman who's manned the bar practically since the potato blight, recognized us instantly—he recognized Biggie, I should say—just as he has every time we've stepped in there for the last fifteen years. PJ knows Columbus is five hundred miles away, but he never seems surprised to see us. "Michael McDermott," he says to Biggie. "What'll ya be havin'?"

Several Guinnesses and Jack-and-Cokes later, Ripps and Ben were ready to call it a night. A Westchester lawyer and a Manhattan corporate slug, both of them are fathers, with wives and good homes, too old and accountable to be drinking past last call on a winter Monday—just like the rest of us. But Biggie was tour managing the bar crawl, and he wasn't letting anyone go just yet. So we said goodnight to PJ, made our usual deli stop at 57th and 9th for brown bag beer, and now we're walking up to the ballfields—which are fenced off for the winter.

"What do we do?" asks Ben.

"We jump it," says Biggie.

Ben sighs. He's about fifty pounds past jumping fences.

"Look, Ben," I say. "In this life we all have fences to climb. Right now your fence happens to be an *actual* fence. Get your ass over it."

His pants get caught, and he doesn't quite stick the landing. He comes up limping, but smiling.

"Atta boy," I say, knowing that tomorrow he'll show up to work with a hangover and a great story. A night in the barrel with a band. Rock and roll fantasy camp.

A few minutes later Pooch passes out on a park bench, his leather coat pulled up to his belly, his navel exposed to the night air. Ripps and Ben whip out their cell phones and take photos of him. Dave lies down in the grass and makes snow angels, while Biggie and Colin argue about Biggie's bad weather driving.

"I'm just saying we hit ninety twice on the way here," Colin says.

"Shut the fuck up," Biggie says. "You don't want to be told when to eat; I don't want to be told how to drive."

I wander into the borderless zone that the four ball diamonds share. From here I can count the checkerboard window lights of the buildings that ring the park. I can make out the silhouettes of the buildings' cakelike, art deco crowns. The sky is dotted with stars that seem close enough to steal.

There was a time when I thought of New York as mine. Now I'm just another tourist. Visiting from the provinces.

I make a snowball and rear back to throw. It falls apart before it hits the ground.

Fuck. We almost had it. We were right there.

And yet we were impossibly far. Just like the tops of those buildings. Just like the stars.

THE THIRD LEG

9

Left of the Dial
Baltimore, Maryland

THIRTEEN YEARS AFTER BEING DROPPED BY EPIC, WE'RE MOTORING down the Jersey Turnpike, operating on four hours sleep, and Biggie's decided to lay a little Bread on us: "Baby I'm-a Want You." The soft rock assault started back at the Newark Courtyard, when he nudged everybody awake with the drippy ballad "If." This was his way of reminding us that we were doing an in-studio at a Baltimore radio station in a few hours. Now the delicate yearning sweeps us southward ever-so-gently, hearts and rose petals floating from the tailpipe.

Colin and I have decided to one day write the softest song in the world. The working title: "A Satchel Kissed with Daydreams."

Right now my head feels like a burlap sack of hornets. "Fuck this," I say, and I drop to the Spider Hole—which still smells faintly of pepperoni and puke—and I let Bread whisper me a lullaby.

The interview is with John Mathews at WTMD, the Towson University station that recently added a couple of our songs into rotation. Even with the radio play, landing the Baltimore gig was a pain in the ass. Mathews suggested we book the 8x10, a small club we'd played years ago on the Smithereens tour. "We used to be on Epic," Colin wrote to the club's talent buyer. "TMD is going to hype the show like crazy. We're just looking for a Tuesday." The talent buyer wrote back that Tuesday was New Band Nite, and yeah, he'd add us to the five-band bill—if we bought thirty-five tickets in advance, for $3 each. After fronting the $105, we could then sell the tickets for $5 to whomever we wanted, keeping a $2 profit on each. Sell all thirty-five, and our pay would be $70. Sell none and we'd make nothing—less-than-nothing, actually, because we'd be out the original $105.

"You believe this snake?" Colin said. "Bands actually agree to this?"

It was the old pay-to-play routine, a scam we thought had gone the way of Sunset Strip hair-metal. Five bands put up $105 each, and before the doors open, the club has banked $525. We didn't expect to make money at this show, but paying $105 to play? Unacceptable.

Colin wrote back: "As a national touring band, we won't front money for tickets."

The talent buyer answered that without the pre-sale, he wouldn't risk booking an out of town band, even one with radio support.

"What a dumbass," Colin said. "Doesn't he want his bar promoted on the radio?"

Colin eventually convinced our current label, Idol Records[45], to front the $105. "But," he wrote to the club, "we must go on stage at 9 p.m. and have at least a 45 min slot." An early set time was crucial, so as not to make WTMD listeners sit through four pimply high school bands—with their indifferent tuning, on a school night—just to get to us.

The talent buyer wrote, "I'll work on getting you a good spot, but the whole point of the night is to have everyone SHARE their audiences. We insist you advertise the 7 p.m. <u>door</u> time."

"For fuck's sake," Colin said to Biggie and me. "This is the hardest fought Tuesday in the history of rock."

Now, as we approach the Towson campus, we're laughing like idiots at the irony of old-ass Watershed playing New Band Nite. *This* is the huge show we've come to the radio station to promote. I'm suddenly remembering a store in Manhattan I once saw, the kind of place that sells lead-based toys and knock-off purses. There were three Chinese symbols on the store's sign. Underneath the Chinese lettering was the English translation: HAPPY-FUNNY-CRY.

After load-in we prep for the interview by watching a DVD of KISS's Halloween '79 appearance on Tom Snyder's *Tomorrow* show. Ace Frehley and Peter Criss are rip-roaring drunk; Gene Simmons gets steaming mad at their unprofessionalism; and Snyder, the consummate TV pro who's just trying to steer the ship, loses hold of the conversation—all of which makes for spectacular television.

Snyder starts by introducing Gene Simmons as the *bass* player. He accidentally rhymes *bass* with *ass,* like the fish. Frehley cackles at the gaffe and then introduces himself as the *trout playa.* When Snyder later asks about Ace's spaceman costume, Frehley, in his native Bronxian, says, "Actually, I'm a *plumba.*" To which Snyder deadpans, "If that's the case, then I've got some pipe you can work on backstage." I'm laughing hard enough to tweak a groin. What you see in that footage is a band whose K-factor is spiking. Not even kabuki-painted rock monsters are immune.

Like most of our generation, Colin, Dave, and I grew up wanting to be the KISS characters. Even now, almost middle-aged, we sometimes slip into KISS alter egos: Dave is The Catman, sensitive-but-medicated drummer. Pooch is Space Ace, the drinks-till-he-pukes guitarist. Colin—pretty boy front man—is a natural Starchild. And I'm the Demon bass player who takes everything a hair too seriously and gets irritated when the other guys don't. For Dave, the *Catman* nickname has stuck. At the country club, when the leggy waitresses poke into the kitchen to drop off their tickets, they say, "Order-in, Catman."

Now Mathews points us to four stools, hands out headphones and mics, and makes the *we're rolling* sign. "We've got very special guests in the studio today," he says. "Columbus, Ohio's Watershed. In town for a big show at the 8x10. Here with me are Colin, Joe, Dave—"

"Catman," Dave says into his mic.

I shoot him a look. Not here. Not now.

Mathews laughs and says, "Sorry, Dave—"

"It's Catman."

Yep. Here. Now.

"You got it," Mathews says. "Catman it is."

"And he's Starchild," Dave says, pointing to Colin, who is supposed to be doing the talking. When we're on the air, it's Colin's show. But today Dave has commandeered the radio tower. He turns toward Pooch. "That's Space Ace."

"I'm the trout playa," Pooch says.

"I see," Mathews says.

Dave looks my way. "And that's The Demon. He plays bass." Like the fish, rhyming it with *ass,* as in *jackass,* the one word the Baltimore listening public is now clearly associating with Watershed.

This asinine exchange reminds me of a gig a few years ago at the Dewey Beach Pop Fest, when in our K-factor–fueled drunkenness we decided it would be hilarious to steal a bit from Elvis, from his Louisiana Hayride days. The plan was for Colin and me to take the stage without Dave. We'd announce to the crowd that our drummer was sick and couldn't make the show. Does anyone know how to play drums? Can we get a volunteer to sit in? Please? Somebody? From the raised hands we'd pick Dave—the shill, the plant. Sitting behind the kit he'd look nervous and uncertain. But we'd encourage him. We'd get the crowd to encourage him. Suddenly he'd cut loose. He'd have the songs down cold, and the audience would go ape-shit. That's how it worked for Elvis, anyway.

When Colin asked for volunteers, thirty hands shot up. *Every*body could play drums because nobody came to the Dewey Beach Pop Fest *but* musicians. As planned, Colin chose Dave, who acted shy and confused. The audience spurred him on, and after a few minutes, Dave was bashing away like a proper member of the band. But when the musician-stacked crowd figured out they'd been hoodwinked, they turned on us. They booed and flipped us the bird and chucked cups and bottles our way. We bobbed and weaved and threw down whiskey shots between songs.

Colin got so drunk he played the last two songs flat on his back, slurring like a campfire hobo. Soon there was nobody left watching but Biggie and the soundman. To the disappointment of both, we played an encore. Finally Colin, who'd caught a second wind, brought the set to a close by spitting beer into the lights and kicking over the mic stand. The soundman was so livid, he ran on stage and grabbed Colin by the neck, screaming, "What's with all the *spitting* and the *kicking?*" Biggie wrestled the guy to the ground and sprung Colin loose.

That sound guy was a meathead prick who deserved to get his microphone busted, but I too was choking-mad at Colin. Why drive all the way from Ohio to Delaware just to suck? We took the argument to the bar, and Colin and Dave tried to convince me that the gig had been twice as good as a standard Watershed show precisely because it was such a pickled wreck. The Replacements, after all, had built a career on playing solid one night, stumbling drunk the next. Let's face it, professionalism doesn't rock. The way Colin and Dave saw it, the show had transcended rock and risen to the level of conceptual art. I'm still not entirely sold, but I do see a certain elegance in sacrificing a show every once in a while for the sake of an inside joke. It's happening right now, in fact, live on the radio.

"I know Colin owns a coffee house," Mathews says. "But what do the rest of you guys do for day jobs?"

I'm trying to decide if I should admit to being a college professor, when Dave leans into the mic and says with utter sincerity, "I own a bikini shop."

We all bust out laughing at this reference to *Runnin' Down a Dream*, Peter Bogdanovich's Tom Petty documentary, wherein we learn that Petty's original bass player, Ron Blair, quit the Heartbreakers to sell swimsuits.

"No kidding," says Mathews. "You got a name for your store? Let's give it a plug."

"Catman's House of Thong," Dave says.

When our hooting and snorting finally dies, Mathews turns the discussion toward *Three Chords II*. "Tell me about the process of reinterpreting the songs for a live audience," he says.

"I'm so glad you asked that, John," Colin says, "because most DJs just want to talk about all the starlets we've had sex with. It's so refreshing to discuss our *art* for a change."

Most DJs would have written us off as assholes by now, but Mathews is a longtime friend and fan. He knows we're not mocking him. It's just that tonight's gig has us bucking under the weight of our failed expectations.

"So, Catman. Thong impresario," Mathews says as a way of shutting the interview down. "Got any advice for young musicians out there?"

Dave looks at Colin, Pooch, and me—perched on our stools like the very kings of New Band Nite—shakes his head and says, "Quit."

We knew we'd be dropped someday. Unless you're U2 or Springsteen, you're going to get dropped, certain as death and taxes. Willie Phoenix, The Toll, and the R.C. Mob had all been cut loose. Even the Smithereens, a band with certifiable hits, lost their deal. We knew our stint in The Pros could end any time. We expected it. Just not so soon.

Sonenberg called to deliver the blow. "Epic's not picking up your option."

We didn't know what that meant. We figured *not picking up your option* was just another phase in our roller-coaster relationship with the hot, sexy Epic. She couldn't possibly be dumping us. Not with "How Do You Feel" burning up in Chicago. Not after we'd just played for ten thousand people at Polaris. We'd win her back. We just needed a chance to remind her why she liked us in the first place. The string of summer radio festivals would do the trick.

"You guys don't understand," Sonenberg said. "No summer. No radio. No festivals." Epic had pulled the shows from us and given them to their latest signing, a bunch of Australian sixteen-year-olds called Silverchair. Our hot girlfriend had left us for teenagers. We were has-beens at twenty-five. "You've had a great run," Sonenberg said. "But it's over."

It didn't feel over. We still had bar shows on the calendar. We still had a closet full of CDs with the Epic logo on them. We were fired up, ready to grind. A break here or there, and we could still stumble into a hit. Then the label would get wise, take us back, and the summer shows and Silverchair and *not picking up your option* would all be written off as a horrible misunderstanding.

Fate seemed to turn in our favor when *Billboard* gave "How Do You Feel" a critic's choice star, hailing the song as a "crisply produced rocker that is infused with stomping barroom energy and a juicy pop hook." The *Billboard* critic praised the chorus for its "ballsy instrumental sound that could do the trick in sparking play from album rock and eventually Top 40 formats—given a little promotional TLC, of course." Frankie LaRocka hung copies of the review on every floor of the Sony building, taping them right in front of the elevators, where nobody could miss them.

By lunchtime, security had ripped down every one.

Next we heard from the WRCX program director, who told us he'd been all set to add our second single, "If That's How You Want It," but then he got a call from an Epic radio rep, telling him he was wasting his time, add Silverchair instead. The PD said no thanks, he'd stick with Watershed. The Epic rep said, not if you want those fifty Pearl Jam tickets to give away, you won't. Twenty years in radio and the program director had never once had a label tell him *not* to play one of their bands. "I hate to say this, guys," he said. "But your record company is actively working against you,"

"Fucking *weasels*," Frankie said when we told him about the call. But he was just as powerless to do anything as we were. Epic *wasn't* our record company. Not anymore. And now the rumor was that Frankie's days at Sony were numbered. Everyone at the company seemed to have forgotten that Richard Griffiths, the president, had actually made the decision to sign us—not Frankie. But that no longer mattered; Frankie was the A&R man of record, and in the Spin Doctors and Watershed, he'd engineered two consecutive flops. Major labels don't keep losers on the payroll.

We later found out that the "How Do You Feel" CD singles that had gone out to radio made no mention of Jim Steinman as executive producer. This was Frankie's call (he thought Steinman undermined Watershed's raw and punky credibility), and it was a mistake. Radio was where Steinman's reputation as a hit-maker mattered most. The snub had hurt Jim's feelings, and now he was allegedly intensifying his efforts to get Frankie fired.

A week after Epic dropped us, Sony released Michael Jackson's greatest hits package, *HIStory*. It was a smash by every measure but one: the kingly standard Jackson himself had set with *Thriller* and *Bad*. Sony spent tens of millions promoting it, but *HIStory* was as close to failure as was possible for the pop monarch. Now the company stood deep in a hole. Cuts would have to be made. One day that fall, Sony fired something like 250 people, and Frankie LaRocka was one of them. Our A&R man, lone ally at the company, was gone. It finally hit us that our major-label days were done.

We kept the news to ourselves. The illusion that we were still a major-label band gave us credibility with radio programmers, concert promoters, press, and potential fans.[46] But word eventually leaked. People we barely knew would make funeral faces and say, "Man, what happened with Epic?" We shifted the blame from ourselves, spinning the story like this: Michael Jackson's album tanked, so our A&R man was fired, so we had nobody left within the company to fight for us, so our album was lost in the corporate shuffle, so we were dropped. A caused B caused C caused D caused E.

Stick to the bullshit long enough and you start to believe it. For years I conveniently forgot that Watershed was dropped *before* Frankie was axed. I'd rewritten *HIStory*. *Twister* didn't bomb because Frankie was fired. He was fired, at least in part, because *Twister* bombed.[47]

I worked through denial, anger, bargaining, and depression, to eventually reach something like acceptance. But it took longer still for me to get a handle on *why* we were let go so soon. I blamed our top-heavy management team for their lack of cohesion. I blamed Epic for being fickle and shortsighted. I blamed Michael Jackson for being Michael Jackson.

But here's the simple truth: *Twister* didn't sell enough copies.

Here's the honest truth: *Twister* isn't a great record. I wish we could duck the blame for this, but the fault is ultimately ours.

Here's the pragmatic truth: The *Three Chords* EP came back to bite us. Somewhere in our contract was a section mandating that Epic decide whether to keep us or drop us within eighteen months of our *first* release. This clause was supposed to work in our favor, preventing the company from leaving us in limbo. We didn't know it until it was too late, but *Three Chords* counted as the first release. It had started the clock ticking early, which didn't give *Twister* nearly enough time to catch fire. We'd only been working "How Do You Feel" at radio for six weeks when the deadline hit. Sonenberg had told me the EP was a throwaway, that the company didn't expect it to sell.[48] But when the Epic brass held the mandatory meeting to weigh the pros and cons of shitting vs. getting off the Watershed pot, we were a band with *two* failed albums. Epic got off the pot.

We'd started with a fund of a quarter million dollars. Colin, Herb, Biggie, and I left Epic with about a thousand bucks each.

Here at WTMD, we play a song live on the air, give away two tickets to caller number nine, and then Mathews and his interns wrap the cables and pack up the mics. As Biggie carries gear out to the van, I ask him if I can check my e-mail on his laptop. In my inbox, there's a new message from Kate. Yesterday I left her a few voice mails, but we haven't spoken in two days, not since I called her from outside the Old Town Bar. That conversation had felt like dental surgery. I open the e-mail and see a lot of text. She must be writing to apologize.

Hey,

    I was really startled the other night when you asked, "Are you mad at me?" because I have been mad at you ever since this thing started. And what's making me really crazy is that you simply keep ignoring my feelings and my anger, as if a) they are not important or b) they will magically change or go away if you don't acknowledge them.

    So I will try one more time. I have been unequivocally against this tour since it began. You know that. But instead of trying to come to some sort of agreement that would take my feelings into consideration, you just started lying more and hiding more. A three day tour magically turned into almost three weeks. Band practices sprung up out of nowhere. I mean, seriously, you wouldn't even mention that there was a band practice until maybe a half an hour before you were scheduled to be there, so I couldn't say anything w/o looking like a shrew. That was calculating and rude.

    Now my worst fears about this tour have come true. I have been trying my hardest to do this on my own out here. I have been exercising and inviting people to go out with me, and I still hate it. I've been depressed and having panic attacks and crying and taking myself on walks, and you act as if you're surprised that I'm not HAPPY with you. You can't just keep ignoring my reality and being "friendly," as if your goodwill magically cures all things.

    So, yes, I'm pissed. And, yes, I'm pissed at you. I really just can't believe that we never agreed as a couple on any part of this trip on any

*level. You didn't hear or listen to my voice at all, not in the beginning,
not now. I was simply told repeatedly that you "couldn't" do anything
about it. And now you're surprised that I'm mad. Really?*

Let me be clear: I won't do this again for any reason. I mean it.

Kate

I look over my shoulder. Colin's laughing with Mathews. Dave
and Pooch are flirting with the intern. Biggie's wrestling with my amp.
Everything appears business-as-usual, except that it isn't. I feel like I've
been kicked in the sternum.

Let me be clear: I won't do this again for any reason. I mean it.

Is she asking me not to tour? Not to tour for so long? Not to leave her
alone on the West Coast?

Or: Is she asking me to choose between her and Watershed?

Please. That's ridiculous. We met because of the band. I read the e-mail
three more times. I can't tell if it's an ultimatum or a storm that will soon pass.

"What's the word, Demon?" Colin says. He walks up, reading a text
message on his phone.

I minimize the e-mail window. "Nothing much." I can't talk to
anybody about this until I have a better idea what it means.

Colin looks up from his phone. "Susan's coming tonight."

"Wow," I say. "That's cool." Susan is the girl he kissed in the kitchen
on that New Year's Eve so long ago. He dated her all through the Wire
days, all through the Epic days. They moved in together and got engaged
when he gave her his mom's wedding ring. Then, not long after we were
dropped, she left him for an immigration lawyer.

I once wrote a song called "Anniversary," about a long relationship
that ends suddenly. The chorus goes: *She's telling me now / this thing has
run its course / Eight years for what? / A shotgun divorce.* This May will mark
Kate and my eight-year wedding anniversary. Maybe this e-mail is her
way of cocking the shotgun. Maybe I should be worried.

But now that song "Anniversary" is stuck in my head, and I'm not
even thinking about Kate anymore. I'm thinking: This song is fucking
awesome. How was it not a hit? How were we *not* rock stars?

September '95. Three months A.D. (After Dropped). We left D.C. with the wipers on high and the gas gauge on E. That night we'd opened for Cowboy Mouth at The Bayou in Georgetown. A thousand ball-capped fraternity-types and their dates chanted our name. We added fifty addresses to the mailing list. Sold a few hundred bucks in T-shirts—proof, in our minds, that Epic had been dumb-asses for dropping us.

"Screw 'em," we said, and we cracked open the Budweisers we'd lifted from Cowboy Mouth's dressing room.

Crossing the Key Bridge, the van was making the same death rattle it had been making for two days, the same *clack-clack-clack* we first heard on the Mardi Gras trip two years earlier. Biggie figured we'd thrown another rod. Maybe cracked a head gasket. The engine might take the terminal shit in five miles or five hundred. Still he was betting that with a full tank and the AAA gold card, he could limp us home to Columbus. We squinted through the rain for an open gas station, but the Parkway was as dark as the Pennzoil we were burning by the case.

We were good and drunk when the gas ran out. Biggie coasted to an exit, circled a cloverleaf, and the van coughed to a stop under the overpass. As the wipers squeaked, Herb reached into his backpack and opened a velvet box. A diamond sparkled in the dome light—an engagement ring for Lori, his longtime girlfriend.

Back on the grass near the onramp, we'd seen a dozer and a backhoe. "Of course they run on gas," I told Biggie. "What else would they run on? Love?"

So while the rest of us drank to Herb and Lori, Biggie clipped the ends from a guitar cable. Then, using a razor blade and needle-nose pliers, he stripped out the electronics, leaving a hollow rubber tube. "Bottoms up, Romeo," he said to Herb and everybody else.

Biggie and I walked the tube and the empty beer bottles to the construction site. He snaked one end into the backhoe tank and inhaled on the other. A virgin siphonist, he sucked too hard and got a mouthful. He spat, wiped with his bandanna, and tried again—this time sealing the tube with his thumb to keep from gargling.

We brought six full bottles back to the van. Biggie was tilting the third into the tank when he stepped back and said, "This is goddamn diesel."

"How do you know?"

"I tasted it."

"Diesel's mostly gas," Herb said, grabbing for the bottles. He jammed the last thirty-six ounces down the hole.

We'd siphoned a diesel sixpack into a gasoline engine. What would happen when we turned the key? Would this be the lethal injection that ended the van's suffering? A mercy kill? Would it slip away peacefully or explode like a Mob hit? We stood at shrapnel distance as Biggie cranked the ignition. Nothing doing. Herb pushed Biggie aside and punched the dashboard Fonzie-style. Not a wheeze.

Then headlights came around the bend, and a Plymouth Fury floated up alongside us. The driver, thirtyish and paint-flecked, rolled down the window. "You look like a band."

Somebody tell Epic Records.

The driver said he'd take Herb and me to the station in Frederick. His car smelled like a bar rag, and he kept swerving from shoulder to solid yellow. "You ever have one of those nights where it feels like you're living a Hank Williams song?" he said, working the wheel with two fingers. "But you can't tell if it's Hank Junior or Senior?"

Herb and I laughed. And buckled up. Finally, we saw the fluorescent glow of a Sheetz station. The third-shift clerk charged us eight dollars for the gas can.

Could the 87-octane outmuscle the beery diesel? Biggie pumped the pedal and pumped again and the engine eventually turned over: *Clack-clack-clack.*

We waved thanks to the Fury driver, but he didn't pull away. He sat dark and quiet, smack in the two-lane. "Fuckin-a, fellas," he said. "I'm outta gas."

Biggie hopped down from the van with a fistful of empty bottles. "You take diesel?"

We pushed the Fury off the road and *clack-clack-clack*ed to the Sheetz. No need to buy a gas can this time. Back under the overpass, we got the car running.

A few hours later, the van would crap out anyway. Herb would call Lori and ask her to drive the five hours to Breezewood to pick Colin and him up. Biggie and I would take another long ride in a tow truck. We'd declare the van a lost cause, giving it away to our mechanic friend, Dave Cook, who'd eventually get it up and running with a transplanted boat motor.

But now, with the engagement ring burning a hole in his Levi's, Herb reached into the Fury and handed the guy a Watershed shirt and a Budweiser.

"I'll be listening for you on the radio," the driver said, twisting open the beer. And he weaved into the Maryland night.

Listening to the radio that year was like a lead pipe to the knee. On seemingly every station was a band we were friends with: Ben Folds Five at this frequency, Sixpence None the Richer at that one. Take a spin down the dial and it was Nada Surf and Hoarse and Howlin' Maggie—the band that ex-R.C. Mob bassist Harold Chichester had recently formed. Howlin' Maggie had signed with Sony's Columbia division, and CD101 had added *six* of their songs. Their single, "Alcohol," was getting a *thousand* spins per week at stations nationwide. The more we saw the big rollouts our buddies were getting, the clearer it became that we had never been a priority at Epic.

Dropped makes you a leper. Our own team insulated themselves from us like we were pathogenic, a pox on their careers. First the booking agency bolted. Then Sonenberg called to say he wasn't the man for us. Finally Don, Danny, and Steinman all bailed. Heads hung, we went back to our day jobs: the Vision Center for me, the restaurant for Herb. Biggie limped back to waiting tables. Colin aproned-up as a Subway sandwich artist—a brutally public shaming. It sucks being asked to sign an autograph on the wrapper of a footlong you've just built. Columbus's *The Other Paper* ran a cover story called THE BAND-O-METER: WHO IS RISING AND WHO IS FALLING? Watershed were the falling poster boys. I took to sleeping on the floor, so as not to wake Kate with my sheet twisting.

Yes, the post-Epic year was dark. We lost our record company, our management team, our van, and now, maybe, our drummer. "I can't fucking take it," Herb told me that fall. "This isn't going anywhere. It's not fun anymore." And even though he kept showing up to band practice, he made us pay for every minute with his surly mood.

One day Colin called Slim Dunlap from The Replacements, hoping ol' Slim could give us a little perspective. We had opened for Slim's solo band a few times, and he'd seen us in Minneapolis once or twice. The first night we met him, he crawled beneath our van to inspect the undercarriage. "Looks like you could use some new suspension leaves down there, ya know," he said, accenting the Minnesota "O." Then he brushed himself off and gave us a lesson on why musicians should never clean out their ears. "Wax is nature's earplug," he said. We'd been seeking him out for advice ever since.[49]

Slim told Colin the trick was to look down the ladder at all the bands below, bands who would gladly trade places with you. Take stock in how far you've come, in what you've left behind. Trouble is, Slim said, most bands only worry about who is higher on the rungs than them. "I remember when The Replacements did that tour with Tom Petty," Slim said. "One of the biggest there is, and even *he's* unhappy. 'Cause he's not as high up as, I don't know, The Beatles."

A few years after that phone call, Slim joined Watershed on stage at Comfest, an outdoor festival in Columbus. In front of a crowd of thousands we rocked though "Battleship Chains" by the Georgia Satellites and "King and Queen" from Slim's tragically overlooked album *The Old New Me*.[50] Between songs Slim took the mic, and announced to the audience, "These boys here once asked me what it takes to make it." He looked across the stage at Colin and me. "Looks like they figured it out."

And that's the thing about rock and roll. It beats you down and beats you down, and just when you're curled in the fetal position, bracing for a kick to the head, it offers you a hand. Pulls you to your feet. Gives you a reason to keep going.

The first hand was extended by Frank Aversa, a producer who'd recorded the Spin Doctors' biggest hit, "Two Princes," and was also the man behind the Burger King "I *love* this place" campaign. He had recently helped a Florida band called The Hazies land a deal with EMI. Now EMI was considering giving Aversa his own boutique label, which he would name Thundercreek Records. Aversa asked us to come to his home studio in the Berkshires to record the *Twister* follow-up. If the sessions went well, he said, Watershed would be the first band signed to EMI/ Thundercreek: another major label deal. "Wheeeew!" Colin said, taking Herb by the shoulders. "We're back, baby. We're back!"

The sessions did go well. Thundercreek released the resulting album, *Star Vehicle*, in early 1997, and—with better-crafted songs and more skilled playing—it marked a giant step forward from *Twister.* CD101 added both the title track, written and sung by Colin, and my song, "Black Concert T-Shirt." This radio play went a long way toward tourniquetting our Columbus following. We could no longer pack the Newport, but we could put a respectable two to three hundred into smaller clubs. EMI, however, reneged on the Thundercreek imprint offer, and Aversa, as a one man operation, didn't have the resources to build on the CD101 airplay. *Star Vehicle* seemed destined to sell a few thousand copies then slip quietly away.

But the Watershed way is to slip loudly. So we worked the record ourselves, old-school, just as we'd done before Steinman and Sonenberg and Epic goddamn Records. We pressed CD singles of "Star Vehicle" and "Black Concert T-Shirt" and shipped them off to radio. Sent kits to press and to record companies. Scored a distribution deal to get the CDs into stores. Played eight or ten shows a month. We regained the DIY drive we'd had in the *Carpet Cliff* days, which was its own kind of payoff.

Herb, however, was looking for a more tangible breed of success. He threatened to quit again. "This roller coaster is driving me nuts," he told me. "And I swear. Colin's optimism. All this we're-gonna-get-another-record-deal shit. I tell you, Joe. I'm gonna break his nose one day." Still Herb kept coming to practice.

The next hand was offered, bizarrely, by the Insane Clown Posse, two Detroit rappers whose axe-murdering, killer-clown personas made them demigods of mildly menacing white boys everywhere. Violent J and Shaggy 2 Dope[51] were in the midst of a sold-out tour for the platinum-selling *The Great Milenko* when one of their opening acts, House of Krazees, suddenly dropped off the bill. ICP needed a last minute fill-in. Their front-of-house soundman, a guy who'd mixed us on the Smithereens tour, convinced them to hire Watershed. *Watershed? Yeah, man. Those fuckers'll do anything.* Another break. Another chance to prove Epic wrong.

At the first show, in Scranton, Colin, Herb, and I were waiting in the dressing room, changing into our power-poppy suits and ties, when through the walls came a familiar sound. "Wa-ter-shed! Wa-ter-shed!"

"They're fired up," Herb said.

"Yeah, they are," I tweaked my double Windsor until it was perfect. "They *know* us."

"We got some radio play around here," Colin said. "Didn't we?"

Herb opened the dressing room door so we could bask in the Scranton love. But now we could hear that the crowd was chanting, "Watershed SUCKS! Watershed SUCKS!" I gulped under my tie. "Uh-oh." We hadn't yet taken the stage and we were already being booed off it.

If you know anything about ICP, you know (1) They call their fans "Juggalos"[52] and (2) At their gigs they douse said Juggalos with Niagaric quantities of Faygo soda pop. The Juggalos—who paint their faces clown-style—spend most of the show jerking lasers of pop toward the ceiling and chucking two-liter bottles at each other. ICP must crank through five hundred two-liters in an hour-long set. At the end of the night, the average Juggalo looks like Marcel Marceau shot through a car wash: wet, sticky, and ready to fight. At every tour stop they pelted Colin, Herb, and me with shoes, shirts, paper cups, Jolly Ranchers, popcorn, chewed gum, lighters, batteries, and loose change of all denominations. The stage would look like a piñata after picture—if the piñata had been hung in the alley behind a dollar store. On the upside, the Juggalo median age was probably fourteen; those kids had weak arms and spotty aim. None of the flotsam hurt all that much, and we always made a few extra bucks picking quarters off the stage.

Herb always wanted to track down stray Juggalos and monkey stomp them for good measure, but Colin and I tapped into our inner teenager. We'd fire the shit right back at the little bastards. It's hard to work up a good anger toward kids who've been dropped off in a minivan. Heck, I sympathized with them. I understood how frustrating it was to wait for your heroes to appear. When we were younger Herb, Colin, and I had absolutely booed King Kobra and Black 'N Blue and Saxon—bands that opened for KISS and Aerosmith and Cheap Trick. Herb probably chucked a Nike or two.

Before our set, we'd sometimes hang backstage with Violent J, who's really a thoughtful guy. At the Orbit Room in Grand Rapids he walked into our dressing room, sat down, and said, "I don't know how you get up there and do it every night, man." He smiled under his killer-clown make up. "Our fans fucking *hate* you."

Colin and I laughed. Herb sat alone in a corner, looking baggy-eyed.

"Hate's never stopped us," Colin said.

"I like you guys, man," Violent J said. "You're stubborn as shit."

He then told us a story from when he worked at McDonalds as a kid. He said his manager was a real asshole, always hassling him for not wearing his uniform right, for coming back from break thirty seconds late. One day, after a particularly humiliating dressing down, Violent J ripped off his McDonalds shirt and hopped over the counter.

"What do you think you're doing?" the manager said.

"I'm quitting," said Violent J. He pointed to his civilian undershirt. "I'm a customer now. And, like you say, the customer is always right. So make me a motherfucking Big Mac, bitch."

That night the crowd booed and spat soda pop and chucked stuff at us, just like always. At one point Colin prodded the whole club, all two thousand of them, to shoot us the double-bird. Biggie stood on the stage, next to Herb, and took a photo of four thousand fingers telling Watershed to fuck off.

Back in the dressing room, Violent J thanked us for our service. We'd no longer be needed on the tour. We said we understood. No hard feelings. We were still down with the clown.

After Violent J left, Herb moped in the corner, shirtless and sweaty.

"Fuck it, Herb." Colin said. "Who cares? We'll land somewhere else."

"We always do," I said.

Herb wiped his face with a sweaty forearm. "I can't do it anymore." He dropped his head to his hands. "I'm done." There was no wall punching. Herb was calm. Too calm. That's when I knew he meant it.

Colin, Biggie, and I were crushed. On the way home, Colin tried to talk him out of it. He said Herb should at least stick around to see if *Star Vehicle* stirred up label interest. The record was just gaining momentum. But I could tell this argument wasn't scoring any points with Herb. The guy had been in the band for twelve years, since before any of us could drive. Now he was married, and he and Lori were thinking about starting a family. He no longer needed to take the music business beating. Colin kept talking, fumbling for the right thing to say, but Herb wasn't listening. He'd heard enough of Colin's pep talks. He sat staring straight ahead, looking the happiest I'd seen him in months. He'd jumped to the other side of the counter.

Driving down Baltimore's Greenmount Avenue, it's like we've crashed the set of HBO's *The Wire*. We pass a string of storefronts with barred windows, pawn shops and corner taverns, check cashing and title loans and payday advance, and bodegas selling shirts that tell us to STOP SNITCHING. Down the eerily empty side streets sits an urban ghost town. I hate to let a TV show tell me what to think of a place, but I'm not about to ask Biggie to hang a right so we can see Baltimurder up close.

While I'm considering television's representation of urban America, Dave says, "I'm not playing the show tonight."

"Yeah, Biggie," Pooch says. "Cancel finger." He's referencing The Hazies, that Florida band. Biggie roadied for them for a few months. Whenever their singer was passed out in bed, too hungover to do an early in-store or in-studio, he'd lift the cancel finger skyward.

"Gotta do the show for the radio station," Colin says, even though he knows Dave and Pooch are kidding. Watershed has never bailed on a gig—even when we should have.[53]

"Then I'm going to need more Percocet," Dave says. "You got any left, Pooch?"

"Mark," Biggie says from behind the wheel. "If you give him one, I'm pulling the van over right here and kicking your fucking ass."

Looking out the window at the boarded row houses and shadowy lots, I'm preparing mentally for the day Dave and Pooch quit. They seem beaten down. We all are to some degree; any sane person would be. "Bet we could find somebody around here to sell you a few pills, Dave," I say.

He slumps into his seat. "I gotta get off the drugs."

The 8x10 sits in Federal Hill, near the Cross Street Market. As we pull up, the talent buyer is standing on the sidewalk, waiting for us. His hair is long, kinky—halfway to whiteboy dreads—and tied back in a bandanna. He's wearing cargo shorts in January, hovering near the van like he wants to supervise the load-in. None of this sits well with Biggie.

Colin and I lower a Marshall half-stack to the sidewalk. "Hey, man," Colin says to the talent buyer. "We've been e-mailing back and forth."

The guy crosses his arms and shakes his head. "Nope-nope. That amp is *way* too big for this place."

"It's cool," Colin says. "We turn the cabinets sideways to keep from blasting the crowd."

The talent buyer tells us *he'll* decide the best way to position the amps. "This place is unique," he says. "The stage isn't set back like in a theater. The stage is *in* the room."

"Just like every club we play," Biggie says, rolling the Marshall past him through the load-in door.

I grab Pooch's well-stickered Les Paul and Dave's busted-up snare case. Something about us has already raised the talent buyer's hackles. Maybe it's the irreconcilable tension between rock and hippie. Our Marshalls vs. his dreadlocks. Our love of The Replacements vs. his love of, I don't know, dreadlocks. I can already imagine his hands around Colin's neck.

Load-in complete, the talent buyer asks all five bands to gather around for a little pow-wow. Twenty musicians—all of them twenty years younger than us—assemble at the foot of the stage. The five Watersheds are hanging back by the soundboard, slouching like high school hoodlums.

"Let me tell you about myself," the buyer says. He's standing on the stage. "I've done *everything* in the music business. I've been on tour with Government Mule. Sold shirts for The Dead. I've been to Bonnaroo."

"He's been to Bonnaroo?" Dave stage-whispers to Colin and me. "Who the fuck hasn't?"

"Here's the great thing about New Band Nite," the buyer says. "It's the start of a long relationship between you and the 8x10. This relationship will grow as your careers grow."

"I doubt that," Colin says to Dave and me.

"Tonight you've all bought thirty-five tickets, so a crowd of 175 should show up." He's gesturing broadly, basking in this stage time. "At the door we'll be asking people which band they came to see. And if you don't get at least fifteen people who say they came to see you, then you get bumped down to Mondays. Open Mic Night."

Yikes. Just when you think you can't get lower, the sub-basement opens.

"But . . ." The talent buyer's rolling now. Breaking it down. Teaching us a thing or two about the cutthroat music business. "If you can bring in *fifty* tonight, and if you can do that for *two* New Band Nights *in a row*, then you get promoted to a Wednesday."[54]

The kids are nodding. They've got something to shoot for.

"As soon as you draw 150 on a Wednesday, then, and only then, do you get to headline a Friday."

"What a douche," Biggie says. "This is a guy who got into rock and roll not for the sex and drugs, but because of all the *rules*."

We bust-up laughing, and I'm half-expecting the talent buyer to rap our knuckles for disturbing the class. But he soldiers on. "The beauty of our system is that it rewards the bands that promote themselves. *You* publicize the show. It's up to *you* to make it happen."

"But aren't you the concert promoter," Colin says to us. "Isn't that your job?"

"In my years in the business I've learned that you gotta work hard, and you gotta build relationships," the talent buyer says. "Look around. These are your peers. You'll help each other. You'll grow together. And when you all become as big as Dave Matthews, you'll come back and play the 8x10, right? The place where you got your start?"

Nods and laughter from the kids.

I can't believe we're being made to listen to this crap. Like a smooth politician, he's sugarcoating this patently unfair pay-to-play scheme with a sweet layer of self-empowerment. This is how rich capitalists convince poor folks to vote Republican. We're not fucking you; we're giving you the power to sink or swim on your own—in a system that's rigged to fuck you.

Sadly it could be that pay-to-play is the only way a music venue can survive anymore. Maybe live rock and roll is only viable when reduced to either Heavy Metal Karaoke or New Band Nite. Either shtick or sharecropping. Still I'm offended by the way this guy preys on the ignorance and desperation of the young bands he's allegedly trying to help. I can remember what it's like to want a gig, any gig, so badly that you'd cozy up to a sleazeball like this and only hear the part you wanted to hear: the part where he says you'll get as big as Dave Matthews. This guy is no different from the unscrupulous "promotion companies" that mine MySpace, sending flattering e-mails to virtually every band in existence, telling them all how special they are, how good their songs are, how the company can make them famous—as long as they first send along a thousand dollars. All major credit cards accepted.

Okay, hippie. Here's what I've learned in my years in the music business. Nobody worth dealing with asks for money up front. Legitimate industry snakes are speculators. Buy low/sell high. They only fuck you on the back end.

The first act looks like prep school kids, seventeen and scared shitless, unpolished but catchy. They angle their bodies toward each other, taking a defensive posture against the crowd, which includes John Mathews and a few WTMD interns. Coincidentally, Biggie's wife Jayna is in D.C. on business this week, so the two of them are tabled away in a corner. At the other end of the bar Colin and Susan are laughing, still friends even after the break-up.

I walk outside and stand in front of the club. Biting off my glove, I dig into my coat for my cell phone, dial Kate's number, and start walking down Cross Street. When we played the 8x10 on the Smithereens tour, Federal Hill smelled faintly of Old Bay and crab guts. Seemed like a block where, if you ran crosswise of the wrong fisherman, you might catch a shiv in the neck. Tonight it's obvious that the hipsters have moved their VWs and MacBooks into the neighborhood.

As the phone rings I can picture Kate sitting at her desk, reading the e-mail she sent me this morning, double-checking that she said all she needed to. Her phone is buzzing, and she's debating. Answer and say more—or don't and let the e-mail resonate longer. She picks up the phone and silences it, sending me to voice mail.

Years ago, when Biggie was roadying for The Toll, he got in a phone argument with Liz, his girlfriend at the time. She was lonely and pissed—that he'd been gone for so long and would be gone a lot longer. He tried to explain; she hung up on him. He hangdogged over to Brad, The Toll's frontman, and told him what had happened. "Don't call her back for a week," Brad said. "Teach her not to pull that shit."

Now I'm debating whether to leave a message for Kate or not. What can I say? We've been having the same argument for years. Watershed is a band that tours. I'm tired of explaining. Tired of justifying. The band's been on the road since the day we met. Get fucking used to it already.

You've reached Kate Faber Oestreich. Please leave a message.

I hang up. No message *is* the message. Teach her not to pull that shit.

Behind me on the street I hear a voice say, "Joe, ol' man. How the hell are you?" Even before I turn around, I know this is Lou Brutus, the DJ we met in 1994 when he worked the afternoon drive at WRCX in Chicago. Shortly after Epic dropped us, RCX changed formats from Rock to Jammin' Oldies, so Lou quit to go do mornings at WHFS, D.C.'s legendary alternative station. HFS eventually switched their format to Latin Tropical, but by then Lou had taken a job at XM Satellite Radio, where he works today. As he walks my way, palms up and arms wide, it occurs to me that Lou is probably Watershed's longest continuous-running ally in the industry. We half-shake/half-hug, and then I ask him about the sad state of the radio business.

"A long plastic hallway where thieves and pimps run free and good men die like dogs," he says. His Hunter Thompson is spot-on.

Inside the club, we stand in the back, next to Pooch and Dave. With the addition of Lou, the average age of our group is north of forty, which looks to be nearly the age of the parents who are right now clapping for their kids on stage. Jammin' oldies, the lot of us.

I walk over to one of the dads. "Is your son up there?"

"Yeah," he says, smiling. "The drummer." He cups his hand to his mouth even though the music isn't very loud, the kids too tentative to rock. "Their first show ever."

I'm thinking of my dad, standing in so many crowds, proud as hell. "Wow. You can't tell." I'm being generous, and he knows it. "A band's only as good as the drummer, and you've got a nice one there."

"Thanks," he says. His eyes never leave the stage.

Leaning into the bar, listening to the haphazard rhythm of the high school kids, it hits me that there are two ways this night can go.

One: The Dewey Beach Scenario. We curse the rock and roll gods for stranding us in the minors. Tell ourselves that we're too good to share the stage with green teenagers, that we've been doing this too long to suffer through New Band Nite. We mock this gig by playing just as shitty as this shitty gig deserves.

Two: The *Bull Durham* Scenario. We show we don't belong in the minors by *dominating* the minors. Prove we're too good for New Band Nite by *being* too good. Show we're leagues above these green teenagers by *being* leagues above. We mock this gig by putting on a show a hundred times better than this shitty gig deserves.

I drain my beer knowing we have to go the *Bull Durham* route. If we're even a tenth of the band we think we are, then there's no choice but to blow these pimply virgins off the stage.

None of this gets voiced to Colin, Dave, or Pooch, but I can tell that having to sit through the talent buyer's self-serving discourse on the music industry has put a burr up everyone's ass. They look equally determined. We go through the pre-show tuning and tweaking with the precision of hit men cleaning their pistols.

I usually don't know what kind of show it will be until we're a few songs in. Sometimes I take the stage confident and fired up, and the show sucks. My guitar strap breaks. Or a string pops. Maybe nothing tangible goes wrong, but I'm still bothered by the feeling that something is off. Other times I'm having a crappy day—where even the most mundane task seems impossible as pole-vaulting—but up on stage everything falls into place.

Tonight I've got a bead on the show from note one. We are *crushing*. Everything works, and everything's easy. Sound the bell, boys, 'cause school is in. This is the best show we've played all tour.

Later, after we've helped Biggie clear the stage, Dave and I line up at the urinals. "Good show, Demon," he says.

"Catman," I say, hitting the flush lever with authority, "we wrecked this dump."

We're standing by the sink, laughing about the WTMD interview, when the teenage drummer's dad walks in. "Hey, that was great, guys."

"Thanks, man." I say.

"How long you been playing?"

"This is it. Tonight. First show ever." I look to Dave for backup.

"Yep," Dave says. "Not bad for the first show." He leans into the mirror, worrying over a patch of gray. "Then again, we've been practicing in the basement for twenty-five years. We oughta be pretty good."

The dad looks down at his piss, mulling this. He comes up laughing. "You bullshitters."

We give him the ten-second history of Watershed. He asks what advice we've got for his kid's band.

Slim Dunlap would tell 'em to look down the ladder. Dave would tell 'em to quit.

"Tell 'em they were great tonight," I say.

The dad smiles. Then he starts shaking his head. "No, really. They want to learn."

"Tell you what," I say. "Duct-tape 'em to a chair and don't cut 'em loose until they've heard The Replacements' 'Left of the Dial' ten thousand times." I turn toward Dave. "They'll learn a lot more from that one song than they did in that dumb-ass lecture this afternoon."

"What?" the dad says.

I laugh. "Just tell 'em they were great."

Walking out of the bathroom, I'm smiling goofy, like a teenager lit up on Bartles and Jaymes. I turn the corner and aim for Lou Brutus and Susan—names from our past lives. I start singing "Left of the Dial" out loud. I'm smiling and singing, telling myself to *keep growing up, playing make-up, wearing guitar. Growing old in a bar.*

10

It's a Long Way to the Top
Charlotte, North Carolina

I'M DRIVING US THROUGH VIRGINIA, SUNGLASSES ON, VISOR DOWN. IT'S bright and beautiful and twenty degrees too warm for January. In the rearview I see Dave and Pooch watching an AC/DC video, imitating Bon Scott's maniacal facial expressions, giggling like second graders on a sugar high. Biggie looks ten pounds lighter. He hasn't stopped smiling since we picked him up outside a D.C. hotel, fresh off his conjugal visit with Jayna. He climbed into the van, dusted his hands, and said, "Well, ladies, at least *my* pipes are clean." Next to me in the shotgun seat, Colin's talking to Erin on his cell, laughing a lot. I can tell she's laughing too. Everyone but me seems to have smoothed things over with the wives. They've achieved, as a friend of mine likes to say, *shalom in the home.*

Kate and I are playing a silent game of chicken. We've both issued a cell phone blackout. No calls, no messages. What could I say that would make any difference, anyway? We're fighting because she wants to fight. We'll make up when she's ready to make up. In the meantime I'm trying not to think about her or that e-mail. Bury the whole complaint under some dusty rug in my brain. Better to appreciate what I've got right here, right now: me and my best friends, bullshitting around the country. We've got a stunning lack of responsibility, as Colin says. Don't have to get up for work. Don't have to run errands or pay bills or change diapers. Just have to make it to the next town and hold it together for the forty-five minutes we're on stage.

After Colin hangs up with Erin, he lowers the volume on AC/DC, turns to the back of the van, and says, "So I've been thinking. In rock and roll, there's almost no actual playing, right? But there's a whole lot of standing around, *talking* about playing."

"Okay," Biggie says. "Go ahead."

"And in a lot of ways our fans care less about the show than about seeing *us* at the show. Hanging out. Shooting the shit."

"That's right."

"So there's our answer," Colin says.

I must have missed something. "What are you saying?"

"I'm saying *not* playing is the next logical step."

Dave chuckles. "Not playing."

"Exactly. We book a whole tour where we don't play. Not once."

"What do we do?" Pooch says.

Colin's getting excited. "We do what we already do. Show up. Drink beer. Talk to our fans and try to make new ones. Everything's the same, we just don't play." He's growing taller in his seat, blocking out more of the side window. "How many people came to see us last night, Biggie?"

"Ten or twelve."

"And how many CDs did we sell?"

"One."

"Okay. What if instead of playing the 8x10, we would have just walked into some bar down the street. No stage. No sound. They don't even book bands. A drinking bar."

"Because we're not gonna play," I say.

"We belly up and we start talking, telling people we're a band. They ask if we have CDs out, and yeah, we do. In fact, we've got a whole case right here," Colin pretends to pull a box from under the seat. "Question: would we sell more or less than one CD?"

"I gotta believe more," Biggie says.

Pooch nods. "Couldn't be less."

"Think about it," says Colin. "Nobody wants to sit through a band they've never heard of, but everybody loves *meeting* a band."

"Our fans would get to spend more time with us," Dave says, "which is what they want anyway."

"Win-win," Colin says.

"It's an angle," I say. "No doubt."

"We announce a ten-date tour," Colin says. "Watershed will be in X city, at X bar, at X time."

"Drinking," Dave says.

"Shit," I say. "We could hit three bars a night. Triple our efficiency."

"The press'll eat it up," Colin says. "The band that only talks about playing."

"But never plays."

Colin leans back and crosses his arms. "Never plays."

While everybody hashes the ins and outs of the drinking tour, my cell phone rings. Not Kate. It's Thomas O'Keefe. He asks how the shows are going.

"Last night we sold one CD," I say. "So there's that."

"Don't feel bad," he says. "I'm at Sundance with Pat from Train. Got a front row seat for his solo career slamming into the side of a mountain."

Thomas makes his living shuttling Pat and Train from the luxury hotel to the television appearance to the gig to the tour bus to the charter flight. I look back at Biggie, Dave, and Pooch, squeezed onto two benches, and I think about the difference one hit song would make for us. One hit and you're at the Four Seasons, appearing on the *Today Show*, rolling around in a Prevost. None and you're sneaking six guys past the clerk at the Fairfield. One shouldn't be that hard. It's only one more than none. But as Bon Scott was just singing on our TV, it's a long way to the top.

"Anyway, here's why I called," Thomas says. "I've been talking with Scott at the LC. He's worried about the pre-sale numbers." Three days to the Columbus show, and we've only sold sixty-three advance tickets for a 2,200-seat venue.

When I finally exhale, my cheeks go Louis Armstrong fat. "Here's the thing," I say. "Our crowd isn't used to advance tickets. They pay at the door, like at a bar show. I'm not worried."

"Scott's worried."

"What, is he going to cancel us?"

"He says if *you* want to cancel, it's not too late."

We've been hearing this nonsense since our first headlining show at the Newport. Hell, this tour started with an e-mail from Small's Bar saying the same thing. If we've learned anything over the years, it's that it's never too late to cancel. "Tell Scott we'll see him on Saturday."

"That's what I wanted you to say. And don't worry about the sixty-three tickets. You've already outsold some of the Pat solo shows—but I didn't tell you that." He hangs up.

"What's the good word?" Colin says.

I tell them. Like me, they're worried and not.

"Our crowd'll come through," Colin says. "They always do." He takes a notebook and pen from his backpack. "On to more important business. How do we finance the drinking tour? A sponsorship? From a beer company maybe?"

But I'm still stuck on the sixty-three pre-sale tickets. Then there's the fact that for all our radio play in Baltimore, only twelve people showed up at the gig, and that includes Lou Brutus, Susan, and the WTMD staff. I'm trying to shove it all under that brain rug where Kate and her e-mail are lurking, but it's getting crowded in there.

"I know how we finance the tour," I say. "During the daytime, we make runs to the downtown hotels in whatever city we're in, with a giant sign slapped on the side of the van." I smile into the rearview. Stay sunny on the outside. "Four words. BIGGIE'S. AIRPORT. SHUTTLE. SERVICE."

Axed from the Insane Clown Posse tour, we figured that if people found out Herb had quit, they'd write us off for dead. No label, no drummer, no career. But we still had shows booked in Detroit and Chicago. And in Columbus, where CD101 was spinning "Star Vehicle." In Appleton, play on *The Rockin' Apple* was making us bigger in Northern Wisconsin than we were at home. We needed a quiet transition, so as not to fuel rumors of our demise.

The first few drummers we auditioned were too fat, too old, or too drum corps. Colin and I sounded horrible without Herb, and it seemed certain that we'd have to cancel the shows. Then a letter landed in our p.o. box, written on Little Turtle stationery. "I heard about Herb through the musical grapevine. I think I can help out. Dave Masica."

"Who's Dave Masica?" Colin said.

I didn't know for sure. "Isn't he that long-haired dude that drums in that one band we played with that one time?"

Biggie nodded yeah. Dave's band had opened for us years before.

"Does he suck?" Colin said.

"Don't remember," Biggie said.

I slumped my shoulders. "That's encouraging."

Two weeks before the Detroit show, Colin and I asked Dave to tryout. We couldn't tolerate one more crap drummer butchering Watershed songs, so when Dave showed up for the audition, we asked him if he knew any Cheap Trick. He said yeah. He knew *all* the Cheap Trick, and we spent two hours playing cover tunes.

When we finally stopped for the night, Dave said, "When do we start the audition?"

"Wasn't that it?" Colin said.

Dave was confused. "But aren't we going to play any Watershed?"

I looked at Colin. "Yeah, aren't we?" We'd never had anyone quit before. What did we know about running a tryout?

"If you can play Cheap Trick you can play Watershed," Colin said.

Dave picked up a drumstick and started twirling it. "Does that mean, I'm, uh, you know, *in the band?*"

"Well, yeah," Colin said.

But I wasn't so sure. Dave had the arrangements cold in no time, and he played with touch and swing. Compared to Herb, though, he had no power; the songs sounded limp-wristed. Besides, Herb and I had learned to play together. His stomping right foot had been my compass rose; without him I was lost.

One night after practice, I told Colin and Biggie that Dave was a mistake. "We have to audition other drummers."

"The shows are booked," Colin said.

"So let's un-book 'em."

"No way," Colin said. "We gotta keep up momentum."

Biggie was sitting on the practice room couch, shaking his head. He agreed with me. "Colin," he said. "Do yourself a favor and hold out for a great drummer."

"Seriously," I said. "Getting the *right* drummer is more important than getting a drummer right now."

"Dave will be good enough," Colin said. "Give him time."

Biggie stood up from the couch. "We don't have time to suck."

"And good enough isn't good enough," I said.

"Good enough *is* good enough," Colin said. "Trust me."

Was this optimism? Or was it impatience? Laziness? Desperation? Whatever it was, it was infuriating. How could Colin be so clutch and so skittery at the same time? I was starting to see how his sunny-side-up attitude could have become too much for Herb.

"Look," I said. "My job is to play with the drummer. Trust me when I tell you Dave is no Herb."

"Agreed," said Biggie.

"He doesn't have to be," Colin said.

"But he can't suck either," I said.

"Nobody'll notice."

"What the fuck are you talking about?" Biggie said.

"People don't come to hear the drummer. They come to hear the songs."

This was starting to piss me off. "You think people won't notice when that song they like so much sounds like shit?"

"It'll be good enough."

Biggie was now ready to punch a wall. "But good enough isn't good—"

"It'll be good enough."

I sighed. Biggie slumped back to the couch. We were too exhausted to sustain the back-and-forth. Arguing with Colin is like playing tennis with a goat. He doesn't volley; he eats the fucking ball.

That first show with Dave in Detroit was horrible, and he, Biggie, and I all knew it. But as we packed up the gear, Colin was all back slaps and pep talks. I wished for once he would just admit it when something sucked.

Then I saw John Speck standing back by the pool table. Ever since the *Wallflower Child* tattoo, he'd been my punk rock doppelgänger. He'd been the first guy to tell me he liked my songs better than Colin's, which made him the last guy I wanted to talk to after a lame gig. His band Hoarse was kicking ass, signed to RCA and getting radio play. He'd become a stronger singer than me, with better songs than mine. Honestly, Hoarse was dominating Watershed in all phases of the game. The proof was in the split EP Watershed and Hoarse had just released for Idol Records. We covered a Hoarse song, and Hoarse covered "Wallflower Child." Their version was hot as a blast furnace. With Dave now in the band, we were impotent as an Easy-Bake Oven.

Speck put his hand on my shoulder and said, "Herb'll come back, right?"

I winced. "He's done."

"Let me introduce you to somebody," Speck said. He turned toward a guy who was wearing polyester slacks and a vintage leather jacket, like a Seventies detective. "Meet Tim Patalan."

"Yeeeaaahhh," Tim said, simultaneously laughing and talking. He shook my hand. "Let's take this to the bar."

I'd heard of Tim Patalan, of course. Most every band who'd rolled a van through Detroit had heard of Tim Patalan. He and his brother Andy had taken an old barn on their parents' Saline, Michigan, horse farm and converted it into a studio called The Loft. Up-and-comers from Grosse Point Shores to Grand Rapids recorded with Andy, while Tim handled the big boys, like Hoarse and Sponge, whose album *Rotting Piñata* had recently gone gold.

Tim ordered ten Miller Lites and passed them around. "Dig this," he said to me. "So we're working on the Hoarse record, and John starts playing this 'Wallflower Child' song. And I say, 'Let's track that right now. In fact, that might just be our single.' Then John tells me he didn't write it." Patalan clinked his beer against mine. "He says *you* did." A few beers later, Tim invited us up to Saline to record with him.

The studio was ten miles from Ann Arbor, out where the roads turn to dirt in a hurry. We crunched up the Patalans' gravel drive, past the horse stables, farmhouse, and two strutting peacocks, before stopping at a red barn with a painted sign: THE LOFT, EST. 1988. TIM PATALAN, PROP. He'd said the door would be open. Make ourselves at home. We loaded our gear up the stairs and got right to practicing. We wanted to be ultra-prepared when Tim got there, to show him we were pros. But midnight came and went with no sign of Patalan, so we drank beer, stared at Sponge's gold record, and crashed on the studio couches. No problem. We still had three more days booked—enough time to knock out four or five songs easy.

Next day noon, Tim called to say have a beer ready. But another midnight passed with no producer, so we jammed a lot, petted the horses, sat in the infield of the training track, drinking the twelve-pack we'd bought for him.

On the third day, Tim finally showed. "Yeeeaaahhh, kick-ass," he said.

Time to get to work. We charged upstairs to the studio and broke out the guitars.

"Not so fast, guys," he said. "Dig this. It's dollar coney day at Dan's Downtown Tavern."

By the fourth day, Colin, Dave, and I were hungover and confused. Danny Lawson had run the Power Station sessions like Catholic school. Frank Aversa had recorded on a strict noon to eight schedule. Now, with one day until we would have to go home, we'd each drank about sixty beers and recorded exactly nothing.

Then Tim walked in. "Fire-up, guys." He bounded up the studio stairs.

We played him a new Colin song, "Romantic Noise," quickly, before he could divert us to Team Trivia Night at the UAW Hall.

"Dig that. Dig that," he said, as we ran through the tune a few more times. "Super-sweet. Let's cut it."

The three of us stood in the tracking room, waiting for Tim to give us the *we're rolling* sign, but he came through the talkback saying, "No-no-no. I just need Dave. You two hang loose for a minute. Go pet one of the peacocks or something."

I'd done too much hanging loose that week. I decided to stay and watch.

"Okay, Dave," Tim said. He rolled his chair from the board to the outboard gear and back, tweaking the knobs and faders. "Sounding great. But try something for me. See if you can play this." He sang a beat, which Dave had down in a minute. "Now hit the hi-hat twice as hard and the snare twice as soft," Tim said.

Dave did as asked.

"*Al*most," Tim said. "But don't rush the downbeat. And play it three beats per minute faster."

Again Dave nailed it. I had a new appreciation for the guy. Herb would have thrown his sticks through the control room window by now.

A half hour later, Tim said, "Flawless, Dave. You're done. Come in here and listen to your drum track."

Done? Drum track? Dave hadn't yet played the whole song. But Tim spun a dial and punched a button, and sure enough, through the speakers came four minutes of the new "Romantic Noise" beat—played by Masica, looped by Patalan. We knew about drum loops, but we'd never made one. This was some serious producer kung fu.

We finished "Romantic Noise" sometime after dawn. By then it was barely the same song we'd been rehearsing for three days. Tim had rewritten the bass and guitar parts, rearranged the lyrics, added sevenths and ninths to our chords. He sampled random bits of feedback and dropped them into the track to build suspensions and overtones. The old "Romantic Noise" had sounded like the all-too-human Colin, Dave, and Joe playing together in a room. This new version was majestic. Music from the ether.

Tim Patalan, you crafty peacock-petter. In one day we'd taken the biggest musical step of our career.

Welcome to the New South. Wednesday night and uptown Charlotte is hoppin'. The Bobcats are set to tip off against the Magic in Time Warner Arena. The sidewalks are swimming with hoops fans in replica jerseys and bankers in business suits. Everybody's hustling to the next place they've got to be, stepping around concrete mixers, ducking under scaffolding. Through the van windows I'm looking up at skyscrapers wrapped in Tyvek and cranes angling overhead. The Bank of America Center points the way to heaven, lording over Charlotte like Billy Graham only wished.

Tonight we're headlining a bar called the Alley Cat. The opening band is fronted by a cute, neo–Joan Jett, but I can't stop staring at the guitarist. He's wearing skeleton face paint and playing a pointy guitar. A skeletor'd-up teenager doing dive-bombs on a whammy bar. Heavy Metal Karaoke distilled down to one man.

Dave and Pooch are huddled around a bistro table. The Superfan and Superfan II, who've once again, independently, travelled hundreds of miles to spend a weeknight with Watershed, are circling the table like barracudas, shooting evil eyes at each other as they compete for Dave and Pooch's attention. It'd be easier on everyone if The Superfan and Superfan II would just become friends.

I walk up to Pooch and yell into his ear, "You getting a load of this guitar player?"

"Steve Vai meets Beetlejuice?" He bends with laughter and slaps his thigh. "Was he even alive when whammy bars were cool?"

Dave stares at the stage. "What's that guy thinking?"

After his band finishes their set, I find the Beetlejuice-looking kid at the bar. "Great show, man," I say. "Let me buy you a beer." We exchange a little small talk. He's from Vegas. Hasn't been in the band long. Up close he looks even younger than he did on stage.

Just to keep myself interested in the conversation, I decide to haze the kid a little, toughen him up. Touring veterans are supposed to razz the rookies. Like Ben-Gay in the jock strap, it's initiation into the club.[55]

As the bartender drops off the beers, I say to Beetlejuice, "So it must be hard sometimes, with people, you know, thinking of you as *just* a guitar god."

"Nah, it's cool," he says.

"I mean, your singer's good and all, but you guys are a *band*, right? You're not her *backing* band. You're not *just* the guitar player."

"We're a band-band."

"I know it," I say. "And you're doing more than your share of the heavy lifting."

"I'm trying."

"No need for modesty. I get it. You're putting on a show up there. Working it."

"Yeah."

"And your singer's only 25 percent of the band, but I bet she gets most of the credit."

"Well, yeah."

"Because what? Because she writes the songs? Because she can sing? I bet you can do all those things."

"Absolutely."

"Because she's got a pretty face? Shit, man. You know there's more to it than just standing there looking cute."

"Fuck yeah, there is."

"I mean, seriously, when's the last time she learned one of *your* songs? Or let *you* sing lead?"

"Never."

I set my beer down on the bar, hard enough that it foams over. "Never! Never? Like *zero?* Listen. I know all bands are different, and far be it from me to tell you how to handle your business, but jeez. Something about that just doesn't seem right."

"It doesn't, does it?"

"I'm saying." I take a long foamy sip.

Beetlejuice shakes his head over his beer, worrying cracks into his skeleton makeup. He looks toward the stage, where Dave and Pooch are now standing next to the singer, undoubtedly telling her how great *she* is. She blushes. She laughs. The three of them raise a toast. "I'll be right back," Beetlejuice says. He scoots away from the bar and aims right for her.

I lift my beer to him. "Keep the faith, brother!"

We spent the rest of '98 and '99 making trips to Saline. Tim was ten times more skilled a musician than Colin, Dave, or me, but he never flaunted it. We had to pry to get him to tell us that he'd gone to U.M. on a double bass scholarship and that he'd played in the Michigan Symphony. He eventually quit school, bailed on the orchestra, and plied his classical chops for a heavy metal cover band called Something Wild. On some trips we'd finish a song or two, but sometimes Tim would send us home without recording anything, saying, "Don't come back until the tunes are better." Sometimes he'd leave us alone in the studio for days. "There's one strong line in this song," he'd say. "Figure out which one, then call me when you've made all the lyrics that good." Sometimes Tim just never showed, and we were left to make a record by *not* making a record.

It took me years to figure out what Tim was doing. Most musicians don't cotton to having their genius questioned. They want the producer to get the song on tape and get out of the way.[56] By keeping us drunk and bothered, Tim was crippling our defenses so he could make the necessary arrangement changes most musicians resist. He was ripping us from our comfort zones, knocking us off-axis so we could tap our creative right brains. It was production as basic training. Break us down, then build the songs back up.

Or maybe Tim just liked to drink. He'd lean back on the couch, eyes closed, cradling a highball of Carlo Rossi on the rocks, and say, "*Al*most, *al*most. Everything is kick-ass except for the rhythm, the tempo, and the pitch. Other than that, *flaw*less."

Tim discovered that Dave played with much more power and confidence when drunk, so if a take felt too stiff, he'd say, "Go shotgun three Budweisers, Dave. Let's get some beer on these tracks." Sometimes Dave passed out mid-song, but most of the time, we'd listen back to the take, and, *Flawless!* Dave couldn't walk a straight line, but he could play like Keith Moon.

Between takes, we'd wander over to the farmhouse for Tim's mom's *golumpki* rolls, washed down with shots of the Zwack-Unicum liqueur his dad had brought back from a trip to Hungary. Mr. and Mrs. Patalan were accustomed to a herd of greasy rockers roaming their farm, and they treated everyone like family. The scene was as idyllic as a Hidden Valley Ranch commercial—if you substituted Molotov-tasting Hungaro-hooch for salad dressing. We once found Tim nursing a litter of raccoons from a baby bottle. They climbed his wool sweater like it was a slippery elm. Another time we found Tim standing shoulder deep into a mare, impregnating her with a syringe. You don't forget the sight of your producer fist-fucking a horse.

When that mare foaled a colt almost a year later, we were still working on the album. The results were slow going, but they were in a different universe from anything we'd ever done. We'd keep driving to Michigan, as long as it took, until the record was finished.

Then Tim started sending Colin and Dave home early, saying he and I needed to concentrate on a vocal pass. Or he'd tell me to drive up to Saline alone so the two of us could flesh out the arrangement for one of my songs. I knew Colin and Dave were disappointed when I'd pack my car and head north by myself—maybe even a little jealous—but, hey, I said, Tim was in charge. I played passive, just following orders, but truthfully I figured it was only fair that I get a little extra attention. Watershed had always been Colin's band. He'd straight-up said it to me many times: "We're best when I sing 60 percent of the songs and you sing 40 percent." And where had that ratio gotten us? My songs were poppier, punkier; my voice had more range; and by now it wasn't just John Speck telling me this. Random bar-goers had started pulling me aside after our sets to say, "No offense, but you should sing all the songs." No offense taken. I was beginning to think 60/40 *my* way would be okay for a change.

Tim and I would tinker with chord progressions and vocal melodies. He worked my vocals hard—*al*most, *al*most—getting the kind of takes I'd always hoped for but had never achieved. It was funny: I'd always considered Colin my ideal creative partner, but Tim was driving me like a thoroughbred on a soggy track, and I was having more fun than ever. On the way home from those sessions, I started to wonder what it would be like to front a band all my own. My voice, my songs.

One afternoon, when I was up in Saline without Colin and Dave, I played Tim a tune called "Suckerpunch." Watershed had practiced it once or twice, but Colin never seemed all that interested. Tim, however, said, "Hang on a minute. Let me make a phone call or two."

A few hours later I was setting up in the studio with John Speck and with Vinnie Dombroski from Sponge. Vinnie was Sponge's singer, but drums were his first and favorite instrument, and as he hammered out the beat for "Suckerpunch," his cowboy boot absolutely *stomped* the kick pedal. Speck played guitar with more rhythm than Colin, and with more interesting chord voicings. Recording with these guys was easy as ice cream. Through the studio monitors, the song sounded massive.

Patalan shook the cubes around his empty glass and said, "Kick-ass, right?"

"See, man," Speck said, punching me on the shoulder, "that's how you *should* sound."

After Speck and Vinnie left, Tim and I stayed up smoking pot. As a rule I prefer drinking to smoking, but I was so fired up, if Tim had pulled out a crack rock that night, I probably would have hit it. We drank Busch Light and passed a bong back and forth, and we talked about string theory, quantum mechanics, and the coming invasion of flesh-eating robots. Tim told me my bong hits were too small; I wasn't holding my smoke long enough. Jesus, I thought, this guy is producing my *buzz*.

At some point Tim told me my songs were good. Really good.

"Good enough to get another record deal, you think?"

He exhaled smoke. "Why does that matter?"

"You know. Getting signed. A major label."

"What can a record company do for you that you can't do for yourself?"

"Distribution, publicity, radio promotion."

He put down the bong and shook his head. "A record label is just a bank. They give you a loan. You pay them back with a recording."

I picked up the bong. "But it's easier to get a record made with their money in your pocket."

"You're already *here*. Recording. No company necessary."

I nodded, trying to hold my smoke like he'd told me. "Fair point." I coughed a few times. "But without the company, it's hard to *sell* that album." I handed Tim the bong and the Bic.

"Dig this, man." He took a monster hit. "Try to think of music as something other than commerce."

"Like art, you mean."

"Or apple pie. Call it whatever you want. The point is, make it to *make* it, not to sell it."

"But there's no shame in wanting as many people as possible to eat that pie, right? Everybody wants an audience."

"Dig that. Dig that. But songs find the audience they deserve. The good ones get heard, label or not. If you write something undeniable, it takes care of itself."

We got more and more high, and the silences grew longer. Eventually Tim exhaled and said, "The songs are everything. They're bigger than the individual members of a band. Bigger than egos." He glanced around the tracking room, taking in the drums and guitars, the mics and amps. "We're only here to do right by the songs."

I took a mini-hit and passed back. I was stoned to the bejeezus.

"I know you guys romanticize the idea of a band," he said. "A group of equals. But that's an outmoded concept." He hit the bong like a Hoover and let the smoke out in a slow leak. "A band is nothing more than a construct we build for the listener. A vehicle to carry the songs."

My tongue was thick and heavy, wrapped in a wool sweater. Couldn't lift it.

"Listen, Joe," he said, reaching out and grabbing me behind the elbow. "We have to make sure your songs are riding the best vehicle."

We sat in silence, retreating into ourselves. I *had* romanticized the idea of keeping the band together, fighting the good fight, Watershed against the world. Patalan was right about that. But now I wondered, could it be that some bands were *supposed* to break up, to clear the way for something better? Let's say Springsteen had kept his high school band, The Castiles, together. Would we be talking about him now? Would he have found his audience? What if Joe Strummer had stayed in The 101ers instead of leaving to form The Clash?

Should I stay or should I go?

My super-baked mind refused to land on one side. It kept flipping from point to counterpoint, finding justification for each, finding weaknesses in both, weighing ramification upon ramification spinning out to infinity. It seemed impossible that anyone had ever settled upon a firm decision about anything.

I was still untangling all this when Tim said, "I don't have any more pot."

Thank God.

Then he smiled. "But I've got something better." He raised his eyebrows and nodded. "A blowtorch."

"Wha?"

"So we can cook the resin off this bowl." He stood up. "It's at my apartment. We'll just drive back and—"

"We can't do that." Besides the pot, we'd drunk enough Busch Light to bathe a stallion.

"You're right," he said. "We can't do that. I'm out of butane for the torch. We'll have to go the slow-cook route." With that he fired the Bic under the bowl. Held it so long he burned his thumb. Three times. "Here it comes, baby. Here it comes." Finally the tar bubbled. "A-ha!" He heated the goo a few more minutes, until it was the consistency of blackstrap molasses, then he held the bong out for me, saying, "I've got to warn you. This is going to be a little harsh."

It was a lot harsh, and I coughed like a coal miner. Then I stood up and fumbled downstairs to the bathroom. On the way I got distracted by something in the windows: the moon twinkling on the Patalans' snow-covered fields. I stood there, my breath fogging the glass, until I thought I saw a unicorn galloping though the snow, a rainbow trailing in his wake. Then I panicked and locked myself in the bedroom. As I lay waiting to pass out, I still didn't know exactly what Tim had meant by "We have to make sure your songs are riding the best vehicle," but in the weedy fog, here's what I finally settled upon: Patalan was telling me I didn't need Colin, Biggie, and Dave. Patalan was telling me to break up the band. To go solo.

After Beetlejuice storms off, I get a tap on the shoulder. "Joe!" And a hug from just the sort of beautiful woman you want to walk up, tap you on the shoulder, and hug you.

It's another Kristie, not the one we met for drinks in New York. The last time I saw this Kristie was at her husband, Ronald Koal's, funeral. We'd originally met in college, when she was a small town beauty from Findlay, Ohio, Flag City, USA. A few years after she moved to Columbus, her tits grew twice as big, her hair turned twice as black, and she started dating Ronald, instantly becoming more central to the Columbus music scene than Watershed. In 1992 Kristie and Ronald were married. We played the reception.

Ronald had always been almost famous. In the Eighties with The Trillionaires and in the early Nineties as a Bowie-esque solo act, he was perpetually *this close*—but horseshoes and hand grenades, et cetera et cetera. Ten months after marrying Kristie, he killed himself.

Was getting *this close,* only to fall short, the reason for Ronald's suicide? Hell if I know. How can we ever know what makes somebody put a gun in his teeth? But I do know how Ronald's death struck me: *this close* can break you.

Kristie is now a remarried mother of three, a self-described soccer mom, living in Charlotte. Her hair has softened to auburn, her tits deflated to their original, Flag City size. Somewhere inside she's surely wearing Ronald-shaped scars, but you'd never know that to look at her.

As Kristie and I talk, I wonder if she isn't better off married to a regular civilian. Hitching up with a musician is thankless. I'm thinking about all the nights Kate has spent alone. I'm thinking about how I missed her grandfather's funeral and her sister's wedding—both for forgettable shows in West Virginia. Thinking about all the times she's stood in the crowd, dancing with her friends, while I sing lines like *you're my consolation prize* and *get over me* and *I'm cutting loose the anchor that's hanging around my neck.* Her friends wonder how she can take it. How can she sing along with the very words that seem to slap her? But Kate always defends me. "They're just songs," she says.

Lots of rock widows can't take it. Consider Liz and Susan, Biggie and Colin's Patterson girlfriends. Biggie bought a wedding ring for Liz. She said yes. But the loneliness became overwhelming, and she canceled the wedding. After Colin and Susan got engaged, she moved west to work on a political campaign. I'm not sure exactly what happened after that. Maybe Colin cheated on her, or she cheated on him. Ultimately, however, she left Colin for the lawyer.

Then there's Pooch and his wife, Christy. Pooch had always been a jock, not a rocker. While playing football at Denison, he majored in kinesiology and went on to get a master's in it. He became a professor of sports medicine at Urbana University, and Christy took a job at a bank. They financed a house and planned to start a family. They were so young and suburban, they could have been the faces in an insurance ad. But then out of nowhere Pooch bought a Les Paul and started flirting with a folkie chick who had angel wings tattooed across her back. This girl played acoustic guitar, wrote poetry, and dabbled in hard drugs— so different from Christy the banker. Man, you had to feel for her. At least Kate knew a little bit of what she was getting into when she met me. Pooch sprung rock and roll on Christy. She'd married Mark Borror, a kinesiology professor who'd never shown any interest in the guitar. Then one day he joins Watershed, his friends are calling him Pooch, and he's taking phone calls from a tattooed folkie who smells like cigarettes and patchouli. Rock and roll slipped into their tidy home like radon gas.

Kate once told me that she'd never be my groupie, but I wonder if being the groupie would have been easier than being the wife. A rock marriage is as hard to hold together as a rock band.

About the same time Watershed started working with Patalan, Kate and I got engaged in Vienna, in a park on the banks of the Danube. I was twenty-nine, and she was twenty-four, working her first post-college job, as an admin at an architecture firm. With her real-job money, we'd booked a two-week trip to Austria and the Czech Republic: youth hostels and rail passes. On the flight across the ocean, I stuffed the engagement ring in my jeans pocket, and I palmed it through the denim, praying that the plane wouldn't crash before I got a chance to ask the question. Whenever we hit turbulence I was tempted to whip out the ring and drop to one knee right there in the cabin, but the air smoothed, and I managed to hold out until Vienna. When we got home to Columbus, we moved out of our apartment above the High Street Radio Shack, a place that smelled like piss and institutional food, and moved into a nice half-double in Clintonville, a neighborhood of front porches and peace signs. We felt grown-up, independent. But not too independent. In order to make the rent, we asked Biggie to move in with us. He took the attic bedroom. On the day I drove the "Suckerpunch" CD home from Saline, he was sitting on the couch, watching TV.

"How'd it go?" he said.

"You tell me." I slid the CD into the player.

A minute into the song, he hit eject. "What the fuck is this? Who's playing with you?"

"Speck and Vinnie."

His face went blank. "You cocksucker."

"Tim wanted to work on it. Nobody else was there. What was I supposed to—"

"You're supposed to stick with your band." He lifted the CD from the tray. Held it away from his nose, like an apple gone rotten. "Fucking Patalan."

"It wasn't him."

Biggie pushed the CD my way without looking at me. "He's gonna break you up if you let him."

"Herb already broke us up. It's different now."

"I'm talking about you and Colin."

I held up the CD. "That's not what this is."

"Then what the hell is it?"

I stood in the heat of Biggie's anger, tapping the CD against my thigh.

He walked toward the kitchen, turning when he got to the door. "Do me a favor, huh. Listen to that song in headphones. I don't want to hear it."

Colin called later that day. "Biggie told me," he said. "Not cool, man. Not cool at all." For years Colin had been dropping hints about someday wanting to do a solo record, and he expected my allegiance to him to be so complete that I would agree to let him do it. He wanted commitment *and* freedom. What did I get in the deal?

"It's a demo," I said. "It doesn't have to mean anything."

"But it does mean something." His voice got soft. "It means something."

I was prepared for a mad Colin. A hurt Colin was a hundred times worse.

"*Sucker*punch," he said. "Isn't that cute. Did Speck at least make the guitars sound good?"

"Okay, I guess." I paced the living room, kneaded my forehead with my fingers.

"I don't know what to think about this."

"I don't either." This was the truth.

"So what do we do now, Joe?"

"What should we do?"

"I don't know," he said. "I honestly don't."

Then the line went silent. For the first time since I'd known him, Colin had nothing to say.

For days Biggie and I passed in and out of the bathroom in silence. There was no word from Colin. I was marinating in my own guilt. I'd cheated on him. I'd hurt him. I hadn't felt this bad since the day I broke up with Kate. Now she and I were planning a wedding. Watershed was teetering.

"Am I an asshole?" I said to her one day, about a week after I'd last talked to Colin. We were walking on the bike trail along the Olentangy River, crunching through snow.

"You've felt slighted for a long time," she said. "This is you fighting back."

"You think Patalan wants Watershed to break up?"

"Who cares what Patalan wants?"

"Maybe the industry sees Watershed as damaged goods. Going solo would make me *new*. Everybody wants new."

"What do *you* want?"

That was easy, I told her. I wanted another shot at The Pros. A chance to do it over, to do it better. With my songs having more say in the sink-or-swim. But I also wanted to feel that Watershed-against-the-world momentum again. The days just before Epic, when we were up and coming, were the best. But the days just after we were dropped were special too—the fighting to prove the company wrong, the scrapping to pick ourselves up off the mat. On the day Herb quit, the magic of four Worthington kids working together—*could be a bakery, could be a bait shop*—had gone with him.

"It's not gone," Kate said. "It's just altered. You guys still love each other."

We stopped at an opening in the trees and turned toward the river. There was a thin layer of ice along the bank, but you could see the water flowing underneath.

Kate took off her glove and looked at her engagement ring. "You know you're already married to Colin, don't you?" She smiled. "He's the wife; I'm the mistress."

"Come on," I said.

She laughed. "It's okay. I like being the mistress. All the fun, none of the stress."

It hit me then that there wasn't enough musical success in the world to compensate for how bad it would hurt to leave Colin. Even if I went solo and lucked into some kind of hit song, it wouldn't mean anything unless we had a hit together. Maybe, in order to be a rock star, you have to have the balls to cut people loose. But that wasn't me. I would do it with Colin and Biggie, or I wouldn't do it at all. At the wedding, Colin, Biggie, Dave, and I drank champagne together, danced together, pissed from the roof of the reception hall together. All was forgiven.

As 1999 odometered into 2000, Tim stopped taking our calls. Maybe he was disappointed that I hadn't broken up the band; maybe he was busy with another project; maybe he'd passed out in a Bangkok opium den. Months went by without a word. I was thirty years old, still working my $10/hour job at the Vision Center, with half an album in the can and seemingly no way to get it finished. I was so depressed and frustrated, I registered for classes at Ohio State. Ten years after dropping out, I dropped back in.

While I was busying myself with school work, Colin found us a new manager: Ron Severance—a guy who'd played on the Worthington High football team, before taking his mom's carnival concession business and growing it into a national enterprise, with restaurants in NFL stadiums and along turnpikes. He operated the world's only mobile McDonalds, which was kind of cool, but certainly didn't qualify him to manage a rock band. I complained to Biggie that this was panicky Colin again, grasping at desperate leads. We begged him not to hire Mr. Mobile McDonalds.

"I was right about Dave, wasn't I?" Colin said.

And Dave had become a badass behind the kit. Ironically, his swingy-quick style suited my songs perfectly. With Dave in tow, Watershed's sound was shifting away from Colin's roots-rock and toward my fast, melodic pop.

That fall Ron drove his Mercedes up to Michigan, with a fat roll of hundreds in his pocket. If Tim wouldn't take our calls, we'd send an emissary to him, shake him out of the horse barn. Over drinks at an Ann Arbor bar, Ron pulled out the cash, and said to Tim, "Here's five thousand right now. If you finish the album, there's another five in it for you. If you don't, then we're releasing the record as is, undone, with your name on it."

"Dig that," Tim said. And we went back to work.

As the sun came up one February morning, I walked out of the studio and onto the porch. There was the barn and the farmhouse, the rising light in the east. Then, directly in front of me, so close I hadn't seen it at first, stood a peacock in full bloom. I froze, caught my breath, afraid the slightest movement would scare him into retracting his plume quick as a hand fan snapped shut. Neither of us moved. The morning sun ran through its feathers like wind through a wheat field. Fifty unblinking eyes stared at me from those feathers, and at the center, the bird itself, a fluorescent blue of a color I'd only seen on airbrushed T-shirts.

The display of the plume is for mating, right? Had I interrupted something? Had I peacock-blocked the bird? Before I could get a handle on the *why*, the *what* was over. With a shiver, the feathers folded back against his body. Now the peacock looked like a turkey in drag.

I wanted to tell someone, but Colin and Dave were still sleeping. I'd been up alone, sitting at the mixing board, cranking our new record with as much volume as the playback speakers would handle. We'd finally finished. It took two years and ten thousand of Ron's dollars, but we'd made the album of our career.

Standing on that porch, with the peacock disappearing behind the hay barn, I knew this album was good. I was dead certain of it. In the recording process, something had clicked for Tim. He'd begun to embrace Watershed as we were: complicated. Poppy *and* rootsy. Joe *and* Colin. But mostly Joe. I'd written the bulk of the record. I sang eight of the album's thirteen songs. "Suckerpunch" even made the cut, the Speck/Vinnie version.

It was six years too late to have regrets about *Twister*, but I couldn't help but wish that back in 1994 Sonenberg or Frankie or someone at Sony had said, "Hey, guys. There's this crazy-ass producer three hours up the road from Columbus. Made Sponge a hit." We would have saved two hundred grand and made a much better record. But forward momentum has a way of sewing up wounds.

The album finished, Tim and Ron burned up the phones. Soon DreamWorks was interested. And RCA. And mid-level indies like Time Bomb, Razor and Tie, and Blackbird. "You're getting another record deal," Ron said. "The comeback of the decade." He had a football player's faith that the game was never over.

He and Tim set up a label showcase, in Chicago this time, on our Midwestern home turf. We'd play the Double Door as part of MOBfest, Chicago's version of South By Southwest. The A&R men had spoken: They'd be there, pens in hand.

"It's happening all over again," Colin said. "I knew it."

But this time it was on the strength of my songs, my voice. Watershed had been Colin's band before. We were my band now.

Two months from the showcase, I started to notice a strain in my voice. At first I just couldn't quite hit the high notes. I figured my vocal cords were tired from being worked so hard by Patalan. It would sort itself out, no need to cancel practice. Then my singing got worse. My vocal range shrunk to one shaky octave, and I talked like a three-pack-a-day asthmatic. Colin told me to drink water and breathe steam. Biggie told me not to baby it. I went through tea and honey like a Member of Parliament, but nothing worked. I needed a doctor.

The ENT stuck a fiber optic scope up my nose and through my nasal passages until the camera had a clear shot at my larynx. He showed me the image on a monitor, and there it was, plain as pie, a polyp on my vocal cords. The doctor explained that the two lip-like folds weren't meeting because of that little bump—probably caused by ruptured blood vessels from years of incorrect singing. The first treatment, he said, was silence. Shut the hell up for a few weeks and see if it goes away.

Try not talking. It's harder than you think. I wrote notes to my Ohio State professors explaining that I wouldn't be raising my hand in class. I carried around a reporter's pad and wrote down my questions. When Kate and I went out to dinner to celebrate our first wedding anniversary, we passed notes across the table. We now have a written record of everything I said.

After three weeks, I finally spoke. Nothing had changed. I was hoarse as ever, couldn't sing "Mary Had a Little Lamb."

The MOBfest showcase was five weeks away.

The next week I had surgery to remove the polyp. Recovery: Four more weeks of silence followed by two months of vocal therapy to relearn how to talk. Then voice lessons to learn how to sing properly. This time, the ENT said, it was crucially important that I not speak. Reinjure the cords and I might be hoarse for life.

Four more weeks of silence? No, no, no. The record company showcase was in four weeks.

Writing on my pad, I asked him if I could please-please-please start talking after three. The Chicago gig was too important to miss. I couldn't let everyone down.

"I don't recommend it," he said. "But I can't stop you."

Three more weeks, total fucking silence. I graduated from Ohio State without being able to say thanks to the dean when he passed me my diploma. Once, in the middle of the night, I accidentally whispered to Kate that I loved her. The next day I was sure those three words had doomed the band.

A week before the gig, I finally spoke. "How does it sound?" I asked Kate.

"Beautiful," she said. "It sounds just beautiful." Then she started crying.

But my voice was weak. It hurt to talk. I didn't say much.

The plan was to have one practice, two days before the show. I'd then have a full twenty-four hours to recover before singing in front of the record companies. My performance at that practice didn't exactly inspire confidence. I hadn't used my vocal cords in two months—and it showed. A smart band would have raised the cancel finger, better to cancel than suck. But canceling isn't the Watershed way. Even if the show wasn't perfect, we'd surely get points for being gamers. Watershed answers the bell, motherfucker.

Colin, Dave, and I stood at the side of the stage. The Double Door was jammed. Tim and Ron had drawn up a set list for us in advance, and this time Colin went along with it. There'd be no surprises. Of the nine tunes on the list, I'd sing lead on seven, suspect voice and all. While Biggie gave our gear the once-over, fans who'd traveled from Columbus chanted "Wa-ter-shed!" They knew what was at stake.

"We always pull something out our asses, don't we?" Colin said. If he was upset about getting short shrift, he didn't let on. He'd even volunteered to sing my songs if that's what it took. Or, like a good quarterback, he'd sit out this series. Whatever was best for the team.

"Okay, ladies." Biggie gave us the thumbs up and led us to the stage. "Try not sucking for once."

As Dave counted us into "Black Concert T-Shirt," I prayed to Jesus or Elvis or whoever was listening that when I opened my mouth, the sound that came forth would be strong enough to support everything riding on it.

I wish I could say this prayer was answered. That I sang like a chorus of angels. That my voice triggered a bidding war. That Watershed made the comeback of the decade. In truth my singing was okay. Just okay. We muscled through. Considering I couldn't talk a week before, muscling through was a minor miracle. But it takes a major miracle to get signed, and you don't get points for being gamers. You get points for being undeniable, and undeniable we weren't. We were okay.

After the show, Tim and Ron bought drinks for the suits. We got the usual high fives and pats on the back. We posed for a photo with the MOBfest people, who said they were certain we'd be offered a contract. Tim and Ron said the same thing. We'd crushed, no doubt.

But the phone never rang.

Ron later told us of the following exchange, which took place while we were celebrating backstage.

A&R Man #1: "The singer doesn't sound as good live as he does on the record."

A&R Man #2: "I heard his voice is all messed up. Just had vocal surgery."

And with that, the comeback clock hit double-zero.

Here at the Alley Cat, we close our set with AC/DC's "It's a Long Way to the Top." During the breakdown in the middle, Colin takes off his Telecaster and yells into the mic, "Okay, now. Who wants to play guitar?"

On the floor stand ten people at most: The Superfan, Superfan II, Kristie, three more Watershed fans, and the opening band.

"Come on!" Colin says. "Somebody get up here!"

Beetlejuice jumps onto the stage. He grabs Colin's guitar and tears into a solo, while Colin leaves the stage and heads down to the floor. Pooch hands his Les Paul to a Watershed fan who obviously doesn't know how to play, but that's okay. Pooch slides the guy's hand's somewhere near a barred-A position and lets him loose. Dave passes his sticks to the opening band's drummer, keeping the kick going until the kid is settled. I pull The Superfan up on stage and sling my bass over her hair and shoulders. She makes this exchange look like a sex act.

"What do I do?" she says, plucking the strings like she's picking lint off them.

As I walk away from her, I yell, "Keep hitting the second string over and over. Never stop." It's really that simple.

The misfit hootenanny fumbles through AC/DC, sounding fantastically shitty, and the four of us are standing next to each other on the floor, drinking beer, watching the show with the rest of the crowd. Band has become audience—and audience band.

Later, I open the load-out door to see snow falling on the New South. It's a freak storm, expected to throw four to six inches from Nashville to Savannah. Tonight we're driving to Charleston, where we'll spend an off day tomorrow before heading up to Raleigh for the last show before Columbus. The Superfan—music teacher by day—says her school has already canceled classes. As we shut the van doors and pull away she says, "Y'all be safe."

The Map Slut coaxes Biggie toward I-77, and Dave and Pooch yell for Taco Bell. "There'll be someplace to eat on the highway," Biggie says, squinting through the fat flakes.

On the interstate Biggie's pushing seventy-five, and the big rigs are blowing past us at eighty, cutting through three inches of slush. Not much demand for snowplows down in Dixie. I'm the shotgun seat, and from here I can feel Colin flinching in the back. Nervousness pulses off him in waves. We're all scared. Scared of dying and scared of telling Biggie how to drive.[57]

"Hey, Joe," Colin says. "Can you write down my last words?"

"Let me guess," I say. "*I told you so, Biggie!*"

Dave and Pooch demand that Taco Bell be their last meal.

South of Rock Hill, Biggie angles into a rest area, to quiet the bellyaching more than anything. The snow in the parking lot is ankle deep. I return from the john to find him pecking away on his laptop. "Last will and testament?" I say.

He shows me the screen. It's the Weather Channel—beamed from his home TV to his laptop via Slingbox. Incredible. We're sitting in a South Carolina rest area, snow caked to our shoes, watching Biggie's TV. "Looks like it's gonna let up south of Columbia," he says.

And that's just what happens. By the time we take the left onto I-26, we're dealing with standard-issue rain. Colin's asleep in the Spider Hole. Dave and Pooch are dreaming, no doubt, of double beef burritos. Biggie's driving in a fugue state, steering with the autopilot that lives deep in his primordial lizard brain.

I'm wide awake, thinking about how much I still love all this—the playing and the not playing, the van and the rest area, the piss break and the truck stop, the food run and the shit talk. Even the silence.

11

Celebrating the End of Hope
Charleston, South Carolina–
Raleigh, North Carolina

FIRST, THE HOTEL. AND THE SWEET, SWEET LUXURY OF TUCKING INTO a bed that isn't moving at eighty-five miles per hour. After a few hours sleep, it's every man for himself. Colin hops a ferry and rides to Fort Sumter, looking to do something vaguely educational before the inevitable drinking. Dave and Pooch peel off in search of a seafood lunch. I grab my umbrella, planning to walk the historic district.

"Knock yourself out," Biggie says. He pulls the sheets over his head and falls back to sleep.

There's no snow this far south, just a fine mist and low-hanging clouds. Tacoma weather. The gray skies make a fitting backdrop for Charleston's stately Georgian-Palladians and Italian villas—a reminder that beauty and ugliness are co-dependent. I wander the cobblestone streets, wondering what secrets have been walled over and buried under these old houses. This is a town whose narrative runs from rice fortunes and the slave trade, to secession and Reconstruction, to Hurricane Hugo and re-reconstruction. Maybe Sherman, that old softy, spared Charleston because it was too beautiful to burn. Or maybe he damned it to survive its sins.

At the corner of King and Calhoun, I come across Millennium Music, a mammoth record store and café, and just for the heck of it, I make for the Pop/Rock section. I know where to look: MISCELLANEOUS W. Either that or tucked behind The Waterboys and Roger Waters. What do you know? There we are, with our own tray card and everything. I pick up the one Watershed CD in the bin—a copy of the original *Three Chords* EP, still around fourteen years after its release, despite being long out of print—and I touch the Epic logo on the spine, feeling like an old bush league ballplayer, staring at the baseball card from the lone season I spent in The Pros. So many albums in this store. So many bands. So few customers. In three months Millennium Music will go out of business, gone the way of Tower, Virgin, and all the other big boxers.

Exiting the store, I turn left down King Street—past Pottery Barn, Williams-Sonoma, Urban Outfitters—toward Cumberland's, the bar we had originally wanted to play tonight instead of taking the day off. Over the years we've logged a little airplay on the local alt-rock station, 96 Wave, so Charleston was supposed to be the centerpiece of the southern swing. But five months ago, the station switched to the limp-dicked, we-play-everything, "Chuck"[58] format. Even without radio support, Cumberland's would have been an ideal stop. The club was small but respected, having hosted the likes of Ryan Adams, NRBQ, and Mike Watt. Colin and Thomas put calls in, trying to book the date, only to learn that come New Year's Eve, the bar was losing its lease and shutting down. The record shop, the radio station, the rock club—all belly-up. The rock is dead. God save the rock.

Now a construction-size Dumpster blocks Cumberland's front door. In the dust-caked window hangs a faded sign that reads *Support Live Music*. I catch my reflection in the glass: an old-timer holding an umbrella, staring into an empty storefront, window-shopping for his past.

With hope of a second major-label deal lost after the Chicago showcase, Ron released the Patalan sessions on his own label in March of 2002. We called the record *The More It Hurts, The More It Works,* which was apt considering that the process was so difficult, but the result was so satisfying. The conventional wisdom is that bands get worse with age. You always hear *I like their old stuff better.* But dammit if we hadn't improved.

I was certain we'd made the best album of our career, but I didn't know if anyone outside the band would care. Ron decided to push "Can't Be Myself" as the lead single, a song that was a true collaboration between Colin and me. We wrote the words together. We both sing on the track. "*This* is how Watershed is supposed to sound," Ron said.

The album had been out for about a month when we got a call from Andyman at CD101. He said he loved "Can't Be Myself" and thought it could be a hit. He was going to add it to heavy rotation, which for an unsigned band was almost unheard of, even on an independent station like his. Every morning on my way to work at the Vision Center, and every afternoon on the drive home, I was treated to my own voice coming through the car speakers. I'd roll down the windows and sing along with myself, not caring one whit if somebody caught me.

Then people started telling us they were hearing "Can't Be Myself" on The Blitz. Surely they were mistaken. The Blitz had spun "How Do You Feel," of course, but that was back when we were signed to Epic. The station only played unsigned bands during their Sunday night local show. Our friends, however, were saying they'd heard the song on a Tuesday, on a Friday. Ron called the program director just to double-check, and sure enough, the PD said he was giving the song a shot in regular rotation. Our fans lit up the phone lines, and soon "Can't Be Myself" was the most requested song on CD101 and The Blitz. Tim Patalan's production sounded fantastic on the airwaves[59], right at home alongside U2, Green Day, and everybody else. He'd been right: Good songs do find an audience. *The Other Paper* dubbed it "the monster hit of the summer."

We were all over Columbus radio, but without major label distribution, we had trouble keeping *Hurts/Works* stocked in stores. Colin and I would drive around town with boxes of CDs in the trunk, making almost daily deliveries, as the album continued to surprise store managers by selling out again and again. Soon it hit number twenty on the Columbus SoundScan chart, and it spent eight weeks as a Best Seller at the Virgin Megastore. The record was moving almost as fast as *Twister* had, despite being much harder to find. Colin and I were damn near giddy making those deliveries. Seven years after being dropped, Watershed was back.

So were our Columbus fans. We played Little Brothers to a four hundred person sellout. We played in a parking lot for Cinco De Mayo and drew even more. Next up was Comfest, Columbus's big outdoor festival, where for three days in June, a hundred or so local bands perform on five stages. Bands break out their big guns for Comfest, everyone wanting to impress everybody else with a balls-out set. Ron pressed hard for us to add a second guitar player for the show. He was worried that as a three-piece, Colin, Dave, and I couldn't deliver on the promise of Patalan's studio production. Too many people were now hearing us on the radio, he said, we couldn't risk sounding thin. Enter Mark "Poochie"[60] Borror. With his nerdy glasses and coal-black hair, he had a great look. And even though he'd only been playing guitar for two years, his right hand was Malcolm Young–rhythmic. Pooch brought the beef, and Watershed had never sounded so good.

Our shtick at Comfest was to poke fun at ourselves for upgrading to a four-piece. In the week leading up to the show, we issued a press release announcing that McDonalds had acquired Watershed in a hostile takeover. But no need to worry. We promised to deliver the same delicious rock and roll and timely service you'd come to expect from us over the years. We decorated the Comfest stage with the McDonalds signs and banners we'd stolen from Ron's mobile McDs truck. Biggie hung the golden arches behind Dave's head, turning the "M" upside down to make a "W." From behind the drums, I looked into the crowd. There were a thousand confused faces gathered around the stage, giving each other *what-the-fuck?* looks. Ricki C. then took the mic and said, "Ladies and gentlemen! Will you please welcome, the new, improved, McWatershed!"

Pooch was as shocked as anyone when we took the stage wearing official, orange and yellow McDonalds uniforms. He'd assumed the whole bit was an elaborate scheme to haze the new guy—get him to show up to the gig in funny clothes. Between songs, instead of drinking beer, we ate cheeseburgers and washed them down with orange drink. We played with fries dangling from our mouths. The audience cheered like mad. As we brought the set to a close, I wiped mustard from my chin, and said to Pooch, "We're a weird band. Welcome aboard." Then I threw a sack of burgers into the crowd.[61]

That fall Colin and I scored tickets to Ohio State's football opener against Texas Tech. As we made the tailgate rounds, people called out to us, "Joe, Colin! Colin, Joe!" Buckeye fans would hand us beers, saying they'd heard "Can't Be Myself" on the radio. A guy would elbow his buddy, then nod our way. "Look over there, man. It's the Watershed dudes."

Riding the buzz of beer and recognition, Colin and I headed into the stadium and up the long stairway of the south stands, where we were both meeting our dads. I glanced up a hundred rows of bleachers, and there was my dad, standing in the middle of the aisle, waving his arms in a panic. "Did you hear it?" he said when Colin and I reached him.

"Hear what?"

He pointed toward the field, where the marching band had formed the human tunnel that would guide the players onto the field. "They played your song."

"Who played what song?" I figured he meant the band had played "Hang On Sloopy," a song that everyone in Ohio could claim as theirs.

"No-no," he said. "'Can't Be Myself!'" He raised his hand to give me five. "They played 'Can't Be Myself.'"

Clearly my dad had been drinking. "The marching band played 'Can't Be Myself?'"

"No, the stadium PA. Played the whole song. Five minutes ago."

"The *Watershed* song 'Can't Be Myself?'" Colin said. Just then I saw his dad, squeezing through the crowd toward us. He looked prouder than I'd ever seen him.

"Yes!" my dad said. "'Can't Be Myself.' You didn't hear it?"

Watershed was played at Ohio Stadium before a Buckeye game. I'm surprised I didn't faint and tumble a hundred rows to the field.

In January we decided to gauge the result of the radio airplay and record sales by booking ourselves into the proving ground that is the Newport Music Hall—just as we had ten years earlier, when we knew we'd become too big for Ruby's. "All right," Colin said. "Let's see where the fuck we stand."

CD101 had just released their top 101 songs of the year. "Can't Be Myself" finished number ten. The second single, "Anniversary," made it to seventy-six. Still, we hadn't played the Newport since Epic dropped us, and I was scared, as always, that the place would be empty, that we had overstepped, that we would humiliate ourselves in our hometown.

A local film crew volunteered to tape the show. As the opening band played, one of the camera guys knocked on the dressing room door. "Holy shit," he said. He looked spooked.

"What?" I said. "What's wrong?"

"There's a line stretched down the block," he said, flipping open the camera. "Check it out. I got it on tape."

We gathered around the screen. Hundreds of fans were queued up along High Street. Colin let out a whoop and started dancing the cabbage patch.

More people showed up at the Newport that night than on the night when we'd recorded the *Three Chords* EP. After the first song, they cheered so wildly, all I could do was turn to Colin and laugh. He shot me a look that said, *Can you fucking believe this?* We ended the set with "Can't Be Myself," and the crowd sang along with every word. I stared out at them, trying to burn the image into my memory. The audience that had filled Polaris Amphitheatre so long ago might have been ten times bigger, but this night felt ten times sweeter. Because this time we'd done it ourselves. No longer would we measure our success by the false validation of a record deal. Standing on that stage, I knew Watershed would forever play in the minor leagues. But that was okay: a win in the minors was still a win.

And a loss was still a loss. A few weeks after the Newport show we played a bar in Springfield, Ohio—forty-five short miles from Columbus— and drew exactly two people. This was a harsh reminder of the limits of Watershed's celebrity. Sure, we were now as big in Columbus as we'd ever been, but for how long could one town sustain us?

We spent the rest of that year touring on weekends. I'd come home late on a Sunday night, after driving all day from, say, Marquette, Michigan, and when Kate would ask how the shows went, I'd say something like,

The crowds weren't huge or anything, but it's important to maintain a presence, you know? Plus we sold a couple CDs, so hopefully we've made a few fans for when we go back next month. I needed to believe this, but if I were being completely honest with Kate, I would have said, *It would be one thing if the crowds were a little bigger every time we came through town, but they just aren't. Maybe we're wasting our time out there.* Kate would rub my neck until I fell asleep. Then I'd wake up the next morning and dress for my day job.

By then she had started grad school, and I'd quit the Vision Center. With my political science degree in hand, I got a job researching medical equipment for an architecture firm. It was a fine company, but working there was soul crushing, in part because Watershed was doing so well locally.

One day a co-worker and I were talking, and I let it slip that I played in a band.

"Oh yeah?" he said. "Which one?"

"Watershed."

He raised his eyes at me like I was an idiot. "You know there's already a big national band called Watershed, right?"

"Yeah, I know," I said. "I'm in it."

He looked dubious. "Then, dude," he said, "why the hell are you working here?"

The price of being a dedicated musician (or painter or pro golfer or comedian) is that you have to spend most of your time at a job you despise, in order to pay for the time you spend doing the thing you love. You can't afford to do that thing full-time, but you can't *not* do it, any more than you could not breathe. So you find a way to set up your life so that the music (or the painting, golfing, or joke-telling) gets done. The trouble was that my current setup—sitting at a desk, in an aggressively ergonomic chair, checking off items from my Microsoft Outlook to-do list—was making me miserable.

I'd get even more frustrated when I saw how the life Kate and I had built stacked up against the lives of our non–rock and roll friends. Take Herb, who was now a successful realtor. He and his wife would invite us over for dinner, tour us around their big suburban house—with its vaulted great room and stainless steel mega-grille—and I'd think, *so this is what quitting Watershed gets you.* Herb's house was like a growth chart that measured success, and according to it, Kate and I were woefully underachieving. In our thirties, we should be ascending to upper management; leafing through the real estate section of the Sunday paper; and receiving holiday cards from insurance agents and financial planners—their professional smiles beaming from magnets stuck to a restaurant-grade Frigidaire.

Back in our apartment, I told myself that I would find wealth in our freedom from financial trappings. I told myself that I was better, or at least more righteous, than Herb. But most importantly, I told myself that I was *happier* than him. Because if I wasn't, then where had all this time in Watershed left me?

I now refer to that period as my Early Midlife Crisis. And in a crisis, you go desperate. Some guys buy a motorcycle; some divorce their wives. Kate and I decided to commandeer the Watershed van and drive to Mexico. After she graduated with her master's, I quit my job at the architecture firm. We moved out of our apartment, put all our stuff in storage, climbed into the van, and headed west. For three months we cruised along Mexico's Pacific coast, camping on the beach or checking into cheap hotels. We paid for much of the trip with money we made by sitting through timeshare presentations. We'd tour the facilities, listen to the spiel, say no, and collect the cash incentive. Days I'd write songs, while Kate read the classics. Evenings we'd cook over a beach fire, open a bottle of wine, and talk. It was the happiest I'd been in a long time, but soon the timeshare money would run out, and we'd have to head home. I didn't want to go back to the same life I'd left.

One night on the beach in Sayulita, a village north of Puerto Vallarta, we sat in a grove of palm trees, drinking under a postcard moon. I asked Kate if she thought I could get into Ohio State's graduate program in creative writing. Over the years I'd mentioned that I'd like to try to write someday, but I'd never actually written anything other than term papers. I'd always thought writers were blessed with superhuman talent, as if they'd been beamed here from a faraway planet where everyone wore berets and breathed clove cigarette smoke. Until Kate started graduate school, I didn't know that a person could learn to write. But at her grad school parties, I met most of the writers enrolled in the program, and they were funny, they liked to drink, and there wasn't a beret in the bunch. If they could write, I could too.

"Just start working on something," Kate said. "Maybe write about this." She gestured toward the van, the tent, the beach campground. "Then go ahead and apply and we'll see what happens." We opened another bottle of wine, and she said, "The music life you've been living is brutal. Because you never get a clear sense of how well you're doing. School is much easier, because for better or worse, you always know where you stand. You get a grade."

Back in Columbus, we found a nice apartment, and I started writing an essay about traveling through Mexico. Kate marked up the manuscript with red ink. She told me to write another draft. And another. And another. Writing prose seemed much harder than writing rock songs. In rock and roll, you can bank on the beat, the melody, the sheer volume. In creative writing you've got to build all that stuff on the page, using nothing but goddamn words. I got pissed at Kate. Told her I didn't think I could do it. But she encouraged me through drafts four, five, six.

And Ohio State took me. Opening that acceptance letter, I was happy as hell. But I was also worried. If writing turned out to be something I really, truly liked, then my personal happiness would put Watershed in jeopardy. A musician finding a tolerable alternative to music is pretty much the worst thing that can happen to his band. Let's face it. Structuring your life so that you can play rock and roll (or paint or golf or tell jokes) is a pain in the ass. But as much as you hate the crappy day job that pays for your passion, it's partially that very hatred for Plan B that keeps you so focused on Plan A. Once you acquiesce to Plan B, once you even accept its feasibility, it goes to work on you with the gravitational pull of a black hole.

After receiving the grad school acceptance letter, I broke the news to the guys that I'd be taking classes in the fall. Watershed would have to cut back on gigging. We'd have to stay close to home and save the longer tours for spring and summer break. "And if we want to try to get another album recorded," I said, "we'd better do it right now. Before school starts."

Colin and Biggie agreed. The trick to knocking out another album would be locking down Tim Patalan. He wasn't exactly a deadline-driven guy.

I left a message in his voice mail. "Hey, Tim, man. We just happen to be coming through Ann Arbor next week. Wanna get a drink?"

He called right back and told us to meet him at the bowling alley.

We drove north with three hundred dollars and a three-tiered plan. (1) Get Patalan drunk, (2) Get a studio session confirmed, and (3) Wipe the lanes with his Michigan ass. We scored on all counts. I slid him the three bills and said, "Here's a down payment." He spent most of the money on jalapeno poppers and pitchers of beer.

Staggering out to our cars after the third game, he said, "So what brings you guys through town, anyway?"

I grabbed his arm. "We came to see you, you Polish bastard."

We were so happy that spring, back at The Loft, recording the songs that would become *The Fifth of July*. Back with the peacocks, the horses, the raccoons. Back with Mr. Patalan's Hungarian booze and Mrs. Patalan's stuffed cabbage. After *Hurts/Works*, recording anywhere else would have been a huge disappointment. How you gonna keep 'em down in the city after they've seen the farm?

We'd record all night, sleep all morning, and in the afternoons I'd sweat out the beer by going on a long run. As a way of stomping the Early Midlife Crisis to death, I'd signed up for the Cleveland Marathon. I needed a goal that didn't depend on anybody else's approval. Either I could run the 26.2, or I couldn't. No A&R guys would be waiting at the finish line, whispering to each other that my running form wasn't rock star enough or that I looked too old for the time I'd clocked. Training for a marathon at The Loft was like holding boot camp in a bordello. The place was set up for excess, not discipline. I'd set out on Saline's dirt roads and put in ten or twelve miles, then come back to the studio and crawl into a Busch Light thirty-pack—carbo loading for the next day's run. But the training regimen worked. I finished the Marathon in 4:23, a respectable time considering that two days before the race I drank at least 26.2 beers.

Dave now understood the Patalan booze-on-the-tracks aesthetic, so while I was still stretching my wire-tight hammies, he'd be warming up with a sixpack, watching Keith Moon crush "A Quick One While He's Away" on *The Rolling Stones Rock and Roll Circus*. This time we all knew how Patalan operated, and he us. Tim knew just when to push ("*Al*most. I like everything but the lyrics, chords, and melody—keep working"), and he knew when to go AWOL, giving us space to solve a problem for ourselves. ("I've got to help my brother fix a wheel on the sulky. Have a new second verse written by the time I get back.")

The sessions went alarmingly smooth, the only delays coming when Tim needed to squeeze in time to record with The Fags—John Speck's new band, started after he imploded Hoarse. The legendary A&R man Seymour Stein had recently signed The Fags to Sire Records, the label best known for breaking Madonna and The Ramones. That damn Speck: He blows out Hoarse's RCA contract and comes right back with a new band and a new record deal. But if any band ever deserved a deal, The Fags did. The songs were sugary, and the live show was nails. The question was, could they stay together long enough to get the Sire debut made? The members annoyed each other to no end. They could barely tolerate standing on the same stage. Tim Patalan wasn't just the producer; he was the bass player, and every couple months, I'd get a call from Speck, telling me that he was firing Patalan, that nut-job, and he wanted me to take Tim's place in the band. Then I'd get a call from Patalan, saying Speck had unhinged, that spaz, would I come up and sing the background vocals he couldn't get Speck to do.

One weekend, Seymour Stein was scheduled to fly to Detroit and limo out to Saline to approve the rough mixes of The Fags' full-length record, *Light 'em Up*. But Speck hadn't finished the harmony parts to Tim's liking, so Patalan asked me to hurry up to Michigan to polish them before Stein got there. I sang for two days straight, trying my best to sound like Speck, and an hour before Stein was due to arrive, I pulled out of the The Loft's driveway. We probably passed each other on a dirt road, him the A&R giant, me the unofficial fourth Fag.[62]

Colin and I titled the new Watershed record *The Fifth of July* because we always seemed a day late and a dollar short. The CD was released by Idol Records—twenty years after our first practice in Herb's bedroom and ten years after Epic dropped us. I was five months into grad school when the album hit stores, and I was proud of the good work we'd done. The *Columbus Dispatch* seemed to agree:

> On Watershed's new album, The Fifth of July, *the band has mastered a craft—the craft of creating so-catchy-it should-be-illegal power pop.* The Fifth of July *is the Kinks with muscle, the Ramones with better voices, and Green Day with bigger brains.*
>
> *Like a four-headed Hemingway with musical instruments rather than writing tools . . . Watershed says more poignant things about never-ending summers, dead-end jobs and drinks to go to sleep and to wake up than a more longwinded outfit ever would.*

Bands are supposed to be too cool to care about reviews, but coming from the hometown paper, this felt like a vindication. We'd take it.

Suddenly it seemed like too many good things were happening. The CD was well received by our fans, radio, and the press, and I was digging school: learning how to write and, as a graduate teaching associate, helping my students to write better. It was by far the best day job I'd ever had.

That spring a big-name local restaurateur started hanging out at the coffee shop, and he and Colin got to talking about life, success, and about how hard it is to succeed when life's demands keep getting in the way.

"I love to see what people can do when they don't have to worry about money," the restaurateur said. "If they just concentrate on their thing, whatever that is. How good will they get? How successful?"

"Hard work's a given," Colin said. "But you know how it is. Hard work can only get you so far. Sometimes you need a leg up."

Since the day I met him, what Colin has always been best at—better than guitar, better than songwriting—is selling people on the dream. A month later, the restaurateur handed Colin a check made out to Watershed for twenty thousand dollars.

Meanwhile Ron, like all our ex-managers, had gotten tired of being *this close* without ever scoring the financial payoff, so he went back to the concessions business, and Colin went to work convincing Thomas O'Keefe that he should manage a band of hitless veterans. We'd met O'Keefe years before in Raleigh, talking for hours about our shared love of Cheap Trick.[63] In addition to having tour managed Train, D-Generation, and Whiskeytown, he was smart, logical, and not panicky. He was just the kind of guy I wanted representing us. And O'Keefe was absolutely confident that Watershed was still viable. We had hits in us. He knew it. "We're *not wrong* about this," he said.

Soon he and Colin had booked our whole summer. When school let out after that first year, Watershed had forty shows on the board and twenty thousand dollars in the bank. I'd been beating my head against the brick wall of the music business for ten years since Epic, figuring one of us, me or the wall, would eventually crumble. By going back to school, I'd essentially said, "That's cool, wall. Stand there for all I care." As soon as I turned my back on it, the bricks came loose.

Colin had insisted that *The Fifth of July* close with a song called "The Best Is Yet to Come," an assertion that had once seemed dubious. A few months later, however, his optimism was rewarded. Thomas called with the good news that "The Best Is Yet to Come" would be used as backing music on MTV's quasi-reality program *Laguna Beach*. "This is a *huge* break," Thomas said. "I told you, we're *not* wrong!"

The night the episode aired, I set the VCR, and Kate and I climbed onto the couch. Bag of popcorn, bottle of wine, the whole nine. I'd never seen *Laguna Beach,* but from the essays my students had written about it, I knew that the show purports to document the real lives of a group of California rich-kids. This particular episode focused on Chase's rock band and their quest to land a record deal. I rolled my eyes. Chase and the boys were already TV stars. Kate and I were sitting on a couch in Columbus, watching their TV *show,* for Christ's sake. Now we were supposed to root for them to become rock stars on top of that? Hadn't The Monkees already covered this thematic turf? Anyway, as the episode unfolds, the band's manager calls with great news: he's scored the band a major-label showcase at The Roxy in L.A. "This is far and away the most important show you're ever going to play," says the manager, looking younger and hipper than Don and Danny ever did.

Kate and I sipped wine and laughed about how this big break comes way too easily, too conveniently, with the band paying exactly zero dues, but okay, whatever. We all know reality shows aren't real. In any case, the band—who, no surprise here, look like Abercrombie models—are now all fired up for this, the show that could change everything.

"The guys are like so gonna get signed," says one of the girls from the deck of a speedboat.

So here's the moment: The *Laguna Beach* rock band loads their gear into a black SUV for the trip from Orange County up to Hollywood, knowing that this is *the* show of their young and already charmed lives. And right then, as our heroes pull out of the driveway, motoring toward their musical destiny, we hear in the background Watershed's "The Best Is Yet to Come." Fourteen whole seconds of it.

"Was that it?" Kate said.

I laughed out loud at the irony. Genuine, old, Ohio band, watching the TV, hoping for a break . . . ends up the backing track for fake, young, California TV band's break.

Then came the kicker: The *Laguna Beach* band signs with Epic Records.

Still, Watershed's tour that summer was the most fun we'd had on the road since The Smithereens shows. Most of the gigs were in small clubs in front of small crowds, but it sure helped to have a twenty thousand dollar cushion against gas, food, and lodging. There were highs and lows, of course. But *The Fifth of July* was proof that Watershed always finds a way to keep going, to get a record made, to get shows booked. We've figured out how to subsist in the minors forever. That's the good news and the bad news.

And that's precisely where we stand right now, three years later, touring behind the new live album. Driving and drinking and putting on a rock show. Celebrating the end of hope and hoping like hell there's still more out there to celebrate.

From Cumberland's, I decamp to Kudu Coffee and spend two hours in that alone-togetherness that is the crowded coffee shop. A woman sitting next to me asks if I'd watch her laptop for a minute. "Feel free to check your e-mail if you want to," she says. In my inbox is Kate's *won't do this again* message, a bunch of junk, and—okay-okay, what is this, good news, maybe-maybe—an e-mail from a school in Ohio where I'd applied for a teaching job.

Kate and I are both looking for work for next year. We are, as they say in academia, *on the market*. A few days before this tour started, we flew to Chicago to interview for jobs at the Modern Language Association's annual conference. Every year, in early January, hundreds of English professors and graduate students come to MLA for job interviews. MLA is like the NFL scouting combine, except instead of running the forty or the three cone drill, candidates are made to discuss their pedagogical philosophies and the scholarly promise of their research. Everywhere you look—in the elevator, in line at Starbucks, curled up in the lobby—there are people in new suits, nervously prepping for interviews. Kate met with search committees from schools in California and Pennsylvania. I interviewed with schools in Wisconsin, Texas, South Carolina, and a school in Ohio, in a small town not far from Columbus.

The e-mail is from the chair of the Ohio school's search committee. But I don't open it yet. I'm milking the moment, staring at the subject line, trying to divine a hint of whether the news is good or bad.

Competition for college teaching jobs is fierce, so on the one hand I'm afraid Kate and I won't get offered anything, and we'll both end up mixing mochas at Starbucks next year. On the other I'm afraid that one or both of us will get hired somewhere. What if I end up in Texas, while Kate's in Pennsylvania? As Kate would tell you, we've already spent too much of our marriage in different states: she at home, me on the road. But the thing that scares me most about landing a permanent teaching job would be landing a permanent teaching job. In Tacoma I'm just visiting, so it's easy to convince myself that I'm a band guy first, professor second. But if I land a tenure-track job? Time to get measured for the jacket with the elbow patches, pal.

In Chicago, during a break in the conference, Kate and I went to see the movie *Juno,* and a nightmarish vision of my future slapped me full in the face: the aging, unhip, un-self-aware, suburban ex-rocker, as played in the film by Jason Bateman. Bateman's character is a guy who was once in a band, but has traded his rock and roll aspirations for a paying gig and a swank house—complete with a spare room where he keeps his guitars and recording gear. He's chickened out and bought into the whole forty-hour, fifty-week, forty-five-year grind that Colin and I quit OSU in order to sidestep. I sat in the theater, watching Bateman stumble through his existential crisis, wondering if I was now the chicken, if teaching college was just another way of selling insurance. I thought of The Toll, the R.C. Mob, and Scrawl, and every other band I knew who'd broken up. I thought of Herb and all the other ex–rock and rollers I know, whose music careers have been reduced to dusty closets and basement corners. Then I thought of all the ex-rockers out there that I *don't* know. There must be tens of thousands, hundreds of thousands, maybe. The ex-rocker is now so common that the character is being written into movies, sitcoms, and luxury car commercials. He's an archetype: *Used-to-Play-in-a-Band-Guy.*

As Kate and I walked back to the conference hotel, I told her that what I wanted most in the world was *not* to become that guy. I would stay with Watershed until Colin and I needed walkers if that's what it took not to be the guy who *used* to play in Watershed.

"Is that what you want?" Kate said. "To move back to Ohio, work at Barnes and Noble, and play in dive bars the rest of your life? If that's really what you want, fine. But you can't expect me to do it with you."

"I don't. I won't."

We were standing on a bridge over the Chicago River, the wind whipping Kate's hair. "I didn't marry Willie Phoenix," she said.

And here it was, the opposite of Used-to-Play-in-a-Band Guy: *Doesn't-Know-when-to-Quit Guy.* Which is sadder? Willie is now fifty-five and still slogging along. His steady gig these days is at a bar that used to be a Long John Silver's.

"I'd quit right now if I thought playing a seafood shack was my future," I said. But I wondered if that was really true. I admire Willie precisely because he can't quit, won't quit, not ever. If I refuse to end up like Willie, is it because I'm smart enough to know when to quit or because I don't have the balls to keep going?

"You guys have accomplished so much," she said. "You should be proud."

I am proud. We held gloved hands, and I told her so. But I also know this: There's not enough pride on the planet to keep me from getting pissed off if I ever look in the mirror and see Used-to-Play-in-a-Band Guy staring back at me.

I bite down on the lip of my empty coffee cup and double click the message from the Ohio school. Colin and Biggie know that Kate and I are interviewing for permanent jobs, but I'm not sure they know what that means for Watershed. They've been rooting for me to land the Ohio job. I have too. Teaching gig, close to home. Best of both worlds.

Dammit. The e-mail is too short to be good news. "I regret to inform you that we will not be pursuing your candidacy," it says, which sounds a whole lot like *we've decided not to pick up your option.*

I exhale into the bottom of my coffee cup and close out my inbox. With Wisconsin, Texas, and South Carolina still in the running, I see only two scenarios for next year: I end up working a good job (teaching) far from Colin and Biggie or a shitty job (Starbucks) near them. One scenario is best for my marriage, the other best for my band.

When the woman returns, we thank each other politely. I gather my things and walk out to the street. It's time to call Kate.

She answers after one ring. "Look, Joe," she says, like this is a conversation already in progress. "I've been the dutiful rock girlfriend for eighteen years. All the times you left for weeks, playing shows that turned out to be meaningless—I didn't complain. All the big events in *my* life you missed, because you were on the road—I didn't get mad. Because I knew how important Watershed was to you. Well guess what, it took me eighteen years, but now I'm complaining. Now I'm mad."

I'm walking along upper King, ducking between College of Charleston students and boutique shoppers. "You never know which shows will turn out to be important," I say.

"Okay, so tell me: How important are *these* shows?" she says.

How to answer? Is opening for Heavy Metal Karaoke important? New Band Nite? Yes and no. Playing them isn't important exactly, but *not* playing them would mean Watershed is finished. "Are you saying you want me to stop?"

"I'm asking what *you* want."

"That's not what your e-mail said."

Through the phone I hear cooking noises. It's 11:00 a.m. Pacific; she's no doubt making her ritual ramen noodles. "I'm so sick and tired—"

"Honey, we've been touring since I met you."

"You're not listening," she says. "Let me finish. Please." Back to the boiling water. The spice packet. "I'm so sick and tired of you blaming your frustration on *me*, or on the day job, or even on Colin and Biggie. As if you have no say in your own life. Again, Joe, tell me. What do *you* want? Because I'll tell you exactly what *I* want."

"You want to not go through this again. For any reason. You've made that clear."

She exhales. Long and slow. "I want you to quit half-assing. The band and your writing. You going halfway in two directions hurts. It's hard for me to watch."

I hold the phone away from my head. Look up and down the street. "I know what I *don't* want."

"That's something."

"I don't want to stop."

"Playing or writing?"

"Both."

"Then that's your problem to solve, isn't it." The pot clangs on the stove. "I'm just the mistress here."

I'm silenced. I can neither agree nor disagree. I go for the redirect. "I got an e-mail from the Ohio school today."

"Yeah."

"No go."

Silence from Kate. Then: "That's too bad."

"It's okay. We're not licked yet."

"Who's not?" I can hear her slicing a lemon, knocking a knife on the cutting board.

"You and me."

Now she's opening the fridge to get the Sriracha, working the peppermill, doctoring the ramen. "We're not, huh," she says, and in her inflection I can read just the hint of a smile.

"How's the dissertation going?"

"I wish I could write it in a bar. And every time I finished a paragraph, people would cheer."

I put the phone close to my mouth. Make a cheering sound.

"You guys are so lucky," she says.

"What do you mean?"

"You get to hear that sound for real." The clink of a fork on a bowl. A noodle slurp. Maybe an actual smile.

"You make the best ramen in the world."

"I am pretty damn good."

"Can you see the mountain today?" Mount Rainier only comes out when the sky is clear.

"I haven't been outside yet," she says. Then she laughs. A brothy, wet laugh. "I've been busy being mad at you, you asshole."

I laugh too, trying to widen this crack in her anger. "Being mad at me is a full-time job."

"You gotta understand, Joe. Nothing makes me happier than seeing you happy."

"I know."

"I'm owed one eruption every eighteen years."

"I know, Kate," I say. "I know."

We talk for another half hour. About big and small things. By the time I hang up, we've brokered the peace. It's a fragile peace, but what peace isn't?

I now realize I'm standing in front of AC's, a dive bar we first discovered on the Smithereens' tour. Back then the bar was located near Cumberland's, on lower King, in what has since become the sovereign nation of Williams-Sonomaland. Now AC's has moved north, to a block without national chains. I call Colin on the phone. "Yo, man. You ready to get drinking?"

We settle into a wooden booth, and he tells me the Fort Sumter tour was great. I tell him I found our CD in Millennium Music. I'm feeling better than I have in days. It's ironic that when all's well on the home front, it's easier to enjoy being gone, but there you have it.

"You think anybody gives a shit about this Columbus show?" he says.

"Tough for me to say, you know, not living there." I pick at the label of a High Life. "What'd Scott say? How many advance tickets? Sixty-eight?"

Colin shrugs to say the number doesn't matter. "I'm getting interviewed on CD101 tomorrow afternoon," he says. "Hype the show a little bit."

It's shocking how loyal that station is. They might as well be Watershed's personal propaganda arm.

"Maybe we'll embarrass ourselves on Saturday," Colin says, "but we *had* to try this."

He's wrong there. We didn't have to try the LC. There were at least five smaller places we could have booked. If I'd been living in Columbus, and not feeling so damn guilty about moving away, I would have talked sense into him.

Who am I kidding? Colin would have sold me; he always does.

He puts his lips around the bottle and drinks, inefficiently, sucking rather than leaving a vent opening with his top lip. On his chin is a patch of beard he missed when shaving with his single-blade Bic. Southwest of that patch is a small cut, a tiny piece of toilet paper still stuck to it. Amazing how different we are. And yet I've shared more of my life with him than anyone else.

Two beers later he calls Biggie at the hotel. "Get your ass to the bar, Mr. Biggie."

I call Pooch. "Drag Catman up here. We're practicing for the Drinking Tour." Soon the five of us are huddled together in the booth, bottles filling the table like bowling pins.

"So then Frankie LaRocka lands us a gig at the Sony Christmas party," Biggie says to Dave and Pooch.

"At Sony studios," Colin says. "The big corporate shindig. Everybody's gonna be there."

I nod. "And *Twister* comes out in a month, so we know this is our last chance to win 'em over."

Dave and Pooch sip their beers and nod along. They never got their stretch in The Pros.

"Anyway," Biggie says. "Sony rented us a backline, so we drive out to New York with just the guitars and Herb's snare and cymbals. Day before the gig."

"And it's snowing like mad. Much worse than this morning." Colin has taken over, weather talk being his forte. "They closed I-80 just after we got on it. But no way we can cancel."

"I'm driving," I say. "Northern Pennsylvania white-out. Twenty miles per hour, tops. All the sudden I see brake lights, so I try to stop, too hard, and we go into a 360. Two full spins. We're headed straight into a long line of semi-trucks. Backed up for miles. We're ten yards from crashing into the last truck, when we finally slide to a stop. I check to see if I've shit my pants, then I straighten us out, get us in line, and we wait."

"For like three hours," Colin says. "Freezing fucking cold."

"Running the heater and hoping we don't run out of gas," I say. "We're pissing in Gatorade bottles."

"When we finally get going," Colin says, "the ice on the road is so thick, it's made the road *higher*. The trucks can barely squeeze under the overpasses."

"And we keep hitting these hellacious potholes," I say. "Bam-bam. Feels like the front end's gonna fall off."

"But they weren't potholes," Biggie says. "The trucks had been sitting there for so long, they melted tire divots into the ice."

"Crazy," says Pooch.

Biggie slugs a fresh beer. "So we get to New York at like 4:00 a.m., and we gotta find a place to park. But we don't want to leave the gear in the van, in the city, overnight."

"But!" I say. "The van was equipped with Biggie's security system."

Biggie takes a pen from his Palm Pilot, and on a bar napkin, he draws a diagram of the extra security he'd installed in the van: Two lengths of stainless steel chain—one ten feet long, the other just over a foot. The short chain was padlocked to the van's back doors. The longer one ran from the passenger door handle, through the steering wheel, to the driver's door handle and back to the passenger side.

"All the doors were chained together," I say. "So even if a crook could get a door unlocked, he'd never get it *open* without bolt cutters."

"Genius," says Dave.

"But the parking lot guy . . ." Colin says.

"The parking lot guy," Biggie says, "wants to hold on to the keys. This is one of those tiny-ass lots, and he might need to move the van. But I tell him hell no, there's no moving the van. And he says, 'Then, buddy, you can't park here.'"

"So Biggie chains all the doors except the driver's," I say. "He hands parking dude the key, and we go catch a few hours sleep at Don and Amy's before the gig."

"And when you get back to the van," Pooch says, "the guitars are gone."

I nod. "The guitars are gone."

"Inside job," Colin says.

"Had to be," says Biggie. "I pitched a fucking fit."

"Wha'd you lose?" Pooch says. "A Les Paul?"

"And my bass," I say.

"They should have taken the cymbals," Dave says. "Probably a thousand bucks, right there."

"Losing the guitars wasn't the worst part," I say.

"The worst part," Colin says, "was having to tell Frankie we lost the guitars."

Biggie laughs. "He thought we were corncobs anyway. Always about to be eaten alive by the big city."

I raise my top lip the way Frankie used to. "You podunk muthafuckas really *did* just fall off the punkin truck, didn't ya."

"So wha'd you do?" Pooch says.

"We played the show," I say. "Borrowed guitars from a few of Frankie's buddies."

"And what did Sony think?"

"Colin and I were too busy fawning over Billy Squier to care about Sony," I say. "We cornered Squier in the bathroom. Pants still unzipped. Scared the shit out of him."

"Pooch," Biggie says. "If the company thought we were good, do you think we'd be here right now, telling this story to you two dumb dildos?"

We drink more, laugh more.

Then Pooch says, "Let's get sushi."

"Good by me," I say.

"Me too," says Dave.

"Not me," Colin says. "Eating sushi is like getting your dick sucked by a guy. With your eyes closed it may feel the same, but deep down you know something fishy is up."

I choke on beer. Biggie pounds the table until bottles fall over.

"Most of our record contract went to pay Steinman's fucking sushi bills," I say, barely able to get the words out. "We should have bought him blowjobs instead."

"Everybody would have been happier," Colin says.

"I still don't get it," Pooch says. "You give me 250 grand, I'll parlay it into a mil. Options trading. High-yield bonds. How'd you retards blow through all that money?"

"Little by little and all at once," I say.

"Here's how, Pooch." Colin says. "Perfect example. Frankie had been mixing *Three Chords I* upstate in Mamaroneck. An hour north of the city. One day he wants us to ride up there with him to okay the mixes. We say we'll take the van. 'Screw that,' he says. 'You're rock stars. We'll take a limo.'"

I explain to Pooch that this was a white stretch number—not a Town Car, which is the usual Manhattan ride of choice. It waited for us, long and beautiful, on Madison Avenue. As I climbed in, I imagined that people on the crowded sidewalks were wondering, *Do I know them? Should I ask for an autograph?*

"So we're in the limo," Colin says, "and Frankie says, 'You guys want a beer? A Coke? Champagne? Help yourselves.' So I figured, why not? And I had a Coke."

"Not co*caine,* but Coke," Dave says.

"Coke."

"*Jack* and Coke?" says Pooch.

"A *Coke,* Pooch. A stinkin' Coke," Colin says. "Anyway, months later, we get a statement from Sony, showing where our quarter million went. Here's a bill for sushi. Here's what we spent at the Power Station. Here's what we paid for our apartment. And then it says, 'Limo to Mamaroneck: $1,000.' And below that, 'One Coke: $10.'"

Happy-Funny-Cry.

Twenty-four hours later, we're driving through Raleigh, looking for Slim's Downtown Tavern, last stop before Columbus. With its top-notch jukebox, cheap drinks, and album art on the walls, Slim's is a great rock and roll bar. If I lived in Raleigh, I'd wear a hole in the bar stools.

We load in, and then Thomas O'Keefe shows up, looking just like a tour manager: hooded sweatshirt, Chuck Taylors, BlackBerry. He says the latest advance ticket count at the LC is just shy of one hundred. Doors open in twenty-two hours.

I pull him aside and tell him there's a good chance I'll be living in Wisconsin, Texas, or South Carolina next year. I don't know why exactly, but I expect Thomas to be mad.

"South Carolina would be cool," he says. "You guys play down here all the time anyway. Now you'll just be closer." Then he laughs and says, "But I've got to warn you, in the Pacific Northwest, at this moment, the year is currently 2015. In South Carolina it's still like 1995."

"Awesome," I say. "A chance to do '95 over again."

During soundcheck, Dave again tells us he's quitting. His plan is to play the first song and then walk off stage and take a seat in the crowd, where he'll heckle us. Like the Elvis bit in reverse. "Playing in a band is stupid," he says. But he says it with a smile on his face.

Then Superfan and Superfan II walk through the door, separately, but only five minutes apart.

Colin, Thomas, and I are standing at the bar, talking to Joe the Bartender. "Can somebody please explain to me why Cheap Trick is not in the Rock and Roll Hall of Fame?" Colin says.

"No KISS either," Thomas says.

"I don't get it," says Joe the Bartender. "Every band I know loves Cheap Trick."

"But the hipster New York critics hate them," Thomas says.

Colin says, "You're telling me The Young Rascals, Del Shannon, and, I don't know, Earth, Wind, and fucking Fire are more essential to rock and roll than Cheap Trick?"

"Crazy," Thomas says.

"No doubt," I say. "Gene Pitney and Frankie Lymon sure don't have a bigger hit than 'I Want You to Want Me.'"

"It's the East Coast bias," Colin says. "Just like with baseball. Guys like Dave Concepcion and Omar Vizquel, who played in the Midwest, get overlooked for the Hall of Fame, but dudes like Phil Rizzuto and Pee Wee Reese, guys with worse numbers, get the nod because they played in New York."

Thomas and Joe the Bartender have gone glassy-eyed at the baseball talk, but Colin has me hooked.

"Here's what I'm saying," Colin says. "What if Cheap Trick was from New York and The Ramones were from Rockford?"

"Impossible," Thomas says. "The Ramones *couldn't* be from Rockford. They *are* New York, in musical form. And Cheap Trick *is* the Midwest."

"That Colin's point," I say. "The Midwest is undervalued. New York, Philly, Boston: overvalued."

"I'm just saying," Colin says. "If Cheap Trick was from New York, they're in the Hall of Fame in a second."

"KISS *is* from New York," Thomas says. "And they aren't in."

Colin waves that off. "Bah. Another argument."

Then Biggie rounds us up, and we play the first of two sets to twenty people, but because Slim's is a small place, twenty doesn't look so bad. From the stage I can see that our friend Terry Anderson has shown up. Terry is one of the two or three most underrated lyricists in rock history. He wrote "Battleship Chains" for the Georgia Satellites, and Dan Baird had a minor hit in the early Nineties with Anderson's "I Love You Period," but considering the cleverness of Terry's lyrics and the tunefulness of his melodies, there should be a statue of him floating down a river somewhere. There's not much justice in rock and roll.

We finish the first set, and I'm thinking that if nothing else, this gig is turning out to be a good rehearsal for tomorrow night's show. Then Colin decides to open the second set with five straight Cheap Trick songs. Fuck rehearsing for tomorrow. We play "Oh Claire," "Hello There," "Come On Come On," and "Elo Kiddies," then Thomas grabs Pooch's guitar and joins us on stage for "On Top of the World." Half the crowd stands right in front of the stage, singing every word. The other half looks utterly confused—sort of like when we played as McWatershed.

We say goodnight, then pack up and load out.

The Superfan says, "I'm gonna miss y'all so much." But I fully expect to see her in Columbus in approximately seventeen hours.

Joe the Bartender says, "You guys are my favorite band in the world." At least I think that's what he said. He's so drunk, it came out, *Yhguy ism flacalate bannin thorld.*

When we're all loaded up and ready to roll, Thomas walks over to the van. I crank the passenger window down. He leans his head halfway in and says, "So how's tomorrow going to go?"

"No idea," I say. I look over to Biggie, who's got a dip in and his iPod on. I turn to Dave and Pooch, sitting shoulder to shoulder on the first bench, and Colin, who is already lying horizontal on the second bench. Then I turn back to Thomas. "But I know one thing," I say. "We're not wrong about this."

12

The Best Is Yet to Come
Columbus, Ohio

NORTH OF WINSTON-SALEM, I LEAVE THE COCKPIT TO BIGGIE. "YOU COOL?"
I ask.

The dashboard instruments throw light on his forehead, nose, and mouth. His profile is lit like a waxing moon. "Cool as can be."

"Wake me when you need me." I squeeze between Dave and Pooch, climb over the first bench, and place my toes on the second bench, trying not to wake Colin, who is laid out underneath me. Struggling for balance at eighty miles per hour, I reach over him and grab a pillow and blanket from atop the gear. I drop the ratty linens to the floor and slide into the Spider Hole. My shoulders are just narrow enough to fit between the benches. I lie on my back, knees bent, head pillowed against the van's side molding, my hands linked across my chest like a corpse. After a while my lumbar tightens and shoulder blades ache, so I turn to my side. Now I'm facing the metal bench leg, looking sharp as a guillotine and bolted to the floor precisely level with my neck, If Biggie rear-ends anything, the gear will slam forward, stacking instruments upon guts, upon bone, upon vinyl, plastic, rubber, and glass—like a seven layer dip. I'll surely be decapitated.

As we climb over the Blue Ridge, I dream that I'm sleeping in a van. I dream of potholes and double yellows. Reflective chevrons pointing Biggie through S-curves. Mountain roads so steep, they fold back on themselves like roller coaster loops. Near the apex, the van slows to a stop, then rolls backwards, then falls from the sky.

Then, from deep in my stomach, a feeling too frightening and familiar to be part of the dream: the shudder of brakes. A swerve, a jolt, and the weightless sensation of five tons of steel and humanity skidding across two lanes. The whine of the rumble strips as the tires hit the shoulder. I'm clawing the back of the seat bench, needing to hold tight to anything that's stable. Surely this is it. Finally and inevitably, Watershed goes into the weeds.

I bolt upright. Pull myself to my knees and look out the windshield, certain I'll be staring death in the face. But nothing. Nothing but open road. Up is still up. Down is still down. We're still pushing toward Columbus. Biggie has the van well under control, one hand draped casually over the steering wheel, the other holding a Gatorade bottle. He's chewing Copenhagen, spitting into the bottle, alert and, yes, cool as can be. A driver in the left lane must have slid right into ours, so Biggie swerved out of the way. No big deal. Happens all the time. But when you're down in the Spider Hole, staring at the instrument of your decapitation, any break in the rhythm feels like certain death.

Too soon, I awake again, this time to the clatter of semi-trucks jake-braking. I have to piss so bad, my bladder's squishing like a water balloon. But I can't get up; I'm too tired and too sore. And shit, I left my contact lenses in. The world looks like it's wrapped in wax paper.

"Hey, Joe," Biggie says. He's standing outside the van, possibly at a gas pump. "Ready to do some driving?"

I screw my eyeballs with my fists. Blink like a strobe light. The world is still wax. "Never been readier, Biggie."

We're parked at a travel plaza on the West Virginia turnpike. The Mountain State's roads are beautiful, with top-notch amenities, a testament to the pork rolling success of longtime senators Byrd and Rockefeller. This plaza's got a Starbucks, a TCBY, and a souvenir shop peddling Wild, Wonderful, West Virginia trinkets—like spoon sets and saltshakers. I'm tempted to buy a T-shirt with a fierce-looking wolf on the front, maybe a cap that says MY TWO FAVORITE DANIELS ... CHARLIE AND JACK, but at 7:15 a.m., it's entirely too early for irony.

The map on the wall tells me what I already know: 180 miles to Columbus. In twenty-four hours I'll board a plane for Houston, then on to Sea-Tac, where Kate will be waiting outside the baggage claim.

Between now and then Watershed will play a show that somehow feels too important to fit inside a single day.

"Home crap home," I say, pulling into the practice spot parking lot. In the shotgun seat, Biggie is wrapping up wires and adapters, packing his iPod and satellite radio, and tossing coffee cups and OJ bottles into the trashcan. Dave and Pooch squint awake, patting their jacket pockets for gloves and keys. Colin's morning hair looks as mussed as Springsteen's from the *Darkness on the Edge of Town* cover.

Biggie says he needs us at the LC at 5:00. This means I'll get four good hours of sleep in his attic before soundcheck. No sleep at all for Colin, Dave, and Pooch. It's Saturday. They've got to go home and be dads.

The three of them roll out of the van in a chorus of grunts and *see-ya-laters*, pulling their bags from the back and dragging them across the blacktop toward their cars. Colin roots around his backseat for an ice scraper. The week has left a dusting of snow and a layer of frost on everybody's windshield. Snow is the great Midwestern equalizer: Doesn't matter how tired you are; you still gotta scrape. Biggie and I head for his house, leaving our bandmates at the mercy of their car batteries and defrost systems.

By the time my alarm goes off, Biggie has already gone to pick up Ricki C. for load-in. On the kitchen table, he's left me the keys to his Saturn. As I pull away from the curb, the steering wheel doesn't rotate smoothly, and the left front tire feels wobbly. I roll down the window to get a listen, and the crank knob comes off in my hand. Upon inspection the tire is simply flat and bald. On the way to our career-defining gig, I'll have to track down a gas station air pump.

The Saturn ain't exactly freeway-worthy, so I stick to High Street, tracing the #2 COTA route—the same bus that Colin and I rode to that first Cheap Trick concert. I drive past the site where Stache's (R.I.P.) used to be. It's now a strip mall. I drive past Patterson Avenue, where Watershed was christened in a college-ghetto kitchen. Past Bernie's Bagels, the house that Willie Phoenix built. Past the Newport, where we recorded *Three Chords I* and *II.* Past Apollo's (R.I.P.), the gyro shop where we played our first campus gigs. And past Mr. Brown's (R.I.P.), Little Brother's (R.I.P.), Chelsie's (R.I.P.).

I feel like a grizzled Marine, going back to Khe Sanh, touring the battlefield in a broken down Saturn. I'm driving slowly, partly because I don't want to t-bone this deathtrap into a telephone pole, but also because I'm expecting to divine meaning from the landmarks that have survived—and the ones that haven't. Instead I'm left with a veteran soldier's uncertainty. What exactly were we fighting for? Did we win?

For Watershed the war isn't over. Deep in the most hopeful chambers of our damn-near-middle-aged hearts, we're still convinced that we belong on the big stage, that we should be playing venues like the LC every night. And we're certain that if we can hang together long enough, then somehow, somewhere, we'll get that chance. I don't know if this makes us optimistic or delusional. Even after gutting it out for twenty-plus years, I don't know if the band is a success or a failure.

Down Buttles to Neil Avenue, under the railroad tracks, and into the Arena District—named for Nationwide Arena, home of the Blue Jackets, Columbus's NHL team. Twenty years ago, the gothic Ohio State Penitentiary stood on this site. Now, in the new brick buildings that flank the arena, bars and restaurants occupy the ground floors, while offices and apartments take up the floors above, a shining example of the urban multi-use renaissance. Across the street, the Clippers, our Triple-A baseball team, recently broke ground on a new ballpark, which will give Columbusites another reason to open their wallets. Nationwide Insurance, whose headquarters occupy three nearby skyscrapers, is the primary developer of this part of town, and even though my car insurance premiums helped to build all this,[64] I have to admit the district is pretty damn slick. It's the area that Central Ohio natives show off to out-of-towners. *See? Columbus is cooler than you thought, right?*

The LC anchors the Northwest corner of the Arena District. If the Foo Fighters were headlining, there'd be a security goon standing guard at the loading lot gate, but tonight the gate is unmanned and open, and I pull the Saturn straight on through, parking next to Dave's minivan. No tour busses or semi-trucks tonight. Watershed's Hertz rental sits small and unassuming at the docks.

Opening an unmarked door and walking directly onto the floor, it's like I've stepped into a living diorama: ROCK SHOW SETUP, CIRCA EARLY TWENTY-FIRST CENTURY. Dave is on stage, adjusting his drum hardware and cymbal stands, making changes so subtle, you'd have to be a drummer to notice. Pooch stands next to Ricki C., watching the roadie pull guitars out of their cases. They're both laughing. Biggie, looking serious as a NASA flight engineer, points to the light truss, showing the LC's lighting tech which cans need which color gels. The monitor man frets over his board, chasing down some runaway 16k feedback, while his assistant troubleshoots a bad channel. Down on the floor, bartenders slice limes and lemons and count out their change drawers, while bar-backs ice down coolers and line trashcans. At the merch stand, Ricki C.'s wife, Debbie, artfully displays Watershed T-shirts and CDs. At the front-of-house position, Mike Landolt stands behind the mixing console, swapping mics in and out—57, 58, Beta 58—listening for tonal differences you'd have to be a soundman to hear. To think, all this preparation is happening in service of little songs that Colin and I wrote on the edges of our beds.

From here the LC looks like a hundred other mid-size rock clubs: open floor space with a few tables scattered about and a small balcony ringing the room. Put two thousand people in here, and it's an ideal place to see a show: small enough to be intimate but large enough that something shared and significant might happen. These days rock and roll lives in clubs this size—Bogart's in Cincinnati, First Ave. in Minneapolis, Irving Plaza in New York. Almost nobody can fill a 20,000-seater anymore, not even bands with big radio hits. You can probably count on two hands the acts that would fill Nationwide Arena across the street—AC/DC, Springsteen, The Stones, U2, Green Day, Sesame Street Live, Stars on Ice, The Promise Keepers, a TV mega-churcher or two. The huge outdoor amphitheaters are doing much worse, the camp-and-rock festivals having made them obsolete. The sheds that are still operating have to package three or four classic rockers onto a bill in order to stay afloat. Even so, the promoters usually do two-for-one lawn seats, hoping to make their margin in concessions and parking. Who other than Jimmy Buffett and Dave Matthews can justify a whole tour of cornfield-size venues anymore? Here in Columbus, Polaris Amphitheater, where Watershed played to a crowd of ten thousand a week before getting dropped by Epic, is now out of business.

The LC is built to capitalize on the downsizing of both arena- and amphitheater-rock. It's two venues in one—indoor club and outdoor mini-shed. When the weather abides, the stage's back wall slides open to a grassy hill, with seats and lawn space for 4,500. If it looks like rain, you slide the wall shut and turn the gear around to face the inside. One stage, two configurations. The LC may be a cramped step down for The Doobies and Skynyrd and all the other ex-arena acts that now play here, but I'm worried that for Watershed—and our 125 fans, which is where the advance ticket count currently stands—the LC is going to feel big and lonely as Wyoming.

"Check-two," Mike Landolt is barking into the PA. "Check-two." The sound carries through the room like a basketball dribbled in an empty gym.

"How's she feeling?" I say.

"Like a hotdog down a hallway." He switches again from the 58 to the Beta. *Check-two.* "Get five hundred warm bodies in here and I'll be happy."

I punch him on the shoulder and say, "Me too."

Ricki C. walks up, carrying the money pouch Debbie will use to make change at the merch stand. "How were the shows?" he says, smiling wide. The guy's fifty-five and outfitted with a pacemaker. He's been roadying for thirty years, and still, for him soundcheck might as well be Christmas Eve.

I tell him about New Band Nite in Baltimore. "*You* should have been the one lecturing those kids about rock and roll."

"Rule number one, kiddies," he says, turning toward the merch stand. "Fill your bathtubs all the way up."

Now Colin walks in from the parking lot. He's brought Erin and Owen with him. Four-and-a-half and holding his dad's hand, Owen looks overwhelmed by the hubbub. If he could tuck his head inside his body turtle-style, he surely would.

Colin points Owen toward Dave's drum set, and Erin smiles and walks my way. She's a thin and pretty blonde, which must make her the envy of the other Montessori moms. We hug. "How's Kate?" she says.

"Hanging in there."

"Anxious for you to get home, I bet."

I nod and exhale as slow as the Saturn's leaky tire.

"Yeah," she says. "I know." Then she dials her smile up and says, "What's the latest on the job search?" She seems genuinely interested—and not just because she's a professional counselor who gets paid to be interested. Whenever Colin asks me about the jobs, I get the sense that he's really asking, *What does all this mean for me?* But with Erin there is no subtext; she just wants Kate and me to be happy.

I tell her that I'm still in the running for three positions, but I don't say that they're all five hundred miles from here. Then I ask how her counseling practice is going, and she says fine; it's scary going alone, but she's excited. I'm sure it *is* going fine, but Colin has told me enough about their finances to know that with two struggling small businesses—the coffee shop and the practice—money is tight. Neither of them brings home a steady paycheck. Colin eventually went back to OSU and graduated with a communications degree, but the idea of him working a nine-to-five job is laughable. I can no more see Colin manning a cubicle at Nationwide than I can see Willie Phoenix processing annuities. Still I wonder if Erin ever says to Colin, *I've supported Watershed for a long time. Now I need you to support my dream. One of us needs to get a job with a consistent salary, and guess what, mister. It's your turn.*

Erin is in no way asking for sympathy, and yet I sympathize with her anyway. I know better than anyone what it's like to be married to Colin. Kate's right: he and I *are* a couple, married so long we lovingly overlook the parts of the other that get on our nerves. Colin's lack of focus, his blindness to detail, his over-compensating optimism—these are as infuriating to me as my wussy pragmatism and occasional disloyalty must be to him. We both know, however, that the relationship is stronger than these petty annoyances, so we put down the toilet seat the other has left up, pick the dirty towel off the floor, and move on, anchored by the depth of experience we've shared. Like all life-partners, we slip comfortably into the roles we've assumed. My role is to sift through the hundred insane ideas Colin has every day and pick out the two good ones. His role is to try to sell me on the other ninety-eight. One of those might be a package sent to a KISS soundman, another might be a drummer that'll get good with a little time.

Being in a band with Colin is always exhausting. Sometimes it's fucking infuriating. If the thirty-eight-year-old Joe were to meet the thirty-eight-year-old Colin now, for the first time, would either of us say, "This is a guy I want to go into business with. This is a guy I want to spend my life with"? I don't know. Maybe not.

I'll always play second fiddle to Colin because he's Watershed's magnetic north, the only personality forceful enough to lead us. The band is and forever will be his, regardless of who sings or writes what. But I'm fine with that now. Like he often says, the best bands have *too much* talent. Think: The Beatles, The Replacements, The Clash. The challenge is binding all that talent together. Eventually musicians, like athletes, get frustrated with their lack of playing time and start to believe, what this band needs is more *me*. But I never would have grown into *me* without him. And even now, if I could go back again to that COTA bus when Colin first said, "We have to start a band," I'd still shrug and say okay and that would be that.

I nod toward the stage, where Owen is armed with two drumsticks, stabbing Dave's kit to death. "What are you going to do when Owen wants to start a band?" I say to Erin.

She smiles. "Oh, Joe. Believe me. He already has." She tells me that Colin and Owen have started jamming together in the basement: Colin on guitar, Owen on drums. They call themselves The Rancors and sound like an out-of-tune AC/DC.

On tour Colin carries a photo of Owen, which he uses as a bookmark. Every once in a while he takes it out and stares at it. After many, many High Lifes at AC's in Charleston, Colin shook his head in wonder and said, seemingly out of nowhere, "Owen Gawel is just the coolest dude."

Then he told us how once, when he was driving Owen home from the zoo, the *Jaws* theme came over the radio. Owen, who'd never before heard the song, said "Uh-oh. That doesn't sound good."

Colin laughed, amazed that the dark melody could convey so much meaning, even to a four-year-old. He then explained that the music was from a movie about a shark.

"Can we watch it?" asked Owen.

"Owen, if I let you watch *Jaws,* I guarantee it: You'd poop your pants." Colin tousled his son's hair and said, "Daddy'd poop his pants too."

Colin and Owen then headed down to the basement and wrote a song called "Jaws." The chorus: *Hungry-hungry-hungry-hungry! Grumpy-grumpy-grump-grumpy!*

As Erin and I talk, we gravitate toward the stage, where father and son are beating hell out of the drums. They've got Biggie, Dave, and Pooch singing along: *Hungry-hungry-hungry-hungry! Grumpy-grumpy-grumpy-grumpy!*

Erin gives me a look that says, *See what I deal with at home?* "Okay, buddy," she says, grabbing Owen from behind and lifting him away from Dave's stool. It's impressive to watch her shift into mom mode. "We've got to get you home. Let's leave the rocking to the big kids."

Five minutes till doors. I wonder if anyone is camped at the entrance, waiting to be let in. High school boys, hidden under their hoodies, listening to "Suckerpunch" on their iPods. Girls huddling together for warmth, with *Watershed* Bic-penned on their jeans, on the soles of their

Chuck Taylors, on the backs of their hands. I wonder if there's a line at all. Of any length.

It's safest to assume not. Mediating expectations is everything.

Colin, Ricki C., and I are hanging around the dressing room. No gold foil star on the door. Instead: a sheet of computer paper that reads *Watershed*, and a shower with five clean towels. I'm temped to rinse off just because I can. Instead I reach into the Budweiser-stocked micro-fridge, drop next to Colin on the leatherette couch, and stare at *SportsCenter* on the flat screen. This dressing room is nicer than Watershed's $1,700/ month New York apartment. A guy could get used to this rock star treatment—but he'd better not.

Biggie walks in, carrying his laptop. "Check this out," he says, tilting the monitor so Colin and I can see. It's an e-mail from Erv at Idol Records telling us that we've been offered a showcase at South By Southwest in Austin.

"Holy shit!" says Colin.

"Okay!" says Ricki C., looking like a proud older brother.

We first tried to get into SXSW in 1991, but year after year we were rejected. We couldn't even squeeze in when we were on Epic. Then, two years ago, we finally made the cut. We figured that would be it. One and done. How great it is to be wrong. But now this has me thinking about Kate's e-mail: "I won't do this again for any reason. I mean it."

Colin turns to me. "We've got to do this, right?"

"I'm in," Biggie says.

Colin pushes himself out of the couch. "I mean, *of course* we're doing this."

Kate needs to understand that SXSW isn't *any* reason. It's *the* reason, like finding your CD in a record bin, like hearing your song in the background of a TV show. Playing an official SXSW showcase is the music business telling you that you *matter*, if only the tiniest bit.

"South By Southwest is in March, right?" Colin says to me. "So it might fall during your spring break."

Besides, playing SXSW will be plain fucking fun. It's like those bumper stickers that say THE WORST DAY FISHING IS BETTER THAN THE

BEST DAY AT WORK. Even if nothing bites at SXSW, we'll still have a hell of a time drinking beer and telling lies. The big break might not be out there, but we *have* to keep going, *have* to keep playing shows like SXSW, in order to make ourselves available for all the little breaks. You've heard the expression "death by a million paper cuts"? Watershed has lived by a million tiny victories.

"Don't worry about spring break," I say, looking from Colin to Biggie and back. "We're playing South By Southwest no matter when it falls." I'll slide the idea past Kate later, from home, after the dust from this tour has settled.

Now Dave walks in, and Colin tells him the good news. I can tell by his reaction that he doesn't necessarily see it as good. He sees another argument over money, time, priorities.

"You've got a slush fund you can pull from, right, Dave?" Colin says. "An account the wife doesn't know about?"

The room goes silent as the weight of this sinks in. "Do you?!" I ask Colin.

Colin laughs. "I got the coffee shop, baby. My money's already laundered."

In walks Pooch, who says no problem, count him in. Soon Dave relents as well. "I'll make it happen somehow," he says.

"Mr. Biggie," Colin says. "Tell Erv we're in. Watershed's coming down to mess with Texas."

Doors have been open for an hour, and as much as I want to walk out to the floor to size up the crowd, I'm too afraid of disappointment to do it. Instead, I slide through the stage door and out to the wings, where I lean against the wall, in a spot where the monitor board and side-fills block my view of the audience. I stand up straight, trying to look like I'm here in support of the opening band, who are now deep into their second song.

Tonight's opener is The Receiver, local guys who practice in the same building as us. They're a young two-piece, a literal band of brothers. One brother drums, the other sings and plays bass, keyboards, and guitar. We're friends with these guys, so I want to like their music, but, man, I just don't get it. To me they sound like Radiohead, but even more experimental and ponderous—all bleeps and bloops and self-indulgent passages that are so damn long, I swear I can see the singer's beard growing.

I wonder if I'm staring into a generational divide. Watershed belongs to the last wave of bands that dreamed big—of signing big contracts, playing big venues, acting larger than life on stage. Our generation modeled ourselves after the arena-rockers we grew up with. We begged our moms for Christmas guitars because we loved Springsteen and Aerosmith, KISS and Van Halen—bands who played to the back row. Our heroes picked up guitars because they'd watched The Beatles on *Ed Sullivan.* And The Beatles did it because they'd heard Elvis and Chuck Berry, Carl Perkins and Eddie Cochran. The Receiver is part of the fifth wave, kids who grew up post-Nirvana and whose worldview is beyond corporate rock. Their heroes, even those like Radiohead who can fill arenas, have always been uneasy with *big.*

Like a lot of bands we've played with lately, The Receiver doesn't seem to be trying to actually entertain anyone. There's no *show* in their *biz.* They're playing their instruments in cocoons of precious concentration, their attention focused on their fingers, rather than on the audience. Their body language gives no indication they're standing in front of an audience at all. The LC might as well be their practice room.

To be sure, in our day there were bands that were too cool (or scared, which is really the same thing) to expose the vulnerability that entertaining requires: shoegazers, art-school hipsters, prog-rockers, punks. But most of these bands still wanted (and expected) to be huge. What's new today, in addition to the passive stage show and thin sound, is the smallness of the career aspirations. Current alt-rock bands set out for niche, rather than mass. They're content to offer up pâté on water crackers, whereas Watershed, for better or worse, wants to dish out a heaping plate of pot roast and potatoes.

Colin and I have always tried to be *transmitters,* rather than receivers. We try to interact with the crowd, making them part of the show, bridging the divide between the stage and the floor. The Receiver is the perfect name for this band, because everything about them points inward. Their songs seem ready-made for earbuds, rather than woofers. They might as well be playing under glass. And yet, when they finally finish the bleeping and blooping song, they get a roaring response. I'm happy because this means the crowd is bigger than I can see from here, but I'm confused. How can an audience care so much about a band that seems to care so little about them? More importantly, how can *our* audience care so much?

All the meat and spuds in the world don't mean spit unless you've got a hungry crowd to dish 'em out to. And by the time The Receiver finishes their set, it's clear that for the first time on this tour, we've got one—an actual crowd. I head back toward the dressing room, and standing in front of the door marked WATERSHED, I take a deep breath.

Inside we crack beers, make repeated trips to the bathroom, take bets on which of the Superfans will show up. Then Biggie walks through the door. "We're set to pop," he says. As he Maglites the way, we follow him to the side of the stage.

Colin hops a few times and says, "This is it, motherbitch."

Dave twists a pair of drumsticks in his hand to warm up his forearms. I grab him by the shoulders. "How you feeling there, Catman?"

"It's not too late to cancel," he says.

Pooch laughs. "Is it too late to quit?"

"You're stuck, fuckers," Colin says. "Watershed is like the mafia. No one gets out alive. Except, you know, Herb." And with that he walks behind the curtain that leads to stage right.

"See you out there," I say to him.

Colin turns around and says, "Always."

Then Biggie flashes his Maglite toward Mike Landolt at the soundboard. The houselights go black. The crowd erupts.

It's showtime.

I walk out of the wings and onto the stage. There's a blast of applause from the audience, and the cheers are thick enough to float on, charged enough to conduct electricity. Colin flips the standby on his amp and lets loose a hundred-watt chord. Pooch fires back. I aim for my bass, drape it over my shoulder. Strap solid, volume knob up, instrument cable sitting tight in the jack, I hit the E-string. Sounds like a shock wave. I look out to the crowd, a silhouetted mass of heads and shoulders. I smile and nod at Colin. Let's crush these motherfuckers. The band is suddenly a spring, wound and hardened, a store of energy.

Then Colin tears into the opening riff of "Obvious," the lead track on *The Fifth of July*, and Pooch and I uncoil, jumping in tandem as we kick-in with Dave on the downbeat. The lights flare at the exact same time. There's a rock and roll show happening here. I head toward the front of the stage, to the lip right in front of the PA stacks. Colin's standing in the same spot on the other side, already sweating like Jackie Wilson. Head bopping to the beat, I point my chin into the crowd. Hundreds, maybe a thousand. Male, female, young and old, with faces I don't recognize. Then Dave pops his snare twice to drop us into the verse, and I slide over to my mic stand. I rest my lips on the ball of the microphone, catch my breath, and start to sing.

I want to slow time, to make this set last long enough to appreciate what it means that after twenty-three years anybody still gives a shit about the band Colin and I started on a city bus. That my mom, dad, and sister are somewhere out in that audience. That this time tomorrow I'll be 2,500 miles from this stage, back to Tacoma and Kate and the life I've constructed in order to make this show possible. But there's no slowing time. Before my brain catches up to my fingers, the set is over.

I'm standing alone by the dressing room door, wiping the sweat from my face with my T-shirt. My right wrist is blistered bloody from pounding against my bass for two hours.

"Thank You!" Colin is saying to the cheering crowd. "Thank You! Thank You!"

I bend over and breathe deeply, like a basketball player grabbing the front of his shorts at the free throw line. I'm thinking what a shame it is that success in the music business is always measured one of two ways: commercial or critical. Bon Jovi or Big Star. Platinum records or indie-cred. How do you gauge a band like Watershed, that doesn't score all that high by either standard? Standing here in the hallway, with the crowd chanting "Wa-ter-shed," I sure don't feel like a failure. But are we a success? There must be some other way to compute it, one that doesn't depend on the acceptance of record buyers *or* rock critics. Staking a career on the capricious tastes of either is like anchoring a boat in Cool Whip.

If you're a real pro, you don't worry about success.

I know this.

You're confident that if you concentrate on the work, the success will come.

I know this.

You do the work for only one reason: because you can't not do it.

I know this. I know this. I know this.

But these platitudes only mean something when they come from the mouths of winners. When losers sling this crap, it sounds like a justification for failure, like saying *the sun got in my eyes.* Winners catch the ball anyway. Their points show up on the JumboTron, not in self-affirmations and excuses. Because in this life we fucking keep score.

There are days when I still get mad that our stint in The Pros was so short. Dammit, if we can draw a crowd like tonight's in our hometown, we should be able to do it in every city, every night. If only our luck had been a little better, then maybe we'd be packing houses from coast to coast. But blaming bad luck is too easy, I guess. It could be that we were missing some intangible *it.* If so, we sure tried to make up for it in hard work, show after show, year after year.

I wonder if we'd be happier now if, on that bus ride home from the Cheap Trick show, the devil would have been sitting in the seat behind us, saying, *You're never going to make it, fellas. Never, ever, ever. Now, tell me. Do you still want to start a band?*

We would have said *fuck you, devil* and formed the band anyway.

Because *making it* for us meant something different than for a lot of other bands. Money and fame would have been nice, sure, but I think what we wanted most of all was to be *included*—in the scene, in the record store, in the critical conversation. We wanted the chance to stick around the big leagues for years and years, like KISS and Cheap Trick. The odds against a career like that were so astronomically huge, I suppose the cause was lost from the beginning. But we were too young to know that, thank God. Now we're too old to stop. Loyal to a doomed mission, fighting a war that's long settled, still blind and battling windmills.

What exactly were we fighting for? Did we win?

Tough to say. If we had played to a 2,200-person sellout tonight, then we would have earned the miraculous come-from-behind ending that the movies tell us we deserve: The underdog Watershed outskates the Russians, outboxes Apollo Creed, outkarates Cobra Kai. Likewise, if we had totally bombed, drawing something like a hundred, that would have put a sad but equally conclusive endnote on the tour, and, maybe, on the career. Watershed crumbles to the mat because a loser is a loser is a loser.

Real life rarely gives you the definitive answer.

A half hour from now Biggie will walk into the dressing room and tell us that tonight's crowd totaled 771, which is, of course, 771 more than a shutout but 1,429 shy of a sellout. I'll be mildly disappointed for about five seconds. I'll say that from the stage the crowd looked bigger. But then I'll take two beers from the fridge, hand one to Colin, and tell him nice job. "Playing the LC was the right call," I'll say. "A total fucking blast."

He'll smile as if I've finally learned something that he's known all along.

Then I'll crack open my beer and settle next to him onto the couch. Maybe Watershed wasn't lucky enough to be in the same league as KISS or Cheap Trick, but my guess is that Joe The Animal and Ken and Kellie and Hot Sandy and a few dozen more fans around the country would call us one of their all-time favorite bands. That makes us awfully damn lucky.

Now Dave and Pooch push through the stage door into the hallway where I'm standing. "Wa-ter-shed!" The crowd is chanting. "Wa-ter-shed! Wa-ter-shed!" They want an encore.

Colin bounds in behind them. "Crushing!" he says, shouldering past us and into the dressing room. He takes four beers from the fridge, passes them around.

Biggie and Ricki C. walk in. "Hey, ladies," Biggie says.

The six of us stand there, circled around Colin, like a meeting at the pitcher's mound.

"So what are we doing?" Biggie says. "Are we done, or are you going back on?"

Colin's buzzing on trucker speed. "Fuck yeah, we're going back on." He breaks the circle and opens the stage door.

I'm the last one out, a few steps behind the other five. As soon as the crowd sees Colin, they go nuts. Dave settles in behind his kit. Pooch flips on his amp. Now I walk into the lights. Another surge from the crowd. I grab my bass and step right to the front of the stage, toes hanging over the edge. I raise my arms, a beer in one hand. With the other I wave the crowd louder, louder still. Then Colin and Pooch launch into the intro for "Mercurochrome." Sometimes rock and roll is like Mercurochrome, that old fashioned anti-septic: the more it hurts, the more it works.

As I wait for Colin to count out the kick-in, I take a swig from my beer, a one-gun salute—*FIRE!*—to all the bands who will lug their amps out of a van and into a rock club tonight. On this night in America, for every band lucky enough to be playing an encore for a chanting crowd, there are a thousand more that will play for nobody. They'll tear down and load out, and they'll sleep on stained carpets and on couches with cigarette holes burned into the upholstery. Tomorrow— just like today, just like yesterday—they'll hit the highway wondering where the gas money's coming from. At the Pilots and Flying Js and T/As, they'll eat beef jerky and three-for-a-buck hot dogs. They'll throw down credit cards for mirrored sunglasses and foam-front Bassmasters hats. In their tight T-shirts and skinny jeans they'll draw stares from the truckers. They'll fish for quarters to get their weight and lucky numbers. Then they'll climb into their rusty Fords and Chevys and Dodges, and they'll barrel down the interstate, counting the miles to the next gig.

After the show, Biggie and Ricki C. drive the gear to the practice site. Dave and Pooch go home to their wives and kids. Colin and I hop into his Impala and head over to Andyman's Treehouse—the bar co-owned by CD101's Andy Davis—to celebrate. The place is a musicians' hangout, and bands play in the back room, where there's a fifty-foot silver maple growing out of the floor and up through the ceiling. Colin and I do whiskey shots with the six-foot-something, three hundred pound Andyman, and we thank him and the station for being so good to us.

"I heard the LC was packed," he says, putting his huge hand around the back of my neck. "A thousand, at least." I don't correct him. He buys another round.

The bar is crowded with people who've just arrived from the LC: our buddies from the Patterson days, Kate's friends, band dudes and scenesters. Colin and I work the room for a while, but eventually we land at the same table. "End of tour party," I say, raising my beer to him.

"Sometimes these things can be so dismal," he answers.

Then somebody mentions that Willie Phoenix is playing in the tree room, so Colin and I head back there and find a spot to stand against the wall. Willie and his band are set up in the corner, rocking though "Gasoline," his most recent almost-hit. His dreads are gone now, and a knit hat covers his bald skull, but his dark skin and elastic body look no different than when we used to open for him at Ruby Tuesday. He's fifty-five, and the room is packed with twenty- and thirty-something women who ogle Willie the way women ogle Prince, and when Willie sings, his voice sounds like a young Rod Stewart, like a young Little Richard. Like a young Willie Phoenix. Here is living proof that a life in rock and roll keeps you from growing old. But that's not why everybody's clapping and singing and staring with mouths agape. We're all clapping and singing and staring because, even if nobody outside Franklin County knows it, Willie Phoenix is a star.

Launching into the guitar solo, Willie immediately breaks *two* strings, but it doesn't faze him. He keeps on rocking, soloing with his teeth, behind his head, between his legs. Then he throws his Strat to the ground and humps it and strokes it. This is a fifty-five-year-old man, wearing tights, rolling around on the dirty carpet of a tiny bar, simulating intercourse with a musical instrument. And it's the single best thing I've seen since I said goodbye to Kate at Port Columbus.

As Willie plays on, I'm thinking about how Kate once asked me if I wanted to end up like him, slugging it out in crap bars into my fifties. I said that that was the last thing I wanted. Said I'd quit right now if that was my future. Thought I had too much pride to hang on that long. But now, watching Willie hop to his feet and lead the crowd in one final, rip-roaring chorus, I see nothing *but* pride. The last thing I want is to *not* be playing at fifty. It takes way more pride to keep going than it does to quit.

Willie says goodnight long past last-call, and Colin and I make for the doors. We're standing in the alley out front, buttoning our coats and pulling on our hats, saying goodbye to the stragglers. This exit-scene reminds me of the night a few years ago when The Smithereens' Pat DiNizio played Andyman's on a solo acoustic tour. After the show I stood in this very spot, helping him load his gear into his car. We talked about the 1995 tour, about how everyone connected to that tour—Ben Folds, Sixpence, Nada Surf—everyone except The Smithereens and Watershed, went on to have big hits. Then we shook hands, and he drove away. Ten minutes later, I was still standing out front, talking to the doorman, when Pat pulled back up.

"What'd you forget, Pat?" I said.

He rolled down the window. "I forgot to tell you something."

I could hear *The More It Hurts, The More It Works* playing on his car stereo: the fourth track, "Over Too Soon."

"Come here, *paisan*," he said.

I leaned against the car door.

"I want you to know that you guys made a hit record here," he said. "It may never show up on the charts. Hell, you might not sell another frickin' copy. But I can't leave tonight without telling you that whatever happens, you and your boys should be proud. This record is a fucking hit." He reached up and smacked me on the side of the head. "*Kapeesh?*"

From the bar, Colin drives me to Biggie's. We sit in the car in front of Biggie's house, proud, both of us.

"Fucking good show," I say.

"Maybe our best ever," Colin says.

I'm gathering my duffel bag and looking for my keys, feeling like I should say more. But then headlights appear in the rearview. We have to make the goodbye quick.

"All right, man," he says. "Have a safe flight."

I get out, stand in the street. "Keep Dave and Pooch from flaking out, okay."

Colin nods, points between me and him, and says, "*This* is the band. Right here. You and me."

Four hours later, Biggie finally gets his chance to be an airport shuttle service. We stop at the LC, pick up the Saturn, then head to Port Columbus, where I have a plane to catch and he has a rental van to return.

We stand in the lot outside the Hertz counter, and he says, "What's it gonna take to get you and Colin to make another album together?"

"I don't know," I say. "Time, maybe."

"That's cool," he says. "Time's the one thing we got."

We hug, hard, and then he stuffs himself into the Saturn and tears off. I walk toward the terminal and board a jet for home, for Kate.

By the time I land at Sea-Tac, the sun has already set. I ride the escalator down to baggage claim and the arrivals curb. The sliding doors part, and there's Kate, pulling up in our Accord. I smile and wave. She pops out of the driver's seat and hustles around the car to the sidewalk.

"Hey, honey," I say, spreading my arms.

She pulls my bag off my shoulder, lets it fall to the ground, and wraps her arms around me. She nestles her head against the side of my face. "I'm so proud of you," she says.

I take off my gloves and run my fingers through her hair. "You don't know how good it feels to hear that."

"I love the band, Joe. I *love* it." She hugs me tighter. "I just miss you."

"I miss you too," I say, and we stand there on the sidewalk, holding a long embrace, until the airport cop whistles us onward.

Two months later, Kate and I are again at Sea-Tac, where she's dropping me off for a flight to Austin and South By Southwest. For this trip she didn't need any convincing. "This is the kind of meaningful show I want you to play," she said, demanding only that I have fun.

Colin, Biggie, Dave, and Pooch make the 1,200-mile trip in a rented minivan, and three hours before the show, we gather in a motel room and have one stripped-down practice. I play an acoustic guitar. Dave slaps his sticks on the guitar case. And that night, in front of a nice crowd, we tear the place up. It's comfortable and easy—as if we'd played the LC the night before, rather than back in January.

Later, on Sixth Street, Colin, Biggie, and I are sitting in the open front window of a bar called Shakespeare's. We're drinking PBR tall boys and eating pizza slices, trying to talk over the combined racket of fifty bands, leaking from fifty clubs up and down Sixth. The street is blocked off to traffic, filled curb to curb with musicians either hurrying toward a gig or winding down from one. Wrist-banded fans scan their programs and plot their next move. Through the open window we watch the bearded, tattooed, and shaggy-haired swim past like fish in an aquarium. Between beers I tell Colin and Biggie that I've accepted a job offer from Coastal Carolina University, just outside Myrtle Beach.

"That's great, man," Biggie says, grabbing my shoulder and shaking my hand. "Congrats."

The good news, I say, is that I'll have summers off, a long winter break, and spring break in March. All told, teaching college isn't a bad day job for a musician. The bad news, of course, is that I'll have to live 650 miles from Columbus in order to do it. "But they've offered Kate a job too," I say. "Which is a real coup."

"We'll make it work somehow," Colin says. "We always do." He takes a pull on his Pabst. "As a matter of fact, this might end up being better. Now we've got a toehold in the Southeast. We should start planning a tour for the summer. Myrtle Beach, Wilmington, Chapel Hill, Atlanta . . ."

As Colin's wheels churn, Biggie pulls a sheet of newsprint from his back pocket and says, "I brought this for you."

It's a copy of *The Other Paper*, a review of the January LC show. I read it right there in the bar, as Sixth Street flows past the window.

Before Saturday, it had been quiet on the Watershed front for quite a while. Even though the band released the live album Three Chords and a Cloud of Dust II *in September. . . for a band that majors in loud, messy, catchy rock and roll and has been known to hit the road for long stretches, one show in 365 days is a distinct change of pace. So Saturday night at the LC was a comeback of sorts, a chance for the band to reacquaint itself with hometown fans who have been (im)patiently waiting for a triumphant return. But the question that seemed to be on everyone's minds—the elephant in the room, so to speak—was: After almost twenty years, does Watershed still have it, or is the band finally past its prime?*

Fortunately the time off has only reinvigorated the band, because these seasoned professionals sound as good as ever. It certainly wasn't perfect, but Watershed doesn't really aim for perfection. The band thrives on spontaneity, and there's a certain amount of sloppiness that comes along with that. There were some flubbed chords and missed notes—Gawel's voice in particular seemed to be going towards the end of the night—but Watershed's contagious energy and onstage charisma made the dents and scratches all seem like part of the show. I'll take some minor infractions in exchange for an invigorated performance.

There's nothing sloppy about Watershed's songwriting, though. Taking lessons from Cheap Trick, the Kinks, and the Replacements, the band hasn't written a song that you can't sing along with by the second chorus. But what separates Watershed from the power pop herd is that Gawel and Oestreich actually write good lyrics to go along with those choruses. Neither are afraid to write with sincerity while performing with playfulness.

The two singers use the dual-vocal attack successfully and sound their best when both are contributing. Oestreich showed his impressive range and clarity on "5th of July" and "Anniversary," especially during the latter's refrain. "Suckerpunch" and "Mercurochrome," both fist-pumping rock songs, sounded particularly fresh and vital.

Watershed drew a respectable crowd, especially for a Columbus band, but at a venue like the LC, it still felt sparse. A smaller showcase might have suited the band's return better.

I laugh at this last line, punch Colin on the shoulder and say I told him so.

Then Biggie drains his beer and says, "Let's go-fucking-go." And the three of us step out of the bar and onto Sixth Street, disappearing into the throng of wannabes, shouldabeens, and those who already are.

LINER NOTES

1. All career-making live albums have a sequel. Think: *KISS Alive II, Cheap Trick at Budokan II, Frampton Comes Alive II,* et al. *Three Chords II* is, of course, the follow-up to our 1994 live release, *Three Chords and a Cloud of Dust.* Trouble is the original *Three Chords* wasn't exactly career-making. It was pretty much ignored.

2. The worst? Norm's basement in Lansing, Michigan. Moldy couch cushions on the wet floor, next to the cat litter box. Norm was a great guy, but these accommodations were so horrifying, we'd play Rock, Paper, Scissors for the privilege of sleeping in the van, even in the winter.

3. Biggie always drives first and longest. New York to Detroit? Cincinnati to Minneapolis? It's nothing for him to drive ten hours straight. I'm next off the bench, specializing in big city maneuvers. Colin is the overnight man who'll pull us through the critical 4:00 a.m. to 8:00 a.m. block. The other guys would be happy to pitch in, but like a ballclub in the postseason, Watershed works best on a three-man rotation.

4. We'll later find out that the owner of the Points East has been arrested for viewing child pornography, but I still applaud him for running a great rock club at a time when great rock clubs are as rare as steam-powered trains.

5. A real club named in honor of the fictional Shank Hall from *This is Spinal Tap.*

6. Trucker speed. *See also:* Stingers.

7. Choosing a band name is an infuriating business. All names sound stupid at first, because they haven't had time to signify anything beyond what the words themselves mean. The Beatles sounds perfect and obvious to us now, but that's only because we recognize it as a reference to The *Beatles.* When the lads first adopted the name, it was simply a misspelling of the hard-shelled insect. The Beatles became The *Beatles* over time. This is why most musicians end up choosing not the name that each member *likes best,* but the name that each *hates least.* The Wire looked cool, it sounded cool, and I had no idea what it meant, unless it was a reference to an actual piece of, well, wire. When we found out that there was already a British band called Wire, we yawned. Q-FM-96 didn't play them, so how big could they be? Bigger than Triumph? Bigger than Zebra, even?

8. Most clubs consider their bands' food and drink checks to be a steady revenue stream, the one tab they can count on.

9. Here's the true story Ricki often tells about how rock and roll literally saved his life:

I was thirteen years old in October 1965. Eighth grade just was not working out. I had been a shy, book-reading kid, and now hormones were kicking in. I just knew I would never know how to talk to girls. One really bad Saturday night I decided to kill myself.

I had it all worked out. I had seen a movie just that week about a guy getting electrocuted when a radio fell into the bathtub he was in. So I went around the house and found a radio with a cord long enough to reach the tub. I ran the bath, plugged in the radio, settled into the warm water, said a little prayer of forgiveness, and let the radio drop. But I hadn't filled the tub high enough. Just before the radio hit the water the plug pulled out of the wall. This was an old-fashioned tube radio, so I got a nasty shock, but it didn't kill me. I lifted the radio out and lay there in the water a few minutes to let my head clear. Then I decided to try again. I ran more water until I was sure I had the right level for the job.

When I plugged the radio back in, WCOL-AM was playing "Get Off My Cloud," the new single by the Rolling Stones. I stood there naked, dripping and chilly, eighth-grade skinny, and I listened to the whole song. At that moment I loved that song more than I loved life itself. And then a thought came very clearly into my head: "What if the next Rolling Stones single is even better than this one, and I never get to hear it?"

I set the radio on the sink, got back in the tub, took a bath, and went to bed. If Wayne Newton's "Danke Schoen" or "Red Roses for a Blue Lady" by Bobby Vinton had been playing on the radio, I'd be dead now.

10. A band should, of course, be thankful that *anyone* comes to see them, because there are so many constructive things a person might do rather than spend four hours in a loud, smoky bar: learn to speak German, drain the hot water heater, finally get serious about reading the Russians, etc.

11. As Colin says, hot chicks don't need to be fans of anybody. They have fans of their own.

12. On the day we bought our first van, we made a bet: First guy to have sex in the van with someone other than his girlfriend wins a steak dinner. The prize went unclaimed for nearly ten years. The eventual winner was a friend from Worthington, a mid-level purchasing manager who was along for the ride. And because he earned more in a day than Watershed did in a week, he went easy on us. Sirloin and eggs at Waffle House.

13. The night in Atlanta when we first met Ken, Colin invited him to ride with us to the next night's show in Augusta. We let him crash on the floor of our motel room.

14. My suggested tagline for the Convention and Visitor's Bureau: COLUMBUS? NO SHIT?

15. A local bar that was suing the national restaurant chain for rights to the Ruby Tuesday name.

16. When we started the band, Colin and I had tried to write together. Our first attempt was for English class. We recorded a tune called "Trading Memories," based on *The Grapes of Wrath*. The teacher gave us a C. Our first bad review from a doesn't-know-shit critic.

17. Yes, it does kind of suck to be mocked by another band's sales award.

18. But this brings us back to an argument against touring: The *idea* of fucking Angelina Jolie is probably better than actual, in-the-flesh sex with her (and her hang-ups and attending baggage). The real Angie can't possibly compare to the fantasy Angie that her images have allowed us to create. Similarly, our idea of what a band will sound like in person is often way better than the real thing. Most bands simply aren't that good live, so they use click tracks, drum loops, and sampled backing vocals to augment their sound and thereby inch closer to our idea of them (or *their* idea of our idea of them). Maybe it's in these bands' best interest *not* to tour. They should exist *solely* on the Internet—like Angelina Jolie does, come to think of it.

19. In Athens we played a tiny bohemian bar where our opening "act" was a slideshow called "Demystifying the Penis." It's hard to rock-out-with-your-cock-out after seeing in graphic detail how small your cock is compared to every other mammal.

20. Or maybe this was just a dream. A happy, happy dream.

21. CBs was famous *because* they opened their doors to bands, not because they locked bands out.

22. When we were The Wire, we played Stache's in the pre-Dougan interim, when the place had been owned by Greek Pete. Pete's slogan was STACHE'S—THE HOUSE OF GOOD BANDS. Not Great, just Good. One night, as we tore down our gear, Pete stomped up on stage. He was a bear of a man. "Next time, we dress you guys up like girls," he said.

Colin looked at me. I was just as confused as he was.

"So the fags will come," Pete said. He smiled, waiting for us to acknowledge the brilliance of the plan. "Once the place is asshole-to-asshole with fags, we lock the doors, beat them up, and take their money." He laughed and hit Colin on the shoulder. "Just kidding, guys. We'll stick with what you're doing." As he walked to the bar he turned back toward us and said, "But let me know if you want to try the other thing."

23. Lots of cities were being called the next Seattle, of course. But in Columbus, we believed it. We'd also believed we were #1 on the Russian bomb list.

24. The unwritten rules of scenesterdom dictate that you can't make overt your desire to transcend the scene itself. You need to pretend not to care about building a music career, even as you secretly work toward that very thing (or don't work at all and instead smoke Meigs County weed all day and complain about how nobody is smart enough to recognize your genius).

25. When Ed Hamell walked into the tavern that night, he marched right up to the bartender and said, "Hey, do you guys still smoke crack out by the Dumpsters? Last time I was here, the cook and I got *sooooo* fucking high."

26. Watershed's ex-soundman says that the Toledo Sports Arena was the true home of rock and roll. The general admission floor was not for the faint of heart. A guy could get an eye gouged easy.

27. Cellular technology has rendered obsolete any excuse for not calling, *I couldn't find a payphone, honey* being the old standby.

28. Like Annie Savoy, Susan Sarandon's *Bull Durham* belle, The Superfan was essentially saying to the poor kid, "Would you rather I listen to Watershed and fuck you? Or fuck Watershed and listen to you?" Now that I think about it, the equation works like this: Annie Savoy – Edith Piaf + The Georgia Bulldogs = The Superfan.

29. A flyer has never by itself convinced anyone to come to a show, but it's a tangible thing you can staple your hopes to.

30. Why do bars always schedule all-ages shows for early in the night? Teenagers are better equipped than anyone for staying up late, so why not make the all ages show the *late* show? Let the old-timers go on early, finish up, and be home in time for Letterman. I know that bar owners want to maximize alcohol sales, but surely it makes no difference if you sell that booze at 7:00 p.m. or 1:00 a.m.

31. As the don't-sell-cigarettes-to-minors signs at the convenience stores continually remind me, a kid turning eighteen today was born in the same year Colin, Biggie, and I dropped out of OSU. To a current eighteen-year-old, Nirvana is classic rock. The Clash is dinosaur music. Kinks songs might as well be eighth century Gregorian chants. The average teenager has likely never heard of Cheap Trick or The Replacements; she listens to Lil' Wayne and T-Pain. Watershed and our old fashioned lineup of two guitars, bass, and drums (no keyboards? no computers? no DJ?) might look as dated to her as The Grateful Dead and their silly two drummer configuration does to me.

32. Making good use of off days is surely one of the things that has kept us together for so long. You get tired and cranky on the road, sick of each other. You need to spread out. Do something fun. We'll go hundreds of miles out of our way to spend an off day camping in the Catskills. Or at a Nags Head beach motel. Or a ballgame at Wrigley. We used to think of these side trips as tour sweeteners, like the fruit in PacMan. Now we see the off days as one of the main reasons *to* tour.

33. We never ran into Keith, but once we ran into Jordan and Drayton in the studio lounge. They were carrying crates of champagne. They shared a few sips.

34. *A quarter of a million dollars.* That's how they always said it. Never two hundred and fifty thousand, but *a quarter of a million.* Always.

35. Record companies exist to make money, not art. This is why record reps use the word *product* or *unit* instead of *album* or *song.* And this is why the major labels today fight so hard (and so litigiously) against free file sharing. This is also why our contract with Epic was thick as a phone book. Colin could have sat on it to see better over the dash.

36. I suspect that raw YouTube footage of live bands is changing our sonic palettes. My guess is that many people would now rather hear the real thing than the doctored construct, for the same reason that a lot of people now like amateur porn more than *Playboy.* We're tired of our experiences being mediated—by a slick record producer or by Hugh Hefner.

37. Steinman only stopped by the studio once a week. Usually he had Charles, his driver, chauffeur CDs of the day's recordings up to Westchester. When Jim wasn't around, Danny called the shots.

38. One sample from the collection: To Watershed. Good Luck On Your Upcoming Project! —Vanessa Williams. A second sample: To Watershed. Fuck You. —Jason Bonham. Getting fuck you'd by Angus Young would have been one thing, but Jason Bonham? Come on.

39. If you don't know the song, you certainly know the dancey, prancey, pink-jumpsuit video, which ruined Squier's reputation as a rocker. What makes the video even more of a shame is that the album, the Steinman-produced *Signs of Life,* is really pretty good. History will be kind to Billy Squier. But that jumpsuit and those dance moves are indefensible.

40. The reviews of *Three Chords* were mostly good, as writers gave a nod to our meat-and-potatoes sensibility. But under the headline "Midwestern Simplicity," the *Chicago Reader* wrote that Watershed was "a surly REO Speedwagon meets a castrated AC/DC." No shame in being a surly REO, I guess. And what band *isn't* a castrated AC/DC—other than, you know, the actual AC/DC.

41. In fairness, Colin doesn't think real bands can come from the South either: "You can't be a band if you've never had to load a heavy-ass Marshall up an icy stairwell." Or from the mountains: "You can't rock in Tevas and Patagonia shorts." Now that I think about it, for Colin, all legitimate rock pretty much hails from the Midwest. Or Australia, which is essentially the same thing.

42. Rock truism: Given a choice between a crap gig and a good gig, the people you most want to impress will always show up at the crap gig.

43. Ben Folds is an even more righteous nerd-stud than you'd expect him to be. At one show, he stood atop his piano and introduced "Underground" by yelling into the crowd, "I was never cool in school!" A drunk hillbilly yelled back, "You're not cool now, faggot!" But Folds just dropped to the keyboard and forged ahead undaunted. By the end of the song, the hillbilly had worked his way to the front row, cheering along with everyone else.

44. One of them was named Cha-cha Bass. "And I'm *not* Puerto Rican; I'm Dominican," she said. "I hate that shit."

45. Founded by Erv Karwelis, a guy we befriended when he worked in Sony's Dallas office. Like many major label lackeys, he quit the big boys to go out on his own.

46. In those days a kid might check out a band solely because of the Epic or Geffen or Warner Bros. logo on the flyer. Only the most discriminating scenester faithfully towed the "Corporate Rock Sucks" line.

47. In 2005, at age fifty-one, Frankie died during heart surgery. He was an A&R guy, but he was never a suit. They were moving units for the accountants; he was "making rekkids for the kids."

48. Lesson learned: A record company that tells you they don't expect an album to sell is lying.

49. Slim—besides being a font of knowledge and goodwill—is a world-class storyteller. He once told us the tale of how he'd ended up joining the Replace- ments. Here's how I remember it, in my best imitation of his voice: "Well, after Bobby left, Paulie came and asked me to join the band. You gotta understand. I thought the Replacements were snotty kids. No way was I hitching up with 'em. But Paulie was insistent. So he finally says, 'I'll tell you what, Slim. You and me'll do some drinking. If you outlast me, then I'll leave you alone. But if I outlast you, then you're in the band.' So the two of us go out, and I wake up on my couch the next morning, and I think to myself, Ha! I showed that punk a thing or two. Then I look down and see there's a note pinned to my shirt. It says, BAND PRACTICE 7:30."

50. No song nails minor league rock and roll better than Slim's "The Ballad of the Opening Band." As a matter of fact, you should shut this book right now and track down that song. Seriously. Do it. The book'll be waiting when you get back.

51. Real names: Joe and Joey.

52. Regarding the origin: I have no clue.

53. Like, for instance, the two times we played indoor volleyball complexes. Volleyball and rock don't mix.

54. Bring in fifty people for New Band Nite? Twice? An act that can draw fifty on a Tuesday is in the 90th percentile of all bands. An act that can do that twice is already too big to be playing the 8x10.

55. Watershed first got pranked by Dash Rip Rock on the opening night of a seven show tour. We were driving out of Mobile, aiming toward Tuscaloosa, when a horrific noise came from the driver's side front wheel. Biggie thought we'd busted a bearing or cracked a tie-rod end. Either way we were looking at a $1,000 repair bill. He pulled to the shoulder, jacked up the van, and popped off the hubcap. A guitar pick, two nine-volt batteries, and

three quarters came spilling out of the cap and onto the pavement. That $1,000 noise had been caused by 75 cents and a couple dead batteries. We were mad for about five seconds, but mostly we felt proud to be prank-worthy, proud to have been indoctrinated into the ranks. Biggie soon became an aficionado of the junk- in-the-hubcap gag, adding a Watershed CD as his own personal calling card.

56. Frank Aversa quit working with Spin Doctors after their guitarist said to him, "Shut up and hit the record button."

57. When we were on Epic, a fellow Sony band called For Squirrels had a van wreck, in which three guys died. We never talk about this, but we all know it.

58. *See also:* Jack and Bob. Who wants *everything?* Radio should be a filter, introducing listeners to *good* things.

59. Famous industry quote I've heard attributed to producer/exec Jimmy Iovine: "You know why this song sounds great on the radio?" "I don't know, Jimmy. Something about the compression? The EQ?" "It sounds great on the radio *because it's on the fucking radio.*"

60. Like Poochie from *The Simpsons*—the "extreme" dog character brought on to boost Itchy and Scratchy's flagging ratings.

61. At Comfest the following year, we dressed in corporate suits, hung the stars and stripes behind Dave, and took the stage to Lee Greenwood's "God Bless the USA (I'm Proud to Be an American)." Our set ended with Biggie and Ricki C. lighting $250 worth of truck stop fireworks: screamers, smoke bombs, a brick of firecrackers, and two huge spinning, sparking wheels. Shock and Awe, Watershed-style. This was four months *after* the tragic fire at the Station Nightclub in Rhode Island killed one hundred Great White concertgoers. We're slow learners.

62. Sire dropped The Fags without releasing *Light 'em Up.* Erv at Idol Records eventually put it out, but by then band tension had boiled to hatred, and they were all but broken up. Speck had already formed a new band—his fourth since we'd met him—the riffier, ballsier Skeemin' NoGoods. Watershed opened for The Fags at the *Light 'em Up* CD release party at Small's Bar. It was their last ever show.

63. Liking Cheap Trick doesn't automatically qualify you to manage a rock band, but it doesn't hurt.

64. Which makes the Arena District like the Vegas Strip. Neither was built on winners.

CREDITS

Portions of this book originally appeared, in slightly different form, in *Barrelhouse*, *Iron Horse Literary Review*, *Swink*, *Cimarron Review*, and *Pindeldyboz*.

"Left Of The Dial"
Words and Music by Paul Westerberg
© 1985 NAH MUSIC (ASCAP)/Administered by BUG MUSIC.
All Rights Reserved. Used by Permission.
Reprinted by Permission of Hal Leonard Corporation.

"I Want You To Want Me"
Words and Music by Rick Nielsen
© 1977 (Renewed 2005), 1978 SCREEN GEMS-EMI MUSIC INC. and ADULT MUSIC.
All Rights Controlled and Administered by SCREEN GEMS-EMI MUSIC INC.
All Rights Reserved. International Copyright Secured. Used by Permission.
Reprinted by Permission of Hal Leonard Corporation.

"Summer Of '69"
Words and Music by Bryan Adams and Jim Vallance
Copyright © 1984 IRVING MUSIC, INC., ADAMS COMMUNICATIONS, INC.,
ALMO MUSIC CORP., and TESTATYME MUSIC.
All Rights for ADAMS COMMUNICATIONS, INC. Controlled and Administered by
IRVING MUSIC, INC.
All Rights for TESTATYME MUSIC Controlled and Administered by ALMO MUSIC
CORP.
All Rights Reserved. Used by Permission.
Reprinted by Permission of Hal Leonard Corporation.

"Racing in the Street" by Bruce Springsteen. Copyright © 1978 Bruce Springsteen (ASCAP). Reprinted by permission. International copyright secured. All rights reserved.

ACKNOWLEDGMENTS

A LIFETIME OF THANKS TO THE WATERPUKES: COLIN GAWEL, MIKE "Biggie" McDermott, Dave "Catman" Masica, Mark "Pooch" Borror, and Herb Schupp. I'm lucky to have grown up in the van with you, you old so-and-sos. Thanks for being patient while I did the mostly unrocking work of finishing this book. Likewise a big thank you to the extended Watershed family: Thomas O'Keefe, Ricki C., Rob Braithwaite, Andy Hindman, Erin McHam, Jayna Wallace, Sarah Masica, Christy Borror, Lori Schupp, Deb Cacchione, Mike Landolt, Jared Butler, and Jen Zigler. Thanks also to Watershed's brothers-in-arms: Tim Patalan, John Speck, Erv Karwelis, Willie Phoenix, Joe Peppercorn, Andy Harrison, Mike Sammons, The Dead Schembechlers, Brian Phillips, and Andyman Davis, R.I.P.

Thanks to Mary Norris, Meredith Dias, and the staff at Lyons Press for their vision and enthusiasm, and thanks to John Rudolph at Dystel & Goderich Literary Management for finding the perfect home for this project.

Thanks to Will Allison, Kyle Minor, Heather Kirn, and Jason Skipper for reading early drafts of this book and for steering me toward daylight. Thanks also to Lee Martin, Lee K. Abbott, Steve Kuusisto, Erin McGraw, and the faculty and students of The Ohio State University Creative Writing Program for the camaraderie, support, and guidance.

Thanks to Dan Albergotti, Jason Ockert, and my colleagues at Coastal Carolina University for setting the bar so high. I could not have completed this book without a generous grant from the Edwards College of Humanities and Fine Arts at Coastal Carolina University and a fellowship from the Virginia Center for the Creative Arts.

Many thanks to my family and friends for their understanding as I disappeared into the writing black hole. I promise to call you soon.

Apologies to anyone I've forgotten. I'll buy you a beer next time I see you.

Lastly, my deepest thanks to Kate and Beckett for making home so hard to leave.

About the Author

Joe Oestreich's work has appeared in *Esquire, Sports Illustrated, Ninth Letter, Fourth Genre*, and other magazines and journals. He's been awarded a fellowship from the Virginia Center for the Creative Arts, honored by *The Atlantic Monthly*, and shortlisted for *The Best American Nonrequired Reading 2007, The Best American Essays 2008* and *2009*, and *The Pushcart Prize: Best of the Small Presses 2010*. A graduate of the Ohio State University Creative Writing Program, he teaches at Coastal Carolina University in Conway, South Carolina, where he lives with his wife and son. For more information please visit www.joeoestreich.com.